The Fall of a Doll's House

The Fall of a Doll's House

a Doll's House

*Three Generations of American Women
and the Houses They Lived In*

JANE DAVISON

HOLT, RINEHART and WINSTON   New York

Published by Holt, Rinehart and Winston, 383 Madison Avenue, New York,
New York 10017.

Published simultaneously in Canada by Holt, Rinehart and Winston of Canada,
Limited.

Library of Congress Cataloging in Publication Data
Davison, Jane.
  The fall of a doll's house.

  Bibliography: p. 229
  Includes index.
  1. Housewives—United States. 2. Home—
Psychological aspects. 3. Middle aged women—
United States. 4. Architecture, Domestic—Social
aspects—United States. 5. United States—Social
life and customs. I. Title.
HQ759.D32   643   79-19053
ISBN 0-03-041676-0

"Live the Life of *McCall's*," a letter from Editor Otis L. Wiese, is reprinted by
permission of the McCall Publishing Company from the May 1954 issue of
McCall's.

First Edition

Designer: A. Christopher Simon
Printed in the United States of America

10 9 8 7 6 5 4 3 2 1

I love this house.

Love my house, love me.

You are the house, sort of. You care, is what your house says. You care about many little things.

I've a trivial mind.

No; you're like a plant with a short growing season that has to put out a lot of tiny roots.

That sounds tragic, Jerry.

I didn't mean it tragically. We all have a season of some kind.

John Updike, MARRY ME

Contents

Preface

In the 1930s and '40s we proper little suburban girls played doll house and otherwise rehearsed for the home of our own we assumed was our destiny. Now grown up (at least technically), I for one have found it surprisingly hard to pursue a common-sense reappraisal of an article of faith in my mother's and grandmother's generations: that caring for her house, loving it and keeping it, is a woman's way of expressing herself and her commitment to marriage and family.

As the middle-class, single-family house that has depended on and defined three generations of American housewives becomes more demanding and less rewarding, many women like me are being forced to acknowledge that mere custodian-ship, a sheltered life work, is either not enough or too much. In the outside world the air grows chilly as our summer gardens fade. We are all too aware of the high cost of heating the place where we live.

In this retrospective tour I write as an amateur walking

through some familiar rooms in remembered houses. I'm not equipped to lecture with the authority of a community of scholars, nor am I attempting to be a Spokesman for My Aggrieved Generation. When I resort to the choral voice of the first person plural, it is not polemically, feministically. It is from an individual sense, perhaps mistaken, that I represent a group that shares my puzzled sense of having become, in some mysterious way that I'm trying to unravel, anachronistic—a period piece from the recent past.

The Fall of
a Doll's House

 ONE

Running Away from Home

A room comfortably and fashionably but not expensively furnished. In the back, stage center, a double-width doorway in the Victorian manner leads from the living room to what was once the rear parlor and is now the dining room. To the left, front, another door opens onto the entrance hall and a steep, curved staircase with thirteen carpeted steps. In the middle of the left wall of the living room is a small, open wooden chest filled with rubbery plants of maximum life expectancy, dracaenae and philodendrons, slightly dusty. On either side of the chest are armchairs, one a barrel shape, upholstered in brown corduroy and suffering from either sagging springs or a prolapsed uterus; on the other side is the showpiece, a classy blonde Scandinavian, a Danish adaptation of a Windsor chair. The intaglio on one of its teak arms was the work of an eight-year-old boy with a hacksaw. Opposite, a sofa in tan linen slipcovers, with grease spots punctuating the cushions and funny muted places worn on the arms. On it are scattered pillows in bright patchwork and Marimekko fabric. In the front, stage

1

*center, is a round skirted table with two yellow bentwood chairs
drawn up to it, as if for a fortune-teller and her client. All curtains are
natural open-weave linen. The room contains many books, garaged
aslant in do-it-yourself bracketed bookshelves. The carpet is autumn-
al, russet to be exact, and the traffic pattern is clearly apparent. The
room has tried for an effect but seems to have lost heart along the way.
The time: an evening in late May 1976. The place: an academic suburb
in New England.*

My apologies, for I have taken some license with the set
directions for Ibsen's play *A Doll's House*. More apologies for
trotting out poor Nora once again. Has *any* book concerned
with women and published since 1970 failed to call upon her?
My excuse is that I'm concentrating less on her than on her
relationship to her house. I've translated its style and decor
from 1879 to 1976, its location from Christiania, Norway, to
Cambridge, Massachusetts, much as trendy directors transport
Shakespeare's merchant to eighteenth-century Venice or Mo-
lière's misanthrope to Art Deco London. Nora's own living
room featured engravings on the wall, a what-not with china
and bric-a-brac, and a fire in the stove. My living room—for my
description is not a whimsical time warp but an exercise in stark
realism—contained an abstract collage of scrunched tissue
paper in earth tones on the wall; copies of *The Atlantic*, *The
New Yorker*, and *House & Garden*; a teak bar stocked with
Dewar's White Label, sometimes Jack Daniels, and an occasional flacon of Grand Marnier someone brought us from the
Caribbean.

As a room it had always seemed friendly enough, with its
mite of charm and its invincible seediness. As I sat there alone
that May evening, I was jostled by a crowd of images:
overdressed Christmas trees banked with drifts of discarded
wrappings; demitasse cups beside empty chairs, morning's
evidence of the previous night's high-cholesterol, high-intensity
dinner party; Sunday sunlight in blocks falling through the
windows and across the rug onto abandoned slag heaps of *New*

York Times and Boston *Globe*. All the helter-skelter of an ordinary American middle-class existence.

But that melodramatic evening it was quiet and solitary in the room—just me mourning—though from outside came an occasional shriek of laughter, a call to a friend, from the students who were strolling back to their dormitories down the street after an evening of end-of-term giddiness in Harvard Square or on Massachusetts Avenue somewhere. They were gay and irritating; I was desolate, grudging, rigid with self-pity. There had been a kind of death in the family, or whatever we four were. In retrospect I imagine myself looking stark, like one of those hostile, bitter Appalachian women whom Walker Evans trapped in his photographs, stripped of softness and optimism. And I was so used to being smiling and reliable, the good sport who never failed to pick up the cleaning, deliver the brownies to the bake sale, make the dentist's appointment on time, walk on the sunny side of the street.

Ibsen's Nora had her smiling public self, for her husband and family and society at large. For them she played "the lark," "the squirrel," "the butterfly" of the first two acts of the play. Eventually, as we are not allowed to forget, she revealed herself as the determined and unrelenting character of the third act, the woman who turned her back on husband, children, house (and bric-a-brac), who realized that she must leave home if she were ever to understand herself or anything else. Her husband, Thorwald, asked, "Are you not clear about your place in your own home? . . . You talk like a child. You don't understand the society in which you live." She answers. She exits. Then, according to that most famous stage direction: *From below is heard the reverberation of a heavy door closing.* A housewife resigns.

I wasn't quite as quick on my feet as Nora. I was too preoccupied with rearranging the furniture of my mind, picking up the broken china, straightening crooked pictures. It occurred to me as I worked that, though for years I'd indulged myself in playing the hen, the gerbil, the ant—extremely undemanding roles in a kind of perpetual kindergarten pageant—I was suddenly too old for such juvenile parts. There was little ingenue left in the mama doll in my doll's house.

Good God, you may well ask, *what* had happened? Why all this mid-life, housewifely kvetching? Had my husband had his wires tapped, were the children lost in poppies in the garden, did the Scottish terrier have amnesia?

My answer is unfashionably discreet, stingily watchful of my loose change. I'll say only that as a family our various lines of development had converged to produce a tangled plot indeed. We offered each other touching evenings in the home theater, alternating between situation comedy and Greek tragedy, and this evening's had been a particularly epic performance. Most of the time son and daughter were unrecognizable in their masks of high adolescence; husband at forty-eight was soliloquizing before the mirror; and wife, noticeably slumping at forty-four, was cast as a stock character, tragicomic perhaps, out of a play by William Inge.

It was Gail Sheehy who called mid-life The Forties Crucible, but long before she named it we had recognized its molten casualties around us: the distraught, the divorcing, the dipsomaniacal. Our Bessemer was still set on medium-low, but even so we knew that somehow we had to move off the heat before we began to look as well as feel like candles in the sun.

And then, too, the house was falling down. Gradually, under years of pressure, its spirit had broken. When we called for a celestial carpenter to come raise high the roofbeam once again, like other workmen of my acquaintance he didn't show up to do the job. The ridgepole was sagging, no angle was right, the square container of family life was all askew.

In letting down, the house had let me down, I felt. After all, I'd given it the best years of my life. And so with an unerring sense of justice, I turned against the one party to our confusion who was completely innocent. I turned against the house, in the way a widower has been known to reject his child, because the memories it arouses are too poignant to bear. Besides, it's always fairly safe to blame an inanimate object. When deeply angry or driven beyond endurance, one can kick the wall and it won't kick back. Or one can throw a Lavoris bottle straight at the shower. Then watch with satisfaction the red liquid dribble down the tiles, a stylized blood that makes florid canals of the grouting, coagulating around the shards of broken glass. Then clean the whole mess up. That's good sensible adult behavior.

The poor house, through fifteen years, had been a stalwart friend of mine. It may have been dented in rage, but it never groaned or held a grudge. A silent lay-therapist, it would simply sit there uncritically. It would submit to indignities, such as slipshod amateur redecoration or repair, or abandonments of a temporary nature, summers fraught with casual collegian tenants who neglected it. I thought of it as a supremely placid companion as well as a shelter. I was as close to it as a hermit crab to the conch shell he occupies. Was it a shell to hide within, or was it simply my outermost skin? But now, in crisis, I was a snapping turtle attacking my own tail. How had I gotten myself into this predicament? How had I become so identified with a house?

My husband the book publisher had long been posing subversive and conventionally hostile budgetary queries, such as "Why the hell don't we move, the taxes are ridiculous?" Or "Have you seen the fuel bill this month? Forty-three and a half cents a gallon. Why this time last year . . ." Or "Is that skylight leaking *again*?"

My husband the poet (the same man, I hasten to add) took a different tack. When in really top form he would generalize about the constraints of middle-class life, "our" materialistic values. Defensively I took his "our" as deriving not from the royal but the medical "we," meaning "you," e.g., "How are we feeling today?" "Our" values, he seemed to imply, were not shared, were mine alone. In theory he made sense, but I suspected him of talking a more radical game than he was actually prepared to play. He couldn't *really* be rejecting our joint endeavor, the house he paid for and I kept.

As a counterbalance I edged further and further into the role of Mistress Pragmatism, the peasant to his poet, the Yin to his Yang, or perhaps it was the Yang to his Yin. As he grew more antagonistic toward the house and the sort of life he seemed to think it embodied, I became more defensive of it. I began by representing it, like the counsel for the defense in a never-ending trial, and imperceptibly it began to represent me. Never anticipating the crash of '76, I invested myself in it recklessly, but the dividends grew smaller and smaller. Having tied up my capital, I wasn't free, I thought, to invest elsewhere; I certainly wasn't at liberty to make speculative excursions into the marketplace. Without being conscious of the process, I had become a full-time professional housewife, enmeshed in a job that had to be self-justifying but wasn't quite.

A housewife. Literally, a woman marries a house, or as *Women in American Architecture* views the relationship, there is "a symbiotic association between occupant and object." This association has been institutionalized, as has marriage. But institutions vary: there is the Smithsonian, and there is the state funny farm. Marriages vary, too. Most of them are, we must suppose, emotional relationships of one kind or another, kisses or tears, though a few do cultivate indifference. Some marriages crumble. Others bring out the best or the worst in the partners, and survive for that reason.

So with women and houses. Some women are, from the start, the adversaries of their houses. Some just don't give a damn. And others, the special ones, live symbiotically in houses they cherish and which reflect the affection they receive, like E. M. Forster's Mrs. Wilcox and her beloved Howards End. Such women, lucky in love, deserve another title to describe them, one that trails no clouds of complaint and Drano fumes as does "housewife," today the ultimate putdown for the edgy lady. Maybe some simple adjustment of punctuation could distinguish the love match from the mere *mariage de convenance*. Perhaps "house/wife" would do. The slash encompasses the idea of separation between the inanimate and the animate, suggests the matter of balance between the two—symbiosis and its shadow, the negative possibility of parasitism. The usage is probably a bit precious for everyday wear, as cute and self-conscious as "mailperson," and I will not indulge myself further.

But whatever the terminology, this housewife and her househusband had for some time been denying a severe imbalance, a wavering relationship. If either of us had been able to be completely honest, we would have admitted that the house had for one of us degenerated into a convenient dressing room in which to rest and store costumes between public performances, and for the other it had become the wings, the little nook offstage where the understudy waits fatalistically, passively, for some "big chance" that will offer the opportunity to face the music at last.

In our private lives and for our most private reasons, we loaded so much symbolic weight on the ordinary little structure we lived in that we strained it to the breaking point. When its emotional framing began to creak and groan, its dangerous structural deficiency could no longer be ignored. It wasn't long after that evening in May that we knew we had to get out and quickly, before the roof really fell in and crushed the whole doll family inside: Mummy, Daddy, Big Brother 'n' Little Sister.

I once saw a marvelously ironic typographical error in a Long Island newspaper editorial on the atomic age. A dire warning was issued against the horrors of "unclear" holocaust. I think a cautionary attitude about the *unclear* family is in order as well. As one cornerpost of a foursquare unit, I had long been unclear about the structural weaknesses of the nuclear family, but it couldn't have been for lack of information, digested and undigested, offered by both the popular press and the academy.

Whether by Christopher Lasch or Dr. Joyce Brothers ("ninth most admired woman in the world," according to one suspect poll), "expert analysis" must and does generalize from its access to the world outside a single home. A docile reader like me can parrot the experts glibly and convincingly in cocktail forums on what should be happening to solve the problematic American family. I can then act out some contradictory, deeply personal, unspoken (and therefore unchallengeable) preconception absorbed in childhood. There is a domestic unconscious that controls all sorts of homely rituals and tastes, and it is usually conservative. A woman can assume a feasible intellectual position, based on The Facts, and then deny it by compulsively staging a retrospective, like a child's birthday party that has to have pin-the-tail-on-the-donkey and crepe paper snappers and patent leather slippers—none of which the small honoree digs at all. "It's your party, dear." (It's my party, dear.) Housewife and mother often speaks with forked tongue.

Liv Ullmann, who had played Nora on the stage, expatiated in *Changing*, her recent contribution to the genre of mid-life crisis, on her conception of the character. Nora, she says, is "a woman who says one thing and means something quite different . . . she plays her part just as [her husband] plays his. Neither of them gives the other a chance, because they are always in service to the other's role."

Kate Brown, another similarly split female runaway, is the middle-aged heroine of Doris Lessing's novel *The Summer Before the Dark*. Prior to taking off she had become "uncomfortably conscious not only that the things she said, and a good many of the things she thought, had been taken down off a rack and put on, but that what she really felt was something else again."

That summer her husband and children were committed to plans elsewhere, ones that didn't include her, and she had lucked into her first paid job in years. Her initial reaction to work outside the home, in the so-called real world, was incredulity: "Was it that for twenty-five years she had been part of that knot of tension, the family, and had forgotten that ordinary life, life for everyone not in the family, was so agreeable, so undemanding?"

Having leased out her emptied house, she took a room in London, and alone there "before going to sleep, she looked at its neatness, its indifference to her, and thought that, yes, this was much better than her large family house . . . full, crammed, jostling with objects every one of which had associations, histories, belonged to this person or that, mattered, were important."

American women have been particularly successful in emotionalizing not only our role (or occupation, if you will) but the very building where it takes place. We have of course been encouraged in this by cultural and economic forces we often dismiss as too large in scope to be really relevant to little us, anonymous in our individual workshops. Does a miner romanticize his mine, an auto worker his factory, a sanitary engineer his sewer? But those gentlemen do not happen to live over the store. The factory itself does not contain and define life. And in most cases the workers have regulated as a group their right to strike or bargain in an organized way. Women considering renegotiation of their contracts have often been afraid of backing themselves into a corner where the only alternative to knuckling under seems to be a wildcat walkout like Nora's.

I had never realized how deeply and widely the attachment to the ideal of the single family in the single-family house had grown into American soil. The effect has often been, I fear, as destructive as the roots of the linden tree that grew in our back yard. They can choke off and crush buried pipes, heave up solid asphalt, entangle, distort, cut off choices. There's nothing intrinsically wrong with the tree: its shade is pleasant. Nor do I hold some sullen grudge against the single-family house; I appreciate its pleasures and privacies. But too many of us, pale creatures, have dissipated our lives in its dappled shadows.

My husband and I became aware of the tenacity of homeowning's grip on other imaginations than our own when, in the summer of 1976, we impulsively signed a year's lease on an experimental alternative to our shaky old house. Out of a kind of desperation, we committed ourselves to what we thought would be a short trip in a small boat—escape from Dunkirk.

On September 1 we moved from our ten-room Cambridge house, the only home our children had ever known, into a compact and eccentric duplex apartment in a large, newly rehabilitated nineteenth-century granite warehouse on Boston's waterfront.

As a place to live, the Mercantile Wharf Building is in almost every way the antithesis of our conventional former home. It is multiple-unit housing; its tenants have mixed incomes, with a majority of the 121 apartments subsidized for low- and middle-income residents; it's a mélange racially, ethnically, socially, and of ages. It's not a simple private enterprise, but depends on state and federal funding. And it's located in the fibrillating heart of a major city, not snug and smug in a suburb. In conception it seems to challenge both the social and architectural assumptions of the Typical American Home for the Typical American Family, and living in it has raised complicated and unanswered questions in my mind about relative merits.

Apparently our move perplexed some of our peers. We emigrated only a few miles, from Cambridge across the river to Boston, but surprisingly, many friends, liberal survivors of the Kennedy years, found our move as exotic as if we had headed into a trackless Brazilian jungle. I was bowled over when one younger, successful career woman, single, a declared feminist, reacted with, "What a gutsy thing to do!" I felt fraudulent—the deserter posing as heroine.

Perhaps it was simply the fact that our friends were used to seeing us in one setting. Or perhaps, quite unselfconsciously, we were challenging important assumptions. We were vacating the nest before it was empty. And we were choosing social heterogeneity in an urban setting rather than exclusivity in a suburban one.

Adrenaline powered us, but we remained eminently responsible and circumspect and moderate in the way we all ran away from home. Not the loud slam for us. It was as if Nora, Thorwald, and the children had packed their bags in an orderly fashion, canceled newspaper delivery, and then had all left together, quietly double-locking the door behind themselves.

I should add, however, that the house had been for some years running away from us, in bits and pieces. Some of it was simply physical attrition, water dripping on a stone and slowly eroding it. Shingles blew off in high winds, and downspouts were strangled by ice and wrestled to the ground. Fence pickets absented themselves without leave. Shutters disgorged their slats, and window putty chose freedom. Rot carried away risers on porch steps and paint flaked to the grass, which was preoccupied with the process of turning brown and dying, and never noticed anyway.

Not only nature but society was conspiring in the late sixties and early seventies to give us a message. While the house silently crumbled, its contents were taking it on the lam, escorted by an energetic corps of petty burglars who seemed to use our unprepossessing neighborhood as a staging area for basic training. Their first major assault removed most of the jewelry I'd been left by the only grandmother I'd ever known: her girlish brooch, an enameled lavender pansy with a dewdrop diamond in the center; an odd bloodstone signet ring with the seal of the young people's club she'd sponsored in her middle age; a tiny diamond solitaire she'd inherited herself from some shadowy aunt or cousin.

In later forays the forces, anonymous and random, that we grew to acknowledge simply as *they* (as in "*they* have just shot Martin Luther King" or Bobby Kennedy or George Wallace), struck again and again. One of *them* must have smiled contemptuously when, having heard the front door open, I chirped out a cheery halloo from the dinner table not ten feet from the newel post where temporarily hung my husband's suit jacket (and wallet and charge cards). I was probably excessively hospitable under the circumstances. Maintaining a perpetual Open House was quite enough.

The hi-fi's, toolboxes, TVs, and cameras that departed were replaced almost as easily as they streamed out, especially as in the course of a dozen burglaries I became proficient in the red tape of filing insurance claims. We of course became assigned risks and were demoted from a name-brand insurer to something like the Alabama Steamfitters Mutual. Nevertheless the continuing interest of the criminal community in my grandmother's legacies never became less painful: out the door or the window went a Tiffany vase, a Nantucket basket, and, cruelest blow of all, a plain oval Shaker box, with the chain of inheritance handwritten on its bottom, antique signatures of three generations of women. Perhaps the thief has added his name to the list, in the block lettering used for ransom notes or extortion demands.

A sick feeling of personal violation is common the first time *they* enter your house, size up your possessions as if shopping, and have their way with their choices. The usual comparison is to rape, but my imagination fails in further refining that analogy. My main reaction, after seizures of undifferentiated fury, was a kind of specialized paranoia. *They* were slowly but surely deracinating *me*. Time after time *they* removed my lares and penates, the symbolic tokens of my past, my meager dowry. They left me with a houseful of meaningless price-tag objects that could be replaced in an afternoon's visit to the local discount or department store, or even on the phone.

I began to feel that the rejects were somehow as offensive to me as they apparently were to *them*. What was wrong with my flat silver anyway? It was, as they say, a classically simple design from Tiffany's, unmonogrammed, eight place settings, all wedding presents. *They* spread it out on the dining-room table, appraised it, and left it behind. Perhaps it was a little tarnished, but I wouldn't have thought that mattered to professionals. Anyway, I haven't felt the same about the silver since it failed to meet *their* standards.

Another, more unexpected and positive reaction to theft is a sudden sense of liberation from responsibility toward material things. It wasn't in my case a profound spiritual experience of a Gandhi-like nature. I simply felt, Well, there's one less thing to worry about. For some women disaster can virtually throw open the door of the cage, allowing the bird to fly free. In *Daughters of the Promised Land*, Page Smith describes an incident in the life of Margaret Sanger, the pioneer in the birth-control movement. Her husband, an architect, had designed and built a house for her and their two sons. The day before the family was to move in, the new house burned to the ground.

"I stood there amazed," Margaret Sanger said, "but I was certain of a relief, of a burden lifted, a spirit set free. It was as if a chapter of my life had been brought to a close." She claimed that the fire taught her "the absurdity of placing all one's hopes, all one's efforts, involving as they do heartaches, debts and worries, in the creation of something external that could perish irretrievably in the course of a few moments. . . . My scale of suburban values had been consumed by the flames."

The life cycle of a house is no more or less complicated than a person's. Ours flaked away in chips or was carried off by inimical but anonymous forces, but, as E. M. Forster describes the process in *Howards End*, "Houses have their own ways of dying, falling as variously as the generations of men, some with a tragic roar, some quietly but to an afterlife in the city of ghosts, while from others . . . the spirit slips before the body perishes." A house can become "a corpse, void of emotion, and scarcely hallowed by the memories of . . . years of happiness."

Not as spunky or philosophical as Mrs. Sanger in her reaction to the "tragic roar" of her fire, I confronted the collapse of my once symbiotic relationship to my house, and with it my conventional ideal of family life as embodied in it, and found the experience simply painful and diminishing. I just wanted to go away and forget about it. Perhaps fire would have cauterized.

The threat of sudden loss of headquarters has always frightened me. I had my first full-scale, remembered nightmare in glorious technicolor after seeing the original *Wizard of Oz*. What could possibly be more terrifying than the prospect of your own house, your very own room, spiraling up into the sky in the funnel of a tornado? Up, up, and away, never to be found again. And home was where you were supposed to be safe.

In 1976, as we four settled into a stripped-down and compressed life (I can hardly resist the temptation to say "life style"), I began to feel strangely restless in the undemanding routine of apartment life. Instead of never really finishing my chores, just abandoning them, I could zap through them all by ten in the morning. Then what? Explore the outside world?

Venture out to do what? We moved into the Mercantile Wharf Building in September, and by November I was hearing, very faintly, the song of the open road. It wasn't Paris or Pago-Pago that attracted me. It was Omaha and Indianapolis and Tulsa and Amarillo, all of unknown America, that seemed urgently exotic. I'd read about these places in *Time*, heard about them on the evening news, knew about their weather ("The temperatures today in the Plains States will . . . mudslides in Los Angeles are . . . snow swept across the Dakotas . . ."). But I'd traveled more in Europe than in my own country.

The siren song calling me to the interstate highways reached a kind of crescendo late on Election Night 1976. As Jimmy and Gerry slugged it out, David and Walter kept showing huge maps of the United States with areas shaded in schematically according to the vote. My husband had long since fallen asleep and was breathing heavily. On solitary vigil I muttered silently to the tube, whose skim-milk light eeried up the room, "I've never been there . . . or there . . . or there." Kansas and Utah and Oregon all had a sudden allure, but somehow I fixated on Montana. My husband had gone there on business a couple of years before and had suggested at the time in a way that I felt was *pro forma* that I come along. I had responded in an equally stylized mode (the children . . . the money . . . no, I couldn't possibly) and had filled his absence by repainting our bedroom, a chore long overdue. Just think how much money I saved; why a professional painter would have cost, why, who knows how much? At least fourteen doubloons and a ducat or two.

So my husband had seen Montana, had had an adventure all on his own, and I had been deprived, had deprived myself. Or had it been the house that had held me prisoner? Now, by God, I'd escaped and I'd see Montana and die.

As a matter of fact I still haven't seen Montana, and live to tell the tale. But I have fumed through Indianapolis in a blizzard and known Tulsa at dawn. The night Jimmy Carter was being elected, I hatched what a friend calls A Cheap Adventure. The 1977 annual meeting of the Society of Architectural

Historians was being held in early February in Los Angeles, and though I am by no stretch of the imagination an accredited scholar, I decided to go, to use it as an official destination. As architecture groupie and natural camp follower, I tag along whenever I can on the SAH's tours and meetings in order to spy on other people's beautiful houses, swoon like a bobbysoxer while specialists discourse on "Frank Lloyd Wright's Hollyhock House: 1914–24" or "A. Constance Austin's Next Step: A Feminist Architect's Utopia."

Besides, I had been toying with the idea of using my strange liberation from full-time domesticity to try to write a book about women *and* houses, or women *in* houses, or women *on* houses (as in the famous Thurber cartoon). Never having tackled anything longer than a few magazine pieces, I was in the euphoric state of infinite possibilities that exists when not a word has been committed. Today the vision—tomorrow the world. My aspirations smacked more, I hope, of naïveté than of hubris. I assumed that if I just looked, I too could see from sea to shining sea. I was, after all, one of the generation imprinted by the best-seller surveys of the 1950s and thereafter, the overview that sorts society out into bins labeled "Typical Exurbanite," "Typical Organization Man," and most recently, "Typical Housewife with Yeasty Consciousness." The popularity of the genre is understandable. Robert Coles writes in *Privileged Ones* of generalizations and their lure, concluding that they "fail wretchedly to do justice to the varieties of human experience, to the complexities of human life, to the ironies and ambiguities and paradoxes that constantly present themselves to anyone."

Anyway I was full of faith that a brief but panoramic trip away from home would provide "insights" and above all "perspective," that wonderful all-purpose commodity.

My mild-mannered master plan called for me to go coast to coast on a Greyhound bus. The newspapers had been hawking special excursion fares, one-way to anywhere, with infinite stopovers, for fifty dollars. It would be a very, very cheap adventure. I saw the journey in prospect as a vast and whimsical game played on a board composed of the map of the United States in primary colors, very like an educational puzzle my children used to have. Across it I'd move in a blue-and-silver tin bus according to a throw of the dice, a twirl of the wheel. No AAA Triptik would organize my route, no pleas that we stop at the next McDonald's or redolent gas station bathroom or Wild Animal Ranch would come from the back seat, no captain would suggest that his co-pilot take remedial map-reading. I visualized a solitary wending toward the setting sun, the vagabond way; I would linger where the impulse took me, a mid-life cowgirl on the road.

No sooner had I left Boston than I fell asleep. When I woke, near Danbury, Connecticut, it was to gaze on a wintry parking lot filled with second-hand Silver Airstream trailers, abandoned like last summer's cocoons. Our own chrysalis was half empty but cozy, and watching out the window was like looking at television. I didn't have to believe what I saw as we rolled along, that, for example, the gutted, blasted area of Harlem, like some urban Vietnam, was quite real. There, facing the north end of Central Park, stood a convent, the Handmaids of Mary, martyred next to a derelict apartment house sardonically called Sans Souci. Carefree indeed.

As we left Manhattan's Port Authority Terminal (or "Port of Authority," in taxi-driver patois), a blizzard raged ahead of us. A voice like God's came over the loudspeaker: AFTER PHILADELPHIA THE REST OF THE TRIP IS UN-KNOWN. What could possibly be more adventurous, I thought to myself, than Destination Unknown. This might be the first bus to outer space!

By Pittsburgh the wind-chill factor was 45° below. We swooshed through a series of classic midwestern hometowns, straight from the back lot of MGM, frozen in time as well as in fact. They looked as though they'd hardly changed since World War II, were just as our boys fighting in Guadalcanal jungles might have remembered them, along with Mom and apple pie. Zanesville, Ohio, houses on our bus route were the stuff of *The Saturday Evening Post* and Norman Rockwell. They were the dowdy, comfortable all-American homes of the late nineteenth and early twentieth centuries, originally of brick or wood but now often redone in asphalt siding or aluminum, their broad front porches stripped of summer's settee or swing, now dredged with snow. While I contemplated them, a compulsively talkative veteran of both navy and army who was stationed behind me anesthetized the populace with his tales of the South Pacific. There was much talk of Bull Halsey and the fleet.

We rolled on through drifted farmland, past slatternly barns and isolated farmhouses, until suddenly the highway flattened out. At our Columbus rest stop I cased the schlocky souvenir shop, noting among the Last Supper postcards and Buckeye State beer mugs a stabbingly poignant teapot emblazoned "Home, Sweet Home." I slunk back somberly to my seat in the bus. After all, this was my first solo flight in seventeen years and I found myself missing that pure voice in my ear: "Mom, make him *stop* it!"

Gusts of high wind still sent snow rising above fields like chill ground mist. The monuments and obelisks of downtown Indianapolis protruded dingily through the whiteness everywhere. That night, they said, the Mississippi was frozen solid, trapping barges and ships, turning them into houses surrounded by icy land.

I slept and woke to find a new dry brown world outside my window, a landscape of Harris tweed dotted with low schematic trees that looked rootless, like brambles simply fastened to the ground to relieve the bareness. We were outside "Downtown Tulsa Unlimited."

Beside me I found a new seatmate, a sixtyish woman who had boarded sometime during the night. We started to talk, with that instant confidentiality that can spring up among women, the feminine counterpart of military camaraderie and AmVet reminiscences. "My mother was an Indian," she soon told me. "We're Cherokees but poor Cherokees." We both laughed when the bus driver announced, in a triumph of trivia, that we were then entering Sapulpa, "the birthplace of Mrs. Thomas E. Dewey."

We chatted autobiographically of children and house-keeping—I think that we were the only housewives on board. There were backpacking young men, surreptitiously puffing pot in the back of the bus, haggard and baggy-kneed senior citizens, a few remnants of a mysterious counterculture (one father and his motherless son were heading for Sacramento, to a guru with an uncanny ability to determine inner energy level by the number of white half-moons on fingernails). But there were just two of us good ole girls.

My instant friend had had a hard but triumphant life. Her husband had died prematurely, leaving her to support and raise four small daughters, one of whom had brain damage. Through the Depression and World War II she had done baby-sitting on a grand scale, freelance laundry for thirty-nine cents an hour, anything she could to keep her house, feed her children. She'd survived, the house was still hers, and she had a steady and comparatively undemanding job at her local hospital. She was en route to Needles, California, to vacation with a married daughter.

She vouchsafed me a recipe that I'll pass on in the interest of history:

WATERGATE PUDDING

1 PACKAGE INSTANT PISTACHIO PUDDING
1 SMALL CAN CRUSHED PINEAPPLE WITH JUICE
1 CUP MINIATURE MARSHMALLOWS
1 CUP WALNUTS OR PECANS
8 OUNCES DREAM WHIP

Apparently you dump everything in a bowl, stir, and chill.

My friend didn't know why this extraordinary dessert was named for Watergate, but my private suspicion is that it memorialized another big mess with some nuts in it. But don't mistake my point, which isn't that I'm so tasteful a disciple of Julia Child that I can make fun of miniature marshmallows. To the contrary, my point is that we two spoke a common language, and we had a genuine impulse to share experience and recipes.

The bus stopped every four hours day and night all across the continent, at almost identical Post Houses, so called. No coffee spoons for me; I measured out America in rest stops. Mealtime conformed to no conventional schedule, so I'd always have breakfast, Kellogg's Raisin Bran and mini-cans of V-8. Anything was preferable to a breaded cutlet of the species that apparently languishes on every steam table from here to eternity.

Every waiting room had travelers in the state of somnolence or catalepsy described as Terminal Illness. Every newsstand had the same array of mass-circulation magazines, the same mass-market paperbacks. The element of suspense and discovery centered on whether or not the next stand would have last month's or the current issue of *House Beautiful, House & Garden, Ladies' Home Journal, McCall's, Good Housekeeping.*

Having long since finished my hardcover Margaret Drabble novel, I started in on the women's magazines. In the darkened nighttime bus, snores and huffing around me, my little reading spotlight beamed down at the slick four-color photographs of Winter Glory Cake, Elizabeth Taylor and her chins, and mix-and-match separates for *you* to sew. Sleepless and a little lonely, moving inexorably through somewhere (but where?), I began to have a sense, however silly it may seem, of wakeful women in houses across the country, distracting themselves from boredom and solitude as I was, with magazine menus, diet secrets, ten ways to reorganize your linen closet, the Kraft Cheese Sweepstakes. All of us might be sharing, in different degrees of skepticism, some common aspiration, common disappointment. And all of us who were turning the pages were receiving parts of the same message: we *can* make ourselves, our homes, our lives better by working and buying, by caring enough.

The land, that travelogue filmstrip passing by my shatterproof window, was sometimes startling, often simply stark, but it did vary. It was the sameness of the built environment that depressed me more and more: the gas stations, the Post Houses, the main streets, the fast-food joints, the motels. I hadn't expected to be converted to highway culture as art. Advanced architectural critics may groove on Burger King's spontaneity, the Las Vegas strip as kitsch masterpiece, but we genteel philistines will always resist the golden arches of neon heaven. I'm afraid we lack aesthetic distance.

What really got to me was the invincible singleness of the houses in sovereign state after sovereign state. Everywhere they seemed so self-contained, so solitary, particularly after dark, with their lights on, their inhabitants locked in for the night. They might be clustered, as in developments proliferating along the highways of the Southwest, or they might be strung out randomly or cast over the flatland and hillsides like a handful of buckshot. Old-fashioned or contemporary, ugly or picturesque, immaculately maintained or down-at-the-heels, the single-family houses marched on, one by one. And in spite of superficial variations in style, they shared, I was sure, a single assumption. A small stucco bungalow in Erick, Oklahoma, close by Interstate 40, said it all. Beside the front door, where the house number might logically appear, big black letters boldly declared: HERS.

All my broad Tolstoyan musing on national character, houses, and women was disrupted by an increasingly specific sense that if I didn't soon get off the bus and into a horizontal position, my ankles, swollen into two unfamiliar melons, might qualify me for a centerfold in *The National Geographic*. Among the hazards of exotic travel are elephantiasis, bilharziasis, and bus bloat. Albuquerque and Santa Fe provided a two-day cure, and some mild but expensive touristical adventures. Deflated, I reboarded.

We traversed a day's worth of arid ups and downs, and suddenly happened upon the fringe of Los Angeles, a city that trails fronds like a giant colony of jellyfish. Once installed in the newly refurbished Biltmore Hotel downtown, I reveled in fresh avocados stuffed with crabmeat and Grand Ballrooms stuffed

with architectural historians. I was in familiar territory again.
The cross-country game had turned out to be a simple physical endurance contest, and my schematic map of the United States has been superseded. Gone were blithe, unacknowledged expectations that I could diagram or overview or summarize this spacious, spaced-out country, though at times during the bus trip, too much alone with moiling generalizations, I'd succumbed to a kind of mobile megalomania. It didn't take long to realize I'd never warble the song of the open road, but from across the range, and the ridge, and the desert, and the fruited plains did come a low whirring hum. I didn't exactly hear America singing, but I would swear I could hear her vacuum-cleaning.

At least it did seem possible that my own tale of a faltering, changing relationship to the house in which I lived was part of a larger national pattern or trend. Were there many others at home like me? Could I justify my existence, or at least explain it to myself, by registering as a typical case history?

"We are covetous of our niche in history," wrote Joy Wheeler Dow, a conservative architectural critic at the turn of the century; "we want to belong somewhere and to something, not to be entirely cut off by ourselves as stray atoms in boundless space either geographical or chronological." Like so many women of my generation, I have, I think, lived much of my adult life not as a stray but as a neutron within a residential atom, with only a girlish chemistry-class interest in the larger molecular structure, a curiosity theoretical at best. Where did I belong, what was my charge, now that the atom had split? What was my niche in history, my legacy from the past?

My grandmother and my mother have passed on to me more than heirloom jewelry and blue eyes. I've absorbed from them both a sense of "that's how you do it" that often translates itself into "that's who you are." Housewives all, we three women reigned in increasingly solitary, diminishing splendor, not in palaces but in ordinary houses, all-American single-family suburban homes. We handed down our ways through a female line parallel to millions of others. Speaking for the third generation, and the last in which such single-minded middle-class housewives have been the norm, I have perhaps idealized the past out of resentment toward a fragmenting present. As for the future, whose dimensions are of course unspecified, we must all remain uncertain though curious. Will our daughters really be a new breed, disturbingly different from us? Where will they not house the children (our lost grandchildren?) they say they'll probably never have?

A closer look at a shared as well as a personal inheritance may well be therapeutic in mid-life or at other crossroads. I offer one do-it-yourself analysis of a representative domestic unconscious. How often and in what subtle ways do we, against our best interests, conform docilely to circumstances no longer relevant (if they ever were) to the realities of our daily lives? How often are we keeping someone else's house? And why have we continued, often past the point of no return, to feel that keeping a house is a moral duty?

The collapse of my monogamous relationship with my house, as isolated and personal an event as it seemed to me when it happened, seems to be a divorce being replicated all over the countryside, as employment and relocation statistics confirm. Women are being either forced out or lured out of their doll houses. The kind of interior, segregated existence that has dominated the expectations of most American women since 1900 is no longer regarded as universally possible or desirable.

But against all reason, the single-woman, single-family house does continue as the setting for the fantasies of customers and purveyors alike. In 1978 alone, 1,428,300 new single-family houses were started and 3,905,000 resales were transacted. Real-estate developers, manufacturers, advertisers, and magazines are all in cahoots with us the buyers, and together we perpetuate the illusion of business as usual in a changing world. Historically, however, rationality has never characterized our national love affair with a home of one's own.

When Helmer accused Nora of not understanding the society in which she lived, she answered, "No, I do not." (Nor do I.) "But now I shall learn," she continued.

Running away from home in a bus did not turn out to be the mythic odyssey I'd imagined in my more romantic moods—it was no free flight with greyhounds, hunting the lost years in mountains. But it was a symbolic action that did provide a new view, more or less perspective than I know how to use. It did convince me that a wide-angle lens might not be for me. My camera is ordinary, Instamatic, and the snapshots pasted in this album may be too small or blurred to serve as general illustrations. Although I shall focus in on a microcosm—my grandmother's house, the houses of my mother and her contemporaries, and my own contrasting settlements—I hope I include enough of the surrounding landscape so that other women like me will recognize the familiar, our common ground.

None of us is typical, a fact women's magazines often seem to deny but novelists have long acknowledged. Though I may pose as one, I know there is no Typical Housewife, but there are typical houses; for unlike their occupants, these inanimate objects can be exactly reproduced in numbers, in types.

If I have resorted to a familiar back-to-one's-sources approach to personal identity, I have not tried to spade up deep taproots. Instead I have aimed to disentangle the tiny tendrils that have kept us clinging, like English ivy, to the walls of our houses.

Though I have scratched into the topsoil when rooting around at foundations, the actual brick and mortar of the houses in my family's past, in revisiting them and recalling the daily life that took place there, I've uncovered no skeletons or hidden silver. I've simply taken another round trip, not in transcontinental space but in time, backwards through so many everydays, years lit recognizably by the gleam of freshly polished floors, sunset caught in windowpanes, firelight reflected in brass. Years sodden with leaks and mildew and steaming mittens braising on radiators. The more things change, they say, the more they remain the same. Until now?

 TWO

Over the River and to the
Woods, 1900-1907

Outside the iron-hinged, white wooden gate, I looked back through the dusk at the house I'd left. It had once been my grandmother's, and I'd just been inside it for the first time. Its gambrel roof loomed large against the October evening sky, which was still a precisely shaded indigo, transparent below but intensifying above, like the spectrum on a paint-chip card from a hardware store. The huge oaks surrounding the house seemed to be silhouettes, as two-dimensional as if cut out of black construction paper or inked onto cardboard. The scene was a stage set, a draftsman's rendering, a greeting card to me from my grandmother.

The hour was the one gloated over by architectural voyeurs like me, that defenseless interval before shades are pulled down or curtains drawn to shut the occupants in, and to close our kind out. Interiors are wide open, conveniently illuminated, unconsciously hospitable to our uninvited eyes. How many prematurely dark winter afternoons I'd cruised through my Cambridge on the way home from the supermarket, following a route no crow could endorse, the car in second gear, moving just fast enough so I wouldn't be suspected of casing the joints, but not so fast I'd miss any juicy details. Glimpses into other people's houses, other people's lives, from a discreet distance, were the stuff of a mild addiction.

Mixed with the compulsions of the peeper was an element of the magic-seeker. Perhaps I'd catch sight of talismans and amulets, of the secrets of the inner sanctum, that I could use to transform my own straw hut, my Cinderella site. At its most cold-blooded this is the pitch of such shelter magazines of the 1970s as *Architectural Digest*, which lets us into the lairs of minky celebrities and the hangars of jet-setters. Adulation is followed by emulation is followed by disappointment. Our large feet of clay don't fit the glittering glass slipper.

Both curiosity and magic-seeking had brought me to my grandmother's house. Conveniently, my hosts this particular evening, the couple who have lived in the house for over three decades, had been delayed in their usual routines by my reluctance to leave, and had not yet attended to their curtains and shades. I could still see inside to the living room on the left of the large center hall, the dining room on the right. I felt like a movie-goer who lingers after the show, savoring publicity stills in the lobby, prolonging an experience. Before brazening out a dinner for one (plus book) at the Hunt Club Restaurant in the somewhat Anglophiliac Hotel Summit Suburban (in Summit, New Jersey), I surely had a moment more to spare, here at the source, the historic site.

The house I'd just experienced had been my paternal grandparents' for almost twenty-five years—from 1906, when they built it, until the late 1920s, when they moved away, obedient to the corporation that was my grandfather's life. Of course it was *their* house, but I couldn't help thinking of it as *her* house, sensitized as I was by a long nostalgic summer spent reading the diaries, two wooden crates of them, in which she chronicled the life she'd spent with her nine children inside, very much inside, that strange but somehow familiar house.

All her little leather-bound notebooks, filled with a remarkable miscellany, inscribed in her old-fashioned penmanship, added an eerie woman-to-woman, transgenerational directness to oral history, all the family stories that had been the folklore of my childhood. I'd heard my father, his five brothers, and three sisters spin reminiscent yarns every bit as good as Brer Rabbit's and mercifully not in any puzzling southern dialect. Their anecdotes evoked a larger-than-life Edwardian childhood, laced with mischief, local personalities, narrow escapes, animals, and eccentricities. Mum and Dad were the Queen and King in all those fairy tales. Any tragic or sordid elements were censored out for juvenile audiences: the production was definitely G, grandparental guidance always invoked.

I loved hearing the embroideries on life at Lindum (for that is the name my grandmother gave her house), and somehow I absorbed the conviction that if life there had apparently been devoid of avarice, lust, gluttony, and other dark shadows, then life in the house I was destined someday to have would surely be too. A grand illusion took root in my naïveté, and grew.

"How can they laugh so much?" I once asked my father, who was checking in with me at my vantage point on the stairs outside our dining room, where a family wedding luncheon, replete with uncles, was in full swing. I always had trouble associating those confident, hilarious anecdotalists with the somber, dwarfish, positively historic figures of the family photo albums, posed self-consciously and with fearful symmetry on the brick walk that led from the white wooden gate in front of Lindum. The snapshots featured grave little boys in wrinkled black stockings, toddlers morosely enduring voluminous pleated garments (the ironing!), gawky girls in unflattering bloomers and Windsor ties. And always, the house behind, spreading wide to either side of the children in the foreground.

Though I grew up in Summit, a few amoeba-shaped suburban blocks away from Lindum, strangely enough no one had ever taken me inside. My grandparents had sold it a couple of years before I was born, but I'm sure my father would have been welcomed by any of the three families that in turn succeeded his. Somehow for him, as well as for most of my other aunts and uncles, the impulse to revisit was weak. They seemed to prefer that legend take over. Would George Washington have returned to all those houses where once he slept, just for old times' sake? Memorialization is for those who don't have the memories.

One generation later it would be for me an uncomplicated, though not unemotional, matter. I wrote the current owners, explained my interest, and asked if I could walk around the rooms I'd been reading up on, just to get the feel of the space, the look of it. I didn't want to make measured drawings or photograph or do anything intrusive or scholarly. They answered immediately and invited me for drinks and a complete house tour. (I did skip the cellar.) We chatted in the wood-paneled room that had been my grandfather's study, *sanctum sanctorum*.

Now, years after the Thanksgiving afternoons and Sunday night suppers of my childhood, when the "Do you remembers . . . ?" rolled, I had made my pilgrimage at last. Who says you can't go home again? I'd gone—sort of—and I'd been strangely at ease. Even though I'd never been there before, in person, I knew the famous mantelpiece in the living room where they'd all hung their Christmas stockings, the back stairs they'd always sneaked up and down to avoid detection, the nursery where they'd conducted a mass barbering from which no toy emerged unshorn. That tale had been my introduction to life as a sequence of irreversible actions. Imagine having to live on forever afterwards with bald dolls and mangy teddy bears. The site was familiar, familial. The rooms looked just the way I wanted them to look. This was not just a house, this was home itself.

My grandmother had the instincts of a matriarch. She instilled, at least in this susceptible granddaughter, a deep sense of home as a woman's domain, as matrix. One definition of *matrix* is "womb," another is "a binding substance such as cement in concrete." Both definitions apply: while she lived she bound her nine children to her and to each other with an emotional epoxy, one of whose major ingredients was a deep feeling for the sheltering, all-embracing family home.

She fostered a stronger sense of the line of descent from her side of a prolific family. My grandfather's forebears, even his immediate family, seemed to me remote and abstract in comparison. My grandmother's clan was a quintessentially WASP New York mercantile family of Scottish descent, so remarkably diligent in keeping track of itself that a fierce sense of the group prospered and continued. An in-law once described it as being not a family but a land mass, and an articulate member has an aerial view of it as "a spreading genealogical phenomenon."

In December 1977, I attended my first of the clan conclaves that seem to happen every twenty years or so. About 250 assorted relatives, many total strangers to each other, ate, drank, and alternated highland flings to the drone of bagpipes with snappy fox-trots to Cole Porter standards. This Scottish-American fantasy took place at the Connecticut country club founded by one convivial cousin on family land: the nucleus of the clubhouse had once been his father's stables. Besides those present, at least a hundred more kinsmen were scattered across the country.

After seeing this, who could take marriage and motherhood lightly? I thought to myself as I scanned the tables. For these hundreds of people were all the descendants of or were married to descendants of one couple, my grandmother's grandmother Elizabeth and her husband John. When those two wed in 1835, could they possibly have imagined the bunch of us, downing our *Filet Rossini aux truffes* and Château Bouscaut 1970, and speaking of them as the Progenitors? Would they have stepped up to the altar had they known what helter-skelter human ramifications would ensue?

The scale was not mathematically so overwhelming when my grandmother was a girl in Philadelphia, and the great progenitors were simply her grandmother, whom she often visited in New York and Newport, and a deceased grandfather. The family wasn't for her as it was for me sequential biological abstractions on a genealogical chart, William I, William II, William III, a pattern of so many Mendelian green and yellow peas.

Born in 1875, brought up as a proper Victorian young lady, and "finished" at Miss Masters' School, she expected, and so did her world, that she would marry shortly after "coming out" and would then get straight to work on extending the chart. Somehow her life didn't work out quite according to schedule, and she marked time for six years. Perhaps there was a tragic romance, a thwarted marriage, but the diaries for those years are missing. My speculations are based only on my own feverish matinee-audience imagination and the fact that though she was the first to admit she was no great beauty, she had many friends and was eminently marriageable. She did, however, mention that when she was eighteen one dancing partner had predicted she would never be a great success in society because she spoke her mind too plainly. To her credit she was amused, and agreed.

Whether romantic tragedy or plain-speaking was the cause of her lost years, by 1898 she knew she couldn't continue in suspended animation forever, passively waiting for life to begin. In Victorian America, life for a woman officially began with marriage.

"I suppose I can get along, but it's pretty hard work, and I must have more to do," she wrote. Using parental pull she scouted up a job as assistant to the head nurse at Babies Hospital in New York City, working under L. Emmet Holt, the Dr. Spock of his day. She was equipped for this position only by quiet desperation and a strong maternal instinct.

Of her incipient nursing career, she wrote to herself, "I wonder if this is to be my [life] work. I want it for second best certainly." There was no question what her first choice was (the alternative, spinsterhood, was hardly anyone's *choice!*), but she was realistic, even if she did lack an overwhelming sense of mission: "Sent off formal acceptance of position. . . . Ugh! I do hate to feel bound but I suppose it's good for me. Ugh! I've only promised Miss W. until June 1st [1899]. . . . I do trust I will be worth while."

By her June 1 deadline, her future had been settled, and she was happily committed to the life work she most wanted, a conventional marriage. Mr. T., as she called him throughout the early stages of a long-unresolved courtship, had gradually become Henry, and they finally decided to marry. She abandoned her short pediatric career (how could she imagine how much nursing of children she was destined to do?) and began to rehearse vaguely for housekeeping. Some of her early intimate dinners for two, often heavy on the legumes, must have given my grandfather pause, though he is not on record. As she recounted with wonderful pride: "When we came home *I* cooked supper for him and myself. Consommé, toast, omelet, baked beans, lima beans, tea, cut peaches, cookies."

During their engagement the youngish couple (he was twenty-five, she twenty-four) played house in her parents' summer home in Atlantic Highlands, New Jersey. "October 1899: Henry took 7 A.M. train [to New York, for he was a commuter even then]. I prepared a little breakfast, and we sat at table as though at our own home, till Henry got lonely and I came to his end."

Her dry runs in the less romantic aspects of household management were not overeagerly undertaken: "I've taken the housekeeping for a month or so to relieve Mother. I simply hated to do it, I'm ashamed to say." Throughout my grandmother's marriage, the day-to-day mechanics of housewifery (for which she was never really trained) were neither her forte nor her focus. She thrived on emotion, high domestic drama like childbirth or holidays; the ordinary drudgery of repetitive practical work or routine management tended to depress her.

Her wedding day, April 18, 1900, was gray and rainy, yet seemed "like an unusually vivid dream." On the honeymoon in Washington, D.C., the rain continued, but "it mattered not one bit." After only a few days alone, the newlyweds headed north by stages to Summit, where my grandfather's family home was, and where they would spend almost all thirty-seven years of their marriage. They did stop over at her parents' house in Philadelphia for the kind of postnuptial visit that is hardly the custom today. With her mother (who relinquished her own room to the couple) she gloated over the accumulation of wedding presents: "219 already!" But "leaving home was oh so hard," she wrote at the end of her stay, "and I ached all through my happiness."

The next parental visit, contiguous but longer, was to Avebury, the large and almost empty house in Summit belonging to my grandfather's recently widowed mother, who had the tact to depart for a six-week stay in New York the very day after the couple arrived. After all, they had not yet been married a week, and it was proper that they should be left to themselves in her house while they hunted for one of their own.

Avebury was in 1900, as it is now, an imposing, horizontally sprawling house in the Tudoresque early Queen Anne Revival style. Built in 1883, it featured gables galore, a stone first story, shingles above, half-timbering on the third story as well as in the generous entrance porch. When I prowled around the house in the autumn of 1977, I was aware that long ago it, like so many impractically large Victorian homes, had gone the parochial school route and was serving as the priests' residence for a Catholic prep school for boys. I approached the baronial oak door and rang the bell hesitantly. All I wanted was to ask permission to photograph, but I felt strangely embarrassed, somehow florid and uncelibate. Perhaps my grandmother, so recently married after such a long, uncertain wait, had felt somewhat the same sexual self-consciousness on that April evening in 1900 when she arrived at the same door to be greeted by a mother-in-law in black, a veritable Mother Superior.

The bride and groom were made to feel at home. "Our room is exquisite," wrote my grandmother, "all pink and green and white. Everyone is *so* good to me."

House hunting was easy; house finding was a much harder proposition than the two novices had expected. By May Grandmother, christened Jane but known through girlhood as

Jennie, began to sign herself J.A.T., branding herself with the amazing new monogram, the one on all the new linen and silver. By July the territorial imperative was growing exceeding strong in her. She desperately needed some space to call her own, and she took it where she found it. The day before the 4th she wrote: "*From experience*. If staying in husband's home after marriage, ask to be allowed to keep your room in order yourself. Works finely." She was still *playing* house, but not for long. The next day, her wish became reality, and she moved into her own home—a housewife at last.

"We entered our cottage at 20 Hillside Avenue, to stay I trust a long while." She was not, however, entirely on her own. Her mother's maid, one Rebecca, had been dispatched from Philadelphia to help her with the settling in, and both families contributed in other reassuring material ways. One entry in her diary reads: "*From experience*. Nicest thing a father can do for a daughter. Give her $2,000 for wedding present to furnish house and help over first stumbling blocks."

Shortly after moving in, J.A.T. had her first encounters with the dark daily reality that lurks beneath every household. In mid-July of 1900, Summit's inspector of drainage announced that "certain pipes" had to be fixed. Then, at the end of the month, "Rebecca went home—the last gangplank has been drawn in—I'm just a bit afraid." But there was an exciting distraction to contemplate after August 3 when she went to see Dr. H. He said "no doubt about something else . . . [I am] so happy!" Plain-speaking J.A.T., so frank with herself on many levels, could never bring herself to forgo euphemisms when discussing (1) sanitation and sewer pipes, (2) pregnancy, and (3) her own "worldly" ambitions, either social or literary. Three more natural areas of interest for any woman can hardly be imagined, but propriety decreed that they be "something else."

In a mere four months, more had happened to the girl who had feared becoming a gray spinster without a home to call her own than had actually occurred in the previous ten years. Suddenly and simultaneously she was wife, homemaker, mother-to-be. When life began, it really began! Nevertheless she was eager for still more experience, with all the euphoric self-confidence of a comfortably settled young American woman at the beginning of the twentieth century. She knew almost exactly what society expected of her.

That first house of hers was rented. It was what it was, an unpretentious period cottage that combined two prevailing vernacular styles in a kind of homey synthesis. There was a Queen Anne element—such as a picturesque window with diamond-shaped panes here, and there, detail inserted into the clapboard siding to suggest half-timbering. Stick Style accents appeared in the ample front porch or piazza, which was balustraded and had turned posts supporting its roof. The house was probably about twenty years old when the newlyweds signed their lease. J.A.T. could only furnish it, mildly redecorate, and try to learn to run it.

She had far more leeway to express herself in constructing a household ideology of her own, rather original but never really at odds with prevailing standards. In September of that first year of marriage, in one of the experiential pronouncements that punctuate her early diaries, she wrote: *"From experience. There must be a head to a house and the wife must make that headship a success by her tact and ready helpfulness in every thing."*

The subsidiary role of head chamberlain to the emperor was not really congenial to her, though it was certainly the standard pose endorsed by women of her class who were probably better cast for the part. After all, she had been a Presbyterian princess, the cosseted one, cushioned by an older and a younger brother, the favorite of her father, a man described by his peers as "kindly, upright, and honorable in all his dealings, a devoted father, and a Christian gentleman." Gentle he certainly was, and family lore has it that the worst epithet he ever applied to another man in that flamboyant era was to call the offender a skunk.

Given his nature, it was not surprising that he had determined to protect his treasure from unnecessary contact with the skunky side of life. I was skeptical when I first read in Arthur Calhoun's *A Social History of the American Family* that the ordinary woman of the period was "from her cradle to her grave . . . always half-protected even against herself. In her father's house and in her husband's home, she is shielded on every side from temptation and even from the knowledge of it." As Nora would have put it, she was treated as "papa's doll-child."

Calhoun cited as evidence the tale of a woman who once complained to the publishers that her *Ladies' Home Journal* was arriving mutilated, only to discover that her husband had been intercepting it and cutting out items he did not wish her to see. How incredible, I thought, even for a proper Victorian. Later I learned from my mother that J.A.T. had confided that her own father used to clip out of the Philadelphia newspapers anything that, as she quoted him, "might bring a frown to Jen's brow."

De Tocqueville had in 1835 noted the contrast between the high status of an American girl in her father's house and the constrictions of her life in her husband's. As he put it, "an unmarried daughter makes her father's house an abode of freedom and pleasure; the [wife] lives in the home of her husband as if it were a cloister." At the end of the century the situation remained essentially unchanged. The transition between being a blithe guest in one man's house and the mistress, shackled with responsibility, in another's was confusing to young women who didn't have much idea of who they were.

However sheltered she may have been, J.A.T. acknowledged with matter-of-factness a certain headstrong streak, or self-will, or just plain ego. She so described herself during a girlhood visit to her much-admired grandmother, who summered in Newport: "When I get here I do learn how dearly I love my own way and how much my happiness depends on my having it." But a woman of character at the turn of the century would set about suppressing such an inconvenient trait, and that is exactly what J.A.T. did, or tried to do, all her life long. Luckily she was unsuccessful.

Character—how dated a concept it seems now, but it was a commodity that continued to be peddled right through my girlhood. A woman of character didn't do a lot of things: she didn't indulge herself, didn't neglect her duties, didn't put off till tomorrow. Though a negative virtue, it was as socially useful as it was oppressive. Little furrows of character in one's nature were enough to cause chronic guilt when pleasure impinged on duty.

I've dwelled so long on biographical details of J.A.T. and her first year of marriage because the pattern she established then with the materials at hand was so typical of the life of the young middle-class wife in a period of social transition as significant for domestic life, for housewifery, as the 1970s are for us legatees. For the ordinary woman, marriage was not a matter of choice—one either married (success!) or didn't (failure!); careers were "second best." Daddy's girl was transformed into the mistress of her own house with little training and alarming suddenness. Extended families were intimately involved in the process of setting up housekeeping, and could be most support-ive (and openhanded). Home was to be kept pure, a spiritual sanctuary from an ugly world.

Throughout her marriage, J.A.T. maintained that early, officially deferential relationship to her husband as the head of the house while continuing to deal by herself with daily crises and an often troubling conflict within herself about her identity as a person, apart from gender and role. Her need for some means of self-expression, her "own way," was unquenchably strong. Though she was neither innovator nor rebel, she was an original. She was to find her deepest satisfactions conventional-ly in her children and in her house, whose symbolism was later to permeate her attempts to speak out publicly from a private platform.

Though her first little rented house was clearly only a prelude to the major work, J.A.T. practiced on it all her frustrated affections, as young couples rehearse for children by raising puppies. On her twenty-sixth birthday, having just returned from her first visit as a young matron to her grandmother's in

Newport, she wrote: "Dear little home! I do love it so, and we seem so glad to be back." Home again! a ritualistic announcement of hers was handed on through her children to her grandchildren, to me. I remember the muffled crunch of car tires on driveway gravel, my father's voice from the front seat coming through the dark and my sleepiness, "Home again."

The statement was one, in theory at least, my grandfather could have shouted, muttered, or gasped more often than anyone in his family. Week after week, year after year, he returned home nightly from a forty-mile round-trip commute from Summit to his downtown Manhattan office. He was a charter member of the first real generation of twentieth-century commuters; during his first decade of marriage two triumphal arches for his legions were under construction in New York: Pennsylvania Station (1906–10) and Grand Central Station (1903–13). His feminine counterpart, my grandmother, also served, in the first solid generation of wives left behind in houses, those ladies-in-waiting in suburban fastnesses.

Today, bored into acquiescence by the party-line rhetoric of pop lib, a media event, we accept a contemporary assumption that housewifery has always seemed exploitative and confining, that women have somehow always thought of themselves as having been left behind to do the dirty work. Hype and truth combine in this deeply influential cultural cliché.

Weary of it, and its attendant manic-depressive cycle in which indignation alternates with self-pity, I was refreshed to find evidence that once the inverse proposition prevailed. When my grandparents were young, the husband, not the wife, seemed the martyr. He was the poor devil who sacrificed himself for his family, and his wife snug at home soothed and protected him in simple gratitude for her good luck. Or so went that cliché, as documented both in J.A.T.'s diaries and in the popular journalism of the day, particularly the many issues of magazines like *House Beautiful* I have browsed through as if I were my grandmother, casually exposing myself to the assumptions she shared with her peers.

The ordinary upper-middle-class woman of the period seldom had any business experience, even vicariously through her father, and the new suburban wife had less and less traffic with the city to which each morning she dispatched the sacrificial ram. How could she appreciate the compensations of the power and the game? Or the convivial pleasures of a man's work in a man's distant world? As Louis Auchincloss acknowledges in *A Writer's Capital*, his father's office was "his fraternity, his club, almost in a way his church," but a naïve and loving wife, failing to understand this, would feel more guilt than envy. If her part in their joint enterprise was, as she saw it, to maintain the stable to which the tired workhorse hobbled home at the end of the day, by God she'd do it, she'd do her duty.

Auchincloss recalls his boyish awareness of the male share in the *haute bourgeois* division of labor: "I came to think of women as a privileged happy lot. With the right to sit home all day on sofas and telephone, and of men as poor slaves doomed to go downtown and do dull, soul-breaking things to support their families." When he met his father at the commuter train on sultry summer evenings, the boy felt "in the touch of his damp cheek that he was coming back to us, poor driven man, a hostage from the inexorable city that made a dull misery of the lives of men."

Though Auchincloss was writing here of a somewhat later period, he describes a long-established attitude, conventional among mothers and children, not only toward the father's work but also toward the very place where he performed it, "the inexorable city."

Kenneth Keniston in *All Our Children* describes the manner in which the American family had been redefined in the early 1800s by the more prosperous urban classes: "In their thinking—soon accepted as the ideal—the family became a special protected place, the repository of tender, pure, and generous feelings (embodied by the mother) and a bulwark and bastion against the raw, competitive, and selfish world of commerce (embodied by the father) that was then beginning to emerge as the nation industrialized. . . . To be sure an urban father had to venture into [the] streets to earn the family's living, and at times had to dirty his hands. But the pure wife-and-mother stayed at home, in part as a sign of the father's success, but also to protect her children from sin and temptation."

The innate American dislike of cities has been well chronicled. Some historians date its crystallization as the 1830s, the era of Andrew Jackson, when the direction of industrial urbanization became undeniably clear. As comprehensible villages and trading-center towns like Boston grew into true cities, they acquired such "European" characteristics as overcrowding, slums, social unrest, intensifying facts and fantasies of disease and corruption. The poor, especially immigrant foreigners, began to dominate, in numbers at least, the cities' population. Those people were strange and dangerous and could contaminate, and what could one do about their misery anyway? Long-lashed blue eyes were averted, cast down.

Families who could afford to do so had long since isolated themselves from infection in the exclusive areas of cities, such enclaves as Boston's Beacon Hill; but after the Civil War, when urban growing pains seemed increasingly unbearable, many of the privileged prescribed for themselves a private cure. They sought relief in a healthy regime well outside the city limits, in an idealized or at least sentimentalized country landscape. As never before, the rich traveled over the hills and far away, to weekend country seats in the English manner, to summer homes in fashionable resorts like Newport, or Lenox in Massachusetts, or eventually to the wilds beyond Summit, around Far Hills and Bernardsville (called in *Town and Country* "the Lenox of New Jersey"). Those who extracted the most income from the city were able to extract themselves as well, for long periods of time.

During the 1880s, McKim, Mead & White, architects, were building the Queen Anne or Shingle Style retreats characteristic of their early Good Old Summertime, or comparatively unpretentious, phase. Their work was much in demand in prepalatial Newport. And in Summit, my grandfather's parents in the same period and much the same scale were constructing their summer home, Avebury, as their refuge from "teeming" Victorian Brooklyn.

The flight from the city that had begun as an upper-class movement—part individualistic *sauve qui peut*, part simple hedonism—gradually extended itself into the middle class as well as into the middle distance, the quasi-country closer to the city. The pressure to evacuate increased on those dank and feverish creatures who still had not found their way to the light. Some gaudy copy appeared in the cause of converting the city mouse to the country.

In 1902 in an unsigned lead article, "Country Life for the City Man," *House Beautiful* described a specific group of the urban population: "These city men are thin and yellow or beer-bloated and unwholesome; their wives are weak-eyed and pale; their children puny." Did these pallid specimens represent the shame of the cities, foul tenements in slums? No, the yellow, the puny, and the pale were cited as examples of the newly rich, urban professional or business class, the fools who didn't know enough to get out of town.

Not only did the city pose hazards to health; it offered more subtle moral dangers, particularly to women. Its very architecture might corrupt. Hotels and boardinghouses, increasingly popular alternatives to expensive townhouses for young couples, threatened seriousness and the integrity of the family, according to the press, and the "modern flat," a racy idea imported from France and introduced in New York in 1869, was publicly denounced. In 1902 *House Beautiful* reported that "at a recent meeting of the architects of Chicago [a not disinterested group] a paper was read that caused widespread comment. Flats were denounced as unaesthetic and unsanitary, and as demoralizers of the women of the community, leading them into idleness and frivolity."

It fascinates me that American women in the decades around 1900 were so often portrayed as latent moral casualties. Females were prevented, it would seem, from slipping into the abyss only by good healthy doses of occupational therapy, such soul-savers as managing a house and servants or caring for children. On the one hand, women were viewed as wispily ethereal—or as Page Smith puts it in *Daughters of the Promised Land*, "delicate, spiritual creature[s] too fragile for the hard knocks of the world"—and on the other hand, they were suspected of being congenitally lusty, ripe for sensual temptation (nothing really roistering and heroic, just bonbons in bed, the lazy route to perdition). What was all this talk about character and duty? Brainwashing? Were American men really convinced that within a classical *huswif*, wound up for action with her shirtwaist starched and her sleeves rolled, lurked a barely contained alter ego, the *hussy*, a sybaritic courtesan in wrinkled red satin negligée, yawning?

If city flats and hotels symbolized moral flaccidity, the house in the nearby countryside represented an almost irresistible bouquet of virtues. A somewhat loaded description appeared in a 1903 issue of *House Beautiful*, reprinted from *Building Monthly*:

The suburban house differs from the country house and the city house chiefly in what it implies instead of what it is . . . [it] expresses freedom from restraint; it is the home of children; it means purer air; it means more room to move around in; it means gardens . . . an abiding sense of space, of freedom of movement, of ample air and sunlight, of a place to live in.

The writer has omitted only the cherubim and seraphim.

"The suburban house is a structure of good intentions," continued the article; it epitomizes progress, "affords the pleasantest kind of life, and is doing more to humanize humanity than any other single resource of civilization." As Teddy Roosevelt himself warned in 1905, "No piled-up wealth, no splendor of material growth, no brilliance of artistic development will permanently avail any people unless its homelife is healthy."

Considering the global or at least national importance attached to the home environment, it was no wonder that any man who was able was exhorted to ship his dear ones to the suburbs before it was too late. "Buy a small house in the country not too far from one's place of business, on a railroad or boat line that affords good transportation facilities," he was advised, "and keep wife and children in it for six months, while you yourself go out every Sunday if you cannot go and come every day." Many families, however, were understandably reluctant to divide themselves, leaving the men behind as hostages in Sodom. As the history of Summit testifies, "going and coming every day" grew increasingly common.

Summit's evolution from rural area to service stop for the Morris & Essex Railroad to vacation resort and on to the "prestige" suburb of today is a textbook example of the pattern of growth of the species. Known originally only as "the summit of the short hills," the area acquired a sudden identity when a local wheeler-dealer built a successful resort hotel there in 1858. After the Civil War the rate of growth accelerated as prosperous vacationers visited, grew to like the lay of the land, invested in it, and built single-family summer homes of their own. The township of Summit was formed in 1869.

Gradually the hour-long train ride and ferry to the city on the east side of the Hudson River began to seem less and less onerous. Families like my great-grandfather's became more committed to the quasi-rural existence. Summer houses turned into primary residences, weekenders became commuters. New houses rose that were designed expressly for year-round use. In 1899, the year before my grandparents settled there, the town was incorporated as a city. By 1900 the diurnal pattern that we who grew up in suburbs accepted as nature's plan, like sunrise and sunset, had developed. Let there be commuting! The divine order had sounded, and man had responded.

Fathers went into the city at dawn, returned in the evening, exhausted and demoralized, or so the myth went. They were then revived overnight in their happy, healthful, peaceable homes by devoted nurse/wives, and by morning had recouped their forces enough to be able to venture forth again. The emphasis fell more on the departure than on the return, on breakfast rather than supper. As a foreign observer once wrote,

"An Englishman is continually going home; an American is continually going to business." An American man, that is; for a suburban American woman, if her husband was a commuter, was continually not going anywhere at all. She was left to hold the fort. She was left to rule the children. By default the house was all hers. During the day.

In Summit this period at the end of one century and the beginning of another has been described by the local historical society as The Era of Expansive Homes—1870 to 1911. Avebury is cited as a landmark example, among other more imposing productions, distant relatives of the palaces and châteaux then being erected in Newport. The suburban extravaganzas were usually set in the middle of large open spaces that were destined to become today's school campuses or subdivision developments. Other representative but less ambitious houses built on smaller lots in Summit during the era ranged from unpresuming Stick Style cottages to the porchy later–Queen Annes near the center of town. As a child I mistakenly assumed that these dowdy houses had always been the lairs of piano teachers, realtors, and podiatrists, and had *always* been out of style, mustily declassé.

But large or small, unassuming or pretentious, Summit's houses of the period were indeed expansive, in that their common attitude toward suburban domestic life was euphoric. I imagine their owners sitting back in wicker rockers, smiling benignly as they enjoyed, along with lemonade and sugar cookies, the comforts of romanticized country life. Over them spread flora—the majestic shade trees they found on the mountaintop (of the short hills)—and before them scampered fauna, imported at first but soon locally produced, the starched children in white who happily played badminton on dappled lawns rolled out beneath the oaks and maples.

Some of the implications of the suburban house were less Thoreauvian. As Stanley Buder put it in an essay included in Philip C. Dolce's anthology *Suburbia* (1974), the families who chose suburban life were looking for a private environment, with extended personal space, interior and exterior. The famous suburban lawn seems to represent *turf* in the sense a city gang uses the word. "Family territoriality, rather than general use or public need, has been the primary concern."

House Beautiful, again quoting *Building Monthly*, commented with a rather cool, self-serving detachment:

> It is . . . an interesting circumstance that suburbs develop in classes. . . . There is no apparent advantage that would seem likely to accrue by mixing people of various means, or of distributing cheap houses among expensive ones.

No advantage, that is, to builders and realtors. In the suburban sheltered life, participants have usually lived comfortably with the handicap of myopia by focusing on property boundaries, town lines, possibly peering as far as the edge of the county, though smoke and blur obscured the view beyond. The concept of exclusivity, of pushing away or excluding all unpleasant realities, not just those of the city, slyly wove itself into the more humane longing for a better life, for simplicity, all that sun and all those flowers. It was to prove one of several snakes lurking in the gardens of a suburban Eden.

In the summer of 1904, J.A.T. was little concerned with broad social issues. In July my grandfather was desperately ill with typhoid fever, and she served as "second nurse." The next month she gave birth to my father, the third in a run of sons, and eight weeks after that she transferred her loyalty and her family to a newly leased house at 7 Norwood Avenue, still in Summit. According to a photograph pasted on the endpaper of a diary, the new place was larger than the old, but similarly picturesque, eclectic. It featured an open piazza across the front facade, and a three-story hexagonal tower on one corner. It would do, for a while.

"Every man or woman hopes one day to realize his or her particular dream of home," in 1902 wrote that regular *House Beautiful* contributor and suburban architect Joy Wheeler Dow. J.A.T. was no exception, and probably her appetite for a home to her own specifications was whetted by her parents' newly built seaside house in New Jersey's Atlantic Highlands. She loved its large gray-shingled hospitable presence, its many and ample porches, its view of the water. In contrast, she realized that simple physical space was becoming an important issue on Norwood Avenue, one that all the hexagonal towers in the world wouldn't solve.

"Any life must be dwarfing that presses human beings too close together," declared *House Beautiful*, inveighing against apartment life. For small human beings, house room was considered to be even more important: "Of the very greatest importance is the effect of the house, its material conditions and environment on the child, for whom a sound nervous organization is to possess a value past calculation. The crowded life is for him too stimulating for healthful development. He is a little savage, and he must have room."

At the Norwood Avenue encampment, three small savages were on the warpath. When J.A.T. discovered that a fourth was on the way, I suspect that it was her nervous organization, not theirs, that twanged. There was no longer any doubt—her second house would soon be outgrown.

One March day in 1906, J.A.T. recorded, hastily and rather baldly, a momentous occasion in her life: "Mr. Ware out for the day. Placed The House [note the capitals, as in The White House] and then Mr. W. and Henry saw contractors, etc., etc. Things are really started for Our House."

Because Summit's early building records have been destroyed by fire, I can only deduce that Mr. Ware was probably Arthur Ware, of the firm of James Ware & Sons in New York. In 1906, Arthur Ware was thirty and just back from three years in Paris at the Ecole des Beaux Arts. His father's firm had, among other "establishment" buildings and townhouses, designed the Madison Avenue Presbyterian Church (1900), and might well have been recommended to J.A.T. by the presbyters among her New York relatives.

Mr. Ware, later the architect of "many large and costly residences on Long Island, in Westchester County, N.Y., and New Jersey" who taught at the Columbia School of Architecture, would as a junior partner have been a natural choice for a commission on the scale of my grandparents' project, a family house large enough to accommodate a small population explosion but by no means a mansion or wildly expensive. Joy Wheeler Dow, who had designed a similar house built in Summit in 1904, estimated rather coyly, "To build a house like Silvergate one could spend $10,000 very easily." According to calculations published in *House Beautiful*, the cost of a house in a fashionable eastern suburb like Summit would have been around twenty cents a cubic foot.

The site of the new house was suspiciously near Avebury. Probably the land itself was a gift from J.A.T.'s mother-in-law, who had long been trying to find a buyer for her large and empty house. She found a prospect in Carlton Academy, and the deal was finally clinched in 1907, but not before my grandfather had acquired a large tract of land that must have been part of the family property, and several Avebury outbuildings had been dismantled, carted down the carriage road, and reconstructed behind J.A.T.'s new house. These were heirlooms or hand-me-downs of the larger and more permanent variety. It would take a mighty thief indeed to spirit away a hay barn.

During April of 1906 six giant trees with "immense trunks" were felled at The Place, "improving the effect immensely," while, as J.A.T. noted ironically, San Francisco itself was falling down. "Earthquake and fire," she continued, "and 300,000 people homeless. It was appalling." (Homelessness, rather than death or injury, was the disaster she fixed upon.) In May she noted the birth of another son and that the footings were all in for the house. In June she observed with a wry fatalism often acquired by homebuilders, "The House is ready for the carpenters who, however, are delayed by non-arrival of lumber—of course!" By July, "Henry says they are starting on the roof beams"; by August, "House coming on nicely. Most of the shingles on and first flooring down. It is coming out just as we wish."

Finally, on January 10, 1907, husband, wife, and four little boys "moved into the New House. Everything went beautifully and no one caught cold or anything." By May they were truly settled, and the mistress of Lindum mused contentedly, "We love the new home better every day and oh how we do appreciate the space, inside and out! It means everything for health and harmony to have plenty of space in which to be either together or apart as it suits each member of a large family."

J.A.T., who so dearly liked to have her own way, now had it at last. The structure that was to contain her life, her growing family, was completed, though the family was not. (Still to come were five—a first daughter, twin girls, and twin boys.) Her house was exactly to her taste. A fortunate member of a fortunate class at a comfortable time in American history, she had been able to transmit to an architect her own memories and yearnings and aspirations for him to measure and translate into wood and shingle.

A writer in a 1901 *House Beautiful* reflected: "I never see a house-plan, or an unfinished house, that I do not think of the possible unseen influences of which the plans of the house are the visible sign." The many and cumulative choices of design details in J.A.T.'s house were again and again echoes from her past, not an imagined past but a real one. The dominant resonances in it were from her own grandmother's summer world, the clarity and comfortable symmetry of the Georgian Colonial architecture of Newport, which had so often and so happily been visited by a young, romantic, impressionable girl.

There was no shadow of the dark picturesqueness of Avebury, with its roast-beef Tudor masculinity. Nor was there any obvious reflection from her parents' Philadelphia houses, although there are some similarities to their new place at the seashore. Though Henry dealt with Mr. Ware and the contractors—with the men—I think that J.A.T. dealt with Henry, and that the aesthetic decisions were mainly hers.

In a diary for 1903, the year after the death of her grandmother the Progenitor, J.A.T. pasted a photograph of that imposing, solid figure, seated in an open carriage, wearing

widow's black dress and bonnet. In charge of herself and her
family since 1876, when her husband died while on a fishing
trip, she had been a strong and apparently sympathetic presence in the lives of many of her grandchildren. Under her
picture, J.A.T. wrote, in the sentimental verse characteristic
both of the period and of her own literary style:

> Oh that I may each day—each hour,
> Look off to Grandma's Home
> And feel her rest, her strength, her peace
> And hear her voice say "Come."

Something said "Come" to me in the fall of 1977, and one
promising gold-and-blue September day I drove from Boston
down to Newport. I knew that my grandmother's grandmother's summer home had been on Washington Street, in the area
known as the Point. My treasure maps were a couple of
photographs, one reproduced in a family genealogy, another in
a small privately printed leaflet, "Grandma's Recipes" (full of
obsolete ingredients like *saleratus* and measurements like *a gill
of milk*).

In both views the house stood up straight, a solid and
unpretentious but enlarged variation of a bracketed cottage in
the style of A. J. Downing. It was probably built in the 1850s or
'60s, and featured a gloriously dusky porch the full width of the
front of the house, with vine-covered lattice and ornamental
posts supporting its roof, from which awnings extended. A
circular entrance drive was announced by low twin gateposts,
granite sentinels like obelisks, which were flanked by gentler
wooden fences draped with roses. The gates were wide open,
and down to the waters of Newport Bay stretched a long lawn.
(I was reminded of the photographs Alice Austen took of her
own garden, which sloped gently toward the Narrows, off
Staten Island.) In one picture, assorted small sportsmen seem
to be playing croquet.

The Point section of Newport was seriously settled in the
eighteenth century, when Georgian mansions like the Hunter

House (1748) were built, along with blocks of smaller clap-boarded dwellings for the more modest citizens of the town. After a post-Revolutionary decline, Newport revived in the middle of the nineteenth century, not as the commercial center it had once been but as a tourist resort, and, among others, the Progenitors were drawn to it as an escape hatch from New York.

As the older and more traditional section of the watering place, the Point continued to attract a more conservative, "cultured" group of summer residents than the flashy trendsetters on the other side of town. There, on Bellevue Avenue and environs, *nouveaux riches* showed off for each other with an ostentation that by the 1890s had attained a preposterous grandeur architecturally, with the erection of the Vanderbilt palaces, Marble House (1892), and The Breakers (1895).

People who lived on the Point had long since "arrived" and found such display both vulgar and comical. Tongues clucked along Washington Street with each new excess reported. My grandmother recorded one summer's joke, the news that one of the gilded matrons had decreed that the kindly Newport cow assigned to produce milk for her darling child should drink nothing but Poland Water.

Washington Street was then much as it is today, a straight allée along the bay, with houses on both the water and land sides. It was lined with trees whose branches touched overhead to form a green tunnel of shade—the most comforting kind of summer street. Along the sidewalks stretched contrasting permutations of the simple garden fence: some were board-and-batten partitions, with honeysuckle drooping over; some cast the shadow of their pattern of horizontal poles like a musical staff; some matched the elaborate balustrading on the roofs of their elegant parent houses. The fences of Washington Street created a cumulative effect of cozy privacy, of enclosed and prosperous lives. It was a street for slow strolling on a July day, for dreaming and absorbing associations: the fresh sea air, the sunlight, the flowers, the soothing, rhythmic regularity of clapboards and many-paned windows and classical doorways. Symmetry and languor. Peace.

The aura of the past combined with a present sense of being *hors de combat*, out of the frenetic "modern" competitiveness on the other side of town. A walk, a row in the bay in the little skiff *White Cap*, and back to Grandma's for her special molasses ginger cookies and iced tea in the shade of the porch. J.A.T. felt a sense of herself in Newport: it was Grandma's undivided attention and summer and the congenial presence of order and tradition. "Ah, when I get here I do learn how dearly I love my own way." Then, too, there was the living example of her grandmother as both kind and powerful, a woman beloved but essentially alone at the head of her own household.

Following clues in my photographs, I wandered up and down Washington Street under early autumn foliage like some lost Avon lady. The house I sought was clearly no longer standing, and in the likeliest site topographically a large, comparatively recent Carmelite retreat house stood fast. Puzzled, I consulted a lifelong Newporter at the Historical Society, and she confirmed that I'd indeed dowsed my way to the right spot, but not the right structure.

"I remember my father telling me how that house there was torn down by one of the owner's sons. John, I think," she recollected. "It was after his mother's death [in 1902]. He said no one else would ever live in his mother's house."

She scrutinized my pictures. "You know, I think those stone gateposts are still over there somewhere. Why don't you go back and look?"

I did, and *mirabile dictu!* there they were, the two obelisks, one for each Progenitor, still standing guard but undercover agents now, almost out of sight in the midst of the Carmelites' privet hedge. On the other side of the bushes was the bare outline of the old circular drive, transformed into the border of a rose bed, with a cement madonna in the center.

The story of the bereaved son's destruction of his mother's house may be apocryphal, but I like to believe in such an extravagant filial gesture. The Carmelite house does seem to me to be off-side in relationship to the gateposts, but some relatives think that there is a fragment of the original house encased somewhere in the interior of the newer structure.

I was content, however, merely to have found the gateposts, was as excited by the rediscovery of those two ordinary stones, still standing straight, as if I had found the house itself, its front door open. The stones are for me certifications of the legacy. They have survived to testify, and they are, for me, monumental.

 THREE

Home Feeling, 1907-1920

At the same time that my grandmother was moving toward "the architectural crystallization" of her own antecedents and aspirations, the writer/architect Joy Wheeler Dow, whose phrase I have just quoted, was expressing in both words and wood a philosophy remarkably similar to hers. Perhaps *philosophy* is too pretentious a term. *Feeling* or *attitude* would be better.

I met Joy Wheeler Dow initially in the pages of a 1902 *Town and Country*, a chance introduction on one of my strolls through turn-of-the-century women's magazines. The author of many articles and of an enormously influential book, *American Renaissance: A Review of Domestic Architecture*, Dow was as well—and I discovered this coincidence later with the unholy glee of someone who suddenly finds that two of her best friends are lovers—the designer of a number of the so-called Expansive Homes in Summit and other stalwart northern New Jersey suburbs, such properly christened establishments as Kingdor, Eastover, Silvergate, Bow-Marchioness Cottage. With another throw of the dice, Joy Wheeler Dow, instead of Mr. Ware, might well have been J.A.T.'s choice as her architect. Certainly some of Dow's houses belonged to acquaintances in her circle, with its rather short diameter. My own closest direct encounter took place in the architect's faithful reproduction of a Colonial meeting house, Summit's All Souls in the East, the chaste setting of my brief flirtation at sixteen with Unitarianism.

Crotchety and emotional, middlebrow, outspoken, with "a sprightly style" of writing, elitist if not downright snobbish, supremely self-confident, Joy Wheeler Dow rose up from the magazine pages as a vision of the individualistic, bluestocking headmistress types I had known at the Kent Place School (for Girls), or at Smith College (for Women), or in Cambridge, where they strode down Brattle Street, "the mighty maidens," as Helen Howe categorized them in *The Gentle Americans*. Dow appeared to me in the full regalia of the Three-Name Lady, that maritally noncommittal usage popular among women of presence long before the invention of Ms. as a no-strings identification. There were such triple threats as Harriet Beecher Stowe, Julia Ward Howe, Elizabeth Cady Stanton, Olive Tisdale Hobart, Frances Parkinson Keyes— even, *reductio ad absurdum*, Olive Higgins Prouty and Edna Wallace Hopper (respectively, the author of *Stella Dallas* and the originator of the White Clay Pack, both of whom figured large in afternoon radio, i.e. soap opera, during my mid-century childhood).

J.A.T. was, for me, the archetype. When she spelled out with a flourish her full moniker, I as her namesake felt inadequate, a potential forger. How could I ever sign her name as if it were mine? I stashed away my middle name until I might somehow grow into it, when I too would wear navy blue georgette with white organdy ruching at the neck, a cameo brooch, sensible Enna Jettick oxfords with cuban heels, and would sit at the head of a dinner table, serving up conversation and lamb chops dressed in frilled paper panties and escorted by *petit pois* (her life-enhancing designation for the gray-green canned peas we Birdseye beneficiaries now disdain).

It was the architectural historian James O'Gorman who passed on to me his intuition that Joy Wheeler Dow was no lady, was not even a woman. "Why," I asked, "would an architect at the turn of the century choose a woman's name as a pseudonym? That would be like pretending to be black in 1851." O'Gorman was firm: "The voice just sounds like a man, not a woman. That's all."

And he was right. Further research revealed that Joy, as in Joyce Kilmer, was in 1861 born undeniably male, a condition he retained unaltered by art or nature until his death in 1937. His defection from the ranks of the Three-Name Ladies came as no real shock, only a mild schematic disappointment for the writer about women and houses. I realized how very few women were practicing architects during those early decades of the century. Three-named pioneers like Minerva Parker Nichols of Philadelphia, Marian Mahony Griffin, who was handmaiden to Frank Lloyd Wright in Chicago, and Lois Lilley Howe in Cambridge were among the exceptions.

As summarized by Judith Paine in *Women in American Architecture: A Historic and Contemporary Perspective* (1976), the obstacles, psychological, cultural, and practical, that stood in the way of independent achievement by women in the profession were daunting, to say the least. She quotes one contemporary journal that advised women architects to stick to interior detail such as designing "artistic" furniture, decorating mantels and inglenooks, rearranging stairways. Those who didn't limit themselves to such needlepoint often settled for the role of superdraftsman or amanuensis, locking themselves into an office rather than into a domestic interior. An up-front character like Julia Morgan was an exception, almost as remarkable as William Randolph Hearst's estate, San Simeon, her most famous but apparently least representative work.

Housewives like J.A.T. may have exerted considerable influence on the male population—financing husbands and creating architects in particular. They may have resorted to the hammerlock methods of a strong-arming Alva Vanderbilt, she of Marble House in Newport, or may have chosen the more subtle manipulations perhaps practiced by my grandmother. But driving force or meandering indirection, both techniques were approaches to power. In the old days the woman of the house was rarely in frank and open control, and her influence, like the average female architect's, was typically confined to interior rather than exterior matters, to rooms rather than facades or plans. Jill was to rearrange and decorate the house that Jack built. Or, to labor my central metaphor, Papa made the doll house and put it under the Christmas tree; his doll-wife cut scraps of fabric into curtains and tacked them up inside; their daughter watched.

There were some minor exceptions among nonprofessionals. In the early 1900s *House Beautiful* would occasionally run special articles on houses designed expressly for, and sometimes by, women living alone. These solitaries tended to be affluent spinsters of an artistic bent, photographers or painters, who often commissioned small artsy-craftsy bungalows in the no-nonsense Craftsman style. Less frequently the magazine featured houses designed by married women who thought of themselves as working in the tradition of Thomas Jefferson the gentleman amateur, who had "done so well" with Monticello. Unfortunately, these lady amateurs were usually more ambitious than talented, and proceeded with solid financing but minimal architectural training.

For example, Mrs. G. H. Taylor of Chicago studied for a whole year at the Chicago Art Institute "in order to fit herself for the task of housebuilding," and then in 1905 inflicted on her family a "stately drawing room" (in the house she designed) whose dimensions were twelve by thirty-eight feet, roughly the size and shape of a Greyhound bus.

The romantic Mrs. Knowlton Mixer designed her house on the outskirts of Buffalo with Tudor England in mind, and to insure the desired effect stopped at nothing. She even "drew her own plans, designed the interior woodwork, prepared the stains for the walls, and superintended the making of much of the furniture." Except for two reading lights, her house was illuminated solely by candles.

House Beautiful was tolerant of the work of these female phenomena, apparently as amused by them as by talking hens. So what if the biddies weren't great conversationalists, or if Mrs. Mixer produced an eerie Great Hall where Anne Boleyn might well have felt at home? "When a woman achieves [a good] result, it is a matter of remark, for building is not a feminine talent," the journalist covering her work patronizingly explained. "Many women can draw plans, but few can draw elevations that fit the plans—and few women, when it comes down to the fine point, want to be responsible for the exact location of even one closet."

In 1904—the year Mrs. Mixer's Olde English fantasy near Lake Erie was presented to the world, and Frank Lloyd Wright was designing the Larkin Building for nearby downtown Buffalo, and my father was born in a bedroom in J.A.T.'s first rented house—Joy Wheeler Dow's *American Renaissance* was published.

"The book is well worth reading," wrote one reviewer in *Architectural Record*, "and we are convinced that it will be read in many places where the sterner historical material has not yet penetrated." Readers of *House Beautiful* and other popular magazines who might not have seen the book itself were treated to excerpts and adaptations of Dow's basic message: *architecture is history expressed in blocks,* and *the historical note is the measure of the successful architectural style.*

Like Mrs. Mixer, Dow turned back to what he called "the Anglo-Saxon tradition" for the truly authoritative historical note. For him it was a single tone, in perfect pitch, that resonated from ancestral sources through American descendants of Englishmen. "No nation has studied homebuilding so persistently and long as the English, and consequently none has arrived at anything like such general excellence," Dow argued. "Being largely descendants of English colonists, and speaking the English language, our traditions and associations cannot get along half so well with any other architecture."

Like the more blinkered of his suburban clients and readers, Dow never indulged in the broad sociological view. For him, the non-Anglo-Saxon immigrations of the nineteenth century might as well never have occurred.

Unlike Mrs. Mixer, Dow was not drawn primarily to half-timbered Tudor as the quintessential English style, though he did endorse and use it occasionally. He was fond of the small Cotswold cottage, but he was passionate on the subject of the large Georgian house, the embodiment as he saw it of the legacy of classical Greece and Rome transmitted through the Italian Renaissance "Florentine Clearing House" of Palladio and his contemporaries to London and to architects like Christopher Wren, James Gibbs, and Inigo Jones. Both humble cottage and proud mansion had been translated into their American versions in the seventeenth and eighteenth centuries. They were known popularly by the catchall term *Colonial*.

Dow's own designation for the simpler early American houses of the 1600s and early 1700s was Witch-Colonial, his favorite examples the small and puritanically chaste wooden dwellings of Salem, Ipswich, and Danvers, Massachusetts. In writing of the more aristocratic, larger showpieces of the latter eighteenth century, including such elaborate Virginia plantations as Shirley, Brandon, and Westover, he simply adopted the prevailing terminology, referring to them as Georgian or Georgian Colonial.

He was always quick to jump to the defense of Colonial builders whose dependence on English precedents he feared might open them to charges of plagiarism. After all, he argued, the English had themselves drawn upon Italian Renaissance models, which were in turn based on classical prototypes, which were of course perfection, and who can do better than perfection?

"It is extremely doubtful if our American ancestors were ever guilty of premeditated deception. Their material was an honest material: it had to be fashioned in some way, why not after the Renaissance?" (Certainly American Indian "architecture" was unlikely to appeal to the colonist, and what other indigenous models were there for adaptation?) Besides, he added, "Time and history have thrown a glamour over all this . . . and established its right of succession with a hall-mark."

The succession had been interrupted, however, by the nineteenth century, when authentic Colonial houses were fashion's exiles, unbelievable as it may seem now to members of the National Trust for Historic Preservation. Often ramshackle and tumbledown, if not in real ruins, they had become disregarded relics.

Dow, in chronicling the long decades of the Colonial eclipse, was generous enough to admit the validity of the houses of the "transitional" period, 1800–1829. In fact, he doted on Federal mansions, such as Samuel McIntire's in Salem, with their graceful and refined attenuation of Georgian precedents, and he appreciated that the Greek Revival buildings dignifying the landscape through the East, the South, and well into the Midwest did embody classical proportions and details.

Andrew Jackson's inauguration in 1829 was to him "the red flag signal of license for all the vast output of American Jacobin architecture." It unleashed "rabid democracy," whipped up new popular obsessions with such mad "architectural abominations" as improvised and inauthentic versions of foreign imports, the Italianate villa or the mansarded French townhouse. "Young America was not emancipated at all," he spluttered. "Another master was unrelenting expediency, who forthwith usurped the throne of deposed art."

In his jaundiced view, post–Civil War prosperity only encouraged new excesses of bad taste. The 1860s demonstrated, in various elaborate Gothicisms, the "ephemeral and perverted influence of John Ruskin." The seventies saw our "architectural Reign of Terror," when *nouveaux riches*, uneducated to cope tastefully with the money that had "as magic, rolled up while they slept," financed swashbuckling "Scaramouches," topped with the abominable cupola, crusted with jigsaw fancywork or metal lace. (Scarlett O'Hara Butler's Atlanta house is a case in point, and with Tara in her background she should have known better.)

Dow ranted on. Alumni of the Ecole des Beaux Arts had graduated from a "school of material art to which there is no spiritual side" at all. "Newport, with its miserable crowding and elbowing of American pretentiousness," represented the sorry spectacle of the "modern invention type of architecture," which was a "product of the modern brain disenfranchised from all considerations of precedent." No one any longer seemed to regard "veneration for ancestors, and what ancestors knew" as an American virtue.

Ah, these were dark days indeed, but not pitch black, for at least one fashionable mode, the Queen Anne of the early 1880s, seemed to "incorporate the vital spark of Anglo-Saxon home feeling," a quality Dow found sadly lacking in another contemporary genre, Richardsonian Romanesque.

Then, too, public interest in the long-ignored "old-fashioned houses" had been aroused by models constructed for display at the 1876 Centennial Exhibition in Philadelphia. From that time on, according to Dow, "the colonial germ . . . seems to have been in the air and sporadic throughout the country." The small flicker that Dow saw glimmering in American Queen Anne designs blazed up into the white heat of the Colonial Revival. Among its earliest examples were those built in Newport by McKim, Mead & White, who had been converted to Colonialism by a pilgrimage through New England they took together in 1877. In the eighties they made the most of various Georgian details. Dow rejoiced in such right thinking, as he deplored the "efflorescence of commercialism" that for so long had distorted the national heritage.

By the turn of the century, according to John Burchard and Albert Bush-Brown in *The Architecture of America* (1961), "the fashion for domestic Georgian was so pronounced . . . that it threatened to become a national style for domestic architecture and for some institutions as well. . . . *American Renaissance* [documented] the resurgence of good Georgian design throughout the country but especially in New England."

Joy Wheeler Dow, documentarian and practitioner, happily monitored thermometer and seismograph. "Perhaps I am a bit over-sanguine and imaginative, but I fancy I am conscious of the distant detonations of an undercurrent at the beginning of the twentieth century ultimately to come to the surface and overcome the noise of commercialism," he wrote at the time. Another magazine writer concurred, adding that "this harking back to old things is in the main a healthy movement; the people of the U.S. worshipped for too long the god of new things, and for a good many years the highest praise that could be given to anything was to say it was absolutely up-to-date." Dow may not have designed J.A.T.'s house, but he would surely have admired it, embodying as it did both ancestral models and a modified Georgian style. Besides, the finished house was so like his own work as an architect, and as more than one reviewer acidly noted, he was a great fan of that. He featured as illustrations in his magazine articles many antique examples and his own contemporary adaptations of them that shared Lindum's basic plan, its degree of fidelity to decorative details in the originals, its general mood of dignified informality, friendliness. Symmetrical with classical ornamentation, in plan generally faithful to center-hall Georgian great-uncles such as the Hancock House (1737) in Boston and the Hunter House (1748) in Newport, to name only two, Lindum was respectful and pulled none of what Dow disdained as "stunts," unless a bay window or a porch or some other minor adjustment might be so considered.

When I first entered Lindum's neatly centered front door, my sense of familiarity derived not just from the anecdotal legends I'd absorbed but also from the fact that I found myself in space exactly where I thought I'd be, in a large central stair hall that bisected the house. Living room and library opened off it to the left, just as they should, and front dining room and rear kitchen-pantry area obediently occupied themselves on the right. We've all stood at the bottom of stairs like Lindum's, in historic houses or their reasonable facsimiles, or in imagination, in movies (watching Katharine Hepburn run down them toward us, or perhaps a spunky Bette Davis groping her way up them en route to her dark victory). Dow once captioned a photograph of an almost identical hall and stairs "the vista that Americans are preferring more and more at their homecomings." Steps rise to a single landing, dramatized with a large window, preferably Palladian, at the top. The sun streams into the heart of the house.

The symmetry of Lindum's first floor, hall flanked on either side by pairs of rooms, repeated itself with slight variations on the second and third stories. On the ground level, however, a room-sized, one-story roofed porch wing lay beyond French doors opening off the side wall of the living room, typical sunporch usage, a kind of extrusion from the body of the house.

If one were to slice down through the house from side to side, the front section, one room deep and three floors high, would be identical to the classical doll's house, the traditional one with shutters and dormers that lucky ten-year-old girls fussed with in the 1930s and '40s.

When J.A.T. reigned in Lindum, certain rooms were more charged emotionally than others. Her eternal vigilance preserved the library as a retreat inviolate, my grandfather's sacred "den." During his daytime absence a good child might be admitted for the privilege of reading quietly alone, or upon his return an especially bad child might be dispatched there to answer for some epic crime. Otherwise the den was his alone, the most private room in the house. (When nine children had access, even bathrooms tended to resemble public facilities in railroad terminals.)

Nightly she hustled my grandfather into his den, as into an iron lung. The man was neither a tyrant nor so sensitive that he needed the silence of Proust's cork-lined room; I am suspicious that her motives in segregating him from the rest of the family were only partially protective of him. Her own pride may have demanded that he not witness chaos until she had subdued it. When her house was in order, children calmed, dinner ready to be served, then the curtain would go up.

The period's ideal of the exclusively masculine preserve found expression not only in dens at home but also in homes-away-from-home: the gentleman's club in the city, the golf or country club in the suburbs, and the club car on the commuter railroad that shuttled between town and country. The Lackawanna's Billion Dollar Express featured a club car of which my grandfather was a member. One row of wicker "Bar Harbour" chairs ran the length of the car, while facing it was another row of dark leather lounge chairs, the confrontation of styles representing, I suppose, the country versus the town. The car featured a "café" (i.e., bar) and a separate compartment for "wives and daughters."

My grandmother's operational headquarters, her office, was neither private nor exactly a room. At the rear of the second-floor hall, where the large window sent light rolling down the front stairs, J.A.T. set up her command post, there at the hot center of the house. She had a desk and chair, eventually a telephone and typewriter, and her own paraphernalia, such as envelopes for paying household bills from the monthly allotment her husband gave her, and a lifelong supply of Dennison bird and flower stickers, the trademark she stuck on all bland expanses—calendars, notebooks, birthday cards.

From her lookout window, she could oversee the coasting hill, the various outbuildings, the sandbox. Sometimes she smiled down from on high, a guardian angel, and other times she glowered like a guard in a penitentiary watchtower. She was positioned to be a dispatcher ("Jim dear, go find Fred, please, and see if he has his arctics on"); a receptionist for those entering either the front door or one at the rear of the hall ("Oh, Henry, you're home. I hope you're not *too* tired tonight"). She was communications central, a captain on the bridge, an executive in the household. And her post was perhaps the most public space in the house.

In the busiest, child-dominated years, she had no room of her own. The kitchen area was the servants' domain; my grandfather had his den, and shared her bedroom; the remaining bedrooms were amply stocked dormitories or a nursery-playroom, or reserved for guest or live-in maid. (Most of her staff lived elsewhere, in their own homes.) The living and dining rooms were common ceremonial areas for the whole family, for

meals and ritual gatherings and seasonal extravaganzas like
Christmas. When a child was sick (and some child was, it
seemed, always at least mildly indisposed) and J.A.T. wanted
to stay on guard as night nurse, she would turn on the light in a
large linen closet in the second-floor hall and sit in there
reading, one ear cocked, literally closeted.

The welfare of children, not only their physical but their
spiritual "upbuilding," was necessarily the focus of daily life in
J.A.T.'s house. Just containing the moiling activity of such a
large and energetic group—the "circus" one aunt described to
me—seemed to rule out an adult social life that included both
husband and wife, privacy for all but the majority of one, and
much spontaneous experience of or intense interest in the wide
world outside, except as an act of will, part of one's duty to
"keep up." Worldly concerns were desirable luxuries, but
luxuries nonetheless. A woman of character denied herself such
nonessentials and confined herself to her clear duty at home—in
fact, confined herself in her home, alone. Beginning in the late
eighteenth century, middle-class American men and women,
attempting to imitate the forms of British society, increasingly
segregated themselves in a way sophisticated Europeans eventually found incomprehensible. The Countess Russell, writing
for *Town and Country* in 1904, announced that no English
woman would consent to her man "leaving her alone and going
off to some amusement that she could not share." My grandmother not only consented but actually encouraged her husband to spend his holidays swatting golf balls at the Canoe
Brook Country Club. I think she viewed the club as a kind of
adjunct to the home, not a single-family but a multi-family
facility, a complement to the den and its restorative privacy.
Never is there a hint that she felt left out, excluded.

When Joy Wheeler Dow defined architecture as "*history*
expressed in blocks," he might well have added the corollary
that domestic architecture is also "*the family* expressed in
blocks," for that is what he believed. He failed to note,
however, that the structure of the idealized family here had

diverged from its "Anglo-Saxon" models in ways that the structure of the family's house had not. And he seemed oblivious to his own role as an advocate of a fashionable style when he made such proclamations as this in 1911: "Whoever designs a cottage that expresses generations of family devotion and sacrifice, creates successful domestic architecture; while he who follows fashion or tries to invent something, simply strays farther from his aim."

In America, in the first decades of this century, acceptable sacrificial traditions included "devoted mothers watching like lynxes over their offspring; devoted wives looking after the comforts of their liege lords and breadwinners as though they were racehorses; and devoted fathers going through fire and water daily that the inmates of the cottage may remain safe and snug at home." I must admit that I find it easier to think of my grandmother as a lynx than to imagine my solid, circumspect grandfather as a racehorse, but the stereotypes and the devotion ring true.

Dow exhorted architects to remember that clients had "spiritual needs as well as physical ones," and that "the home one builds must mean something besides artistic and engineering skill." Americans are "starving for a little spirituality in the home architecture," he maintained, and for him the equivalent of the architect's aesthetic legacy was the client's inheritance from previous generations of his family of a tradition of the "ethics of the home atmosphere."

According to Dow, the person of Anglo-Saxon descent was genetically equipped to be a particularly "home-loving creature," just as, I suppose, evolution has provided the sloth with three toes in order to be a particularly tree-hanging creature. His variant of Anglophilia crops up elsewhere in popular journalism of the period. For example, Mary Hinman Abel, writing for *House Beautiful* in opposition to the apartment house, quoted from *Anglo-Saxon Superiority*, the work of one Monsieur Desmoulins, who attributed the achievements of the breed to "the independence and privacy of their home life, where are produced men and women strong in themselves, rather than taught to lean on each other, as in the more socialistic communities."

As I remember my English history from the seventh grade, Hengist and Horsa and other associated Angles, Saxons, and Jutes were big movers and shakers in architectural demolition rather than preservation; their talents were for sacking and looting and bashing in Roman installations. These barbarians can hardly be described as having been Keepers of the Flame of Classicism, nor were they exactly home-loving. "Anglo-Saxon" in Dow's context must be shorthand for White Anglo-Saxon Protestant, referring to that prosperous class whose home-loving instincts were at the turn of this century expressed by neocolonizing the suburbs, by constructing "independent and private" single-family homes. A later critic, Henry-Russell Hitchcock, would use a less loaded term: "the Anglo-American house."

Dow was actually more egalitarian than his rhetoric suggests. He even proposed that those without a suitable lineage just pretend, make up some acceptable spiritual ancestors to populate dreams of home, and then start building. "By subtle architectonic expression," he wrote, a house can give the impression that its owner—be he an orphaned, first-generation Polish-American or an eighth-generation Carter of Virginia— "possessed once upon a time two good parents, four grandparents, eight great-grandparents, and so on; that *bienséance* and family order have flourished in his line from time immemorial— that there were no black sheep to make him ashamed—and that he has inherited heirlooms, portraits, miniatures, pictures, and all rare volumes."

His endorsement of the self-made family and instant heritage was expressed on another level by the growing business in historical reproductions, not only of houses but also of home furnishings that capitalized on this taste for ancestry, real or imagined. Home feeling—Anglo-Saxon, American, sentimental, hoked-up, or authentic—was to prove, as Dow once predicted, "no ephemeral fad of the American, but a great national trend . . . the apotheosis of home that is irresistible." When Dow referred dreamily to the "delicious sense of Anglo-Saxon home restfulness that comes to charitable people under the influence of some charming old wooden and brick dwelling houses once upon a time erected in New England," he was indulging in a romanticism far removed from any real social, ethnic, or historical issues. He was musing on the relationship between individual imagination and architectural style, between observer and object, actor and set. He was trying to define "something which shapes itself unconsciously to the mind—something which will neither be coerced nor cajoled, but obeyed," and he concluded that "style is the master, and we are but the students ever observing, listening, trying to understand, waiting for our cue, and finally speaking our lines, according to the histrionic ability there is in each of us, for style is eminently dramatic." He might well have been describing the passive role that many American women assumed for themselves, on stage in their homes, as the century unrolled.

J.A.T. consistently thought of her house in dramatic terms: it brimmed over with home feeling. Lindum was hardly the "laboratory of rational planning" that some forward-looking innovators were envisioning during the period. If she had little ambition to intellectualize her environment, she had even less compulsion to become a chatelaine, a great hostess in a small castle. Home feeling was for her a composite of stylistic nostalgia, a taste for simplicity, and a need for a sense of place. Above all, she valued the security she thought of as coziness. As a young girl traveling abroad in the 1890s, after paying a Henry Jamesian call on the American ambassador to Rome and his wife, she wrote in her diary, "But oh I felt so sorry for them . . . in their magnificent palace. It all seemed so grand and imposing and overpowering. Perhaps they are happy but I'm sure from her face, her manner, that she often longs for her beautiful broad acres at Bryn Mawr, and the dear roomy old house where they could be so very much at home. No, no, no, I do not long for a palace. A home is all I care for."

She would always write about her home in diminutives, as if

speaking of one of her children: "So cozy and happy in this precious little house" or "I enjoyed today, cozily having my Christmaswork and my tea in our dear *dear* sunny parlor." The occasions she treasured were the brief, quiet pauses in her day, the moments of friendly intimacy, miniatures of domestic life to be worn like a locket: "Must write down such a pleasant breakfast. Delicious coffee, fishcakes, scrambled eggs and feather-light biscuits. Henry reading bits of news from the paper. Mrs. V. doing upstairs work, and children blissfully happy with Violet in parlor. A mother's time of joy—and nice to call to mind."

One contemporary magazine that paralleled J.A.T.'s unpretentious tastes in the home was *House Beautiful*, whose subtitle after July 1904 was "The Only Magazine in America Devoted to Simplicity, Economy, and Appropriateness in Home Decoration and Furnishing." As early as 1902 it had come out against Victorian excess, advising "a life free from craven care, but full of incident—not more stuffed chairs and more cushions, and more carpets and gas, and more dainty meat and drink, and therewithal more and sharper differences between class and class." The author of those words, Mrs. Henry Wade Rogers, then posed a hard question: "Is there a real desire for the simple life, a longing 'to double the soul's leisure by having its wants' or is it but a pose, a mood of our complex life? . . . Surely the revived interest in simpler architecture, and in simple and artistic household furnishings marks the beginning of a better time."

Mrs. Rogers blamed women themselves for complicating their own lives, and though her view of women's nature is a little harsh, she does have a point: "Women too often give their precious hours and efforts unstintedly and unwisely, because they are naturally long-suffering, lack courage and well-defined purpose . . . they succeed in burying themselves under trivial obligations and possessions. . . . Most women need courage and purpose for the simplification of life. . . . Life is simpler for men than for women because [men] must and will have it so."

She concluded her excoriation with a quotation from a man:

"The present civilization is harder on women than on men, and riches are harder on her than poverty." In many ways twentieth-century American prosperity was to support her claim. We women in houses were to take an inordinately long time to recognize "human limitations" and to question the validity of a snowballing accumulation of both possessions and duties. Later in life, J.A.T. pasted in her diary a plucky little verse from the literature of simplicity and coziness. Clipped from *The Mother's Magazine*, written by the tripartite Florence Jones Hadley, the poem represents some of the corny excesses of high home feeling:

> A homekeeper am I: this is my task
> To make one little spot all snug and warm,
> Where those so bruised and beaten by the day
> May find a refuge from the night and storm.

But it also explains the psychic rewards of what might otherwise seem a puzzling acceptance of a limited life.

> Gladly I serve—love makes the serving sweet;
> I feel no load—love makes the burden light;
> A happy keeper I of home and hearts—
> Serving I reign—a queen by love's own right.

The message is about power: the monarch of a small principality is nonetheless a monarch. In the best of times J.A.T. could relax upon a throne whose legitimacy was unquestioned. When Elizabeth I's kingdom was secure, the arts did flourish.

"The architecture of the home begins where the architecture of the house ends," and "by common consent . . . woman is preeminently the architect of the home." Or so a 1904 article in *House Beautiful* assigned responsibility for what was widely regarded as an art. "The Art of Everyday Living" in 1910 stated that "the home offers a woman her closest chance of artistic expression," and that any woman who neglected it for frivolous efforts of a showy sort, such as lessons in hammering brass, was foolishly oblivious to what the commonplace offered as the true material of art. "Sunlight and firelight, two of the most magically artistic things in the world, are always at service to the home," and to the adornment of "woman's sphere . . . an atmosphere." Dow himself pontificated that, "animal comfort once attained" the numerous spiritual and ethical considerations involved in the building of a home (as distinct from a house) belonged purely to the realm of art.

Lindum was certainly J.A.T.'s primary medium of self-expression, and she spent herself extravagantly in producing its pageants and legends, in giving it a dramatic identity. One of her first moves was to christen the house. The turn of the century, when so much willed sentiment fueled the hearths of home feeling, was the great era of house-naming, just as development-naming would represent the commercial spirit of the 1950s, with its raw Royal Crest Estates and Tudor Highlands.

Her husband's family had turned for the name of its Summit house to the English village of Avebury, which was as quaint and Anglo-Saxon as could be, and was thought to be the ancestral home. For reasons unclear to me, J.A.T. turned elsewhere in England, to Lincoln, which its early Roman occupiers had called *Lindum Colonia*. Somehow the Latin name connoted to her "Truth, Strength, Kindness and Love." Perhaps unconsciously she was drawing on the character of another Lincoln—Abraham Lincoln—whom she deeply admired and whose portrait I remember seeing in a place of honor in her house.

As her children grew in number and size, J.A.T. continued to provide them with dramatic identities for not only the house but also for the land and the outbuildings on it—her support space, if you will. One section of woods was called Jerusalem Hill (and shall we build Jerusalem in New Jersey's green and pleasant land?), and the brick gateposts in front of the house formed a famous garrison, Fort Bedford.

The full voltage of J.A.T.'s dramatic energies was reserved

for the staging of ritualized celebrations. Christmas was a heyday of home feeling, with high intensity for all, except perhaps my grandfather, whose role often seemed to be that of a kindly, dignified character actor, who carved the roast and read aloud the Christmas story to family and servants assembled in the dining room.

Christmas 1914 was perhaps J.A.T.'s classic celebration. All nine children had been born, and although World War I had started abroad, or perhaps because of that, Lindum seemed especially fortunate, especially cozy and sheltered. My grandmother was thirty-nine when she wrote, with the delight of a ten-year-old, of that epochal Christmas:

Early, early I sneaked down with each little girl first (each took away one gift), then the boys. When we opened the doors of the sitting room the light was dim, but we could see the mantel simply smothered in bulgy stockings and extra toys. On the other side the room was a huge pile of great papercovered parcels just as they came by express. Then as we looked through to the open French doors beyond we saw a glimmering dazzle and much greenness, for The Tree stood in the glass-enclosed piazza and around it were the usual smaller evergreens.

The door was hung with old tinsel in festoons and two red paper bells dropped on each side. The lamp was hidden behind the tree, and among the branches beside all the dangling dazzles were half a dozen tiny electric lights. Oh, it was exquisite—and for the first time I partly carried out the dream I've always had of going in a wood till the sparkles shot towards me through the trees, and I knew I had found Christmas.

But sometimes J.A.T. did feel she had lost her way, and her diaries chronicled those days snarled in discouragement. Dow could afford to pass over the attainment of "animal comfort" as if it were a task too elementary to discuss, and move airily onward and upward to "numerous spiritual and ethical considerations." But the material world of untamed animal comforts, when children whined and milk soured, often seemed to claw at a frazzled J.A.T. and hold her back. During "The Times," as

she called them, "all things animate and inanimate combine,
and from cockcrow to cocksnore one's brain feels bristling with
prickly heat . . . sometimes I feel as though if anyone set me
going at the top of the house as one does a buzzing top I'd whir
and buzz and bang all the way to the cellar and feel better for
the exercise. I'm not a bit fun or philosophical."

Sometimes she would turn for solace to a kind of projection
of herself, similar to the imaginary friends with whom children
share secrets. "Remember, Jane of future years, oh remember
these days and help a young mother whenever you can," she
would write. When I first came across such entries of direct
address I felt timestruck, as if her voice came from another
dimension, beamed to me, Jane of the Present. Her confidences
were telephone calls from the past: "Busy times though, I can
tell you, Jane of the future . . . well, it's no use worrying, not a
bit . . . but running a household is no joke."

"Nails no longer catch the dress, small objects no longer slip
through the fingers. Oh, the peace and joy of home when one of
'The Times' is over." Kismet (on which she perhaps relied more
than a good Episcopalian convert should have), a change in the
humidity, a broken fever sometimes ended it. Often, however,
relief came from other women: servants, the veteran "helpers"
who shared the "Glorified Monotony" of life inside her house,
or friends outside, comfortable matrons like herself, who
offered her refuge in their secluded, walled gardens or the
simple, conventional solace of a shared tea table. She was not
too proud to accept help. She knew when she needed it. "I
might as well say it to myself—it's truly more than one person
can do properly, my job."

From time to time she tried to organize a mutually support-
ive, formal network of women: the Garden Club survived; for a
while so did the Jacot Club ("Just a Cup of Tea"), whose "sole
and commendable aim [was] that of informal, independent
coming together for mutual cheer"; but the stillborn Homemakers Council of Summit had only a single meeting, attended
by four "mistresses" and seven women "helpers" (four black,
one Irish, and two Swedish).

Though she believed in herself and in the validity of a community of women, she was far from a feminist. In her most official position paper on women's suffrage, a letter published in the Summit *Herald* in August 1914, she came out vigorously against the proposed "new burden." She saw it as a threat to the tranquillity of the home, into whose midst "the vote would be thrown like a bomb."

Our real mothers, and they are legion, are not stupid pieces of putty. They are intensely human, and as a rule nowadays deeply interested in the affairs of the time. Could they systematically conceal which way they would vote so as to preserve harmony? . . . All through the ocean of our great people moves this silent current of feeling—silent, because it is against the very principle of our lives, we home-makers, to come away from home into the glare of the open, except in aid of suffering [but] we must join shoulder to shoulder, spirit to spirit, for Peace, Progress, and Protection of the Home.

This "quiet, earnest group of women, this Home Guard of N.J." happily did not prevail. Though, smug in the 1970s, I find my grandmother's *position* antique, I can't really patronize *her*. She was an individual, one of many, caught in an historical style that didn't really suit her, in a period when official self-abnegation in a woman seemed to demonstrate character, not the lack of it, strength, not weakness. And I find her assumption that members of the Home Guard would naturally oppose their husbands' Republicanism both ironic and redeeming.

"The nation is in a bad way," Teddy Roosevelt once told an organization called The Mothers' Congress, "if there is no real home . . . if the woman has lost her sense of duty, or has let her nature be twisted so that she prefers a sterile pseudo-intellectuality to that great and beautiful development of character which comes only to those whose lives know the fullness of duty done, of efforts made, and self-sacrifice undergone."

"Loving service," wrote another advocate of the status quo,

"is the foundation stone of the home," of the happy home, that
is. Even Dow himself rose up and charged the timorous
housewife for her own sake to buck up and get busy: "If you are
unwilling to do for others in countless and endless ways, *not* as a
weakminded but otherwise selfish character, under the influence of some strong and magnetic personality—for that is
pitiful—but voluntarily, joyously, then there is no use bothering
your head about the economy of a cottage, or a castle, for that
matter, for you will not be happy in it." As I read him, he was
saying that a housewife must be self-propelled in her altruism,
not a handmaiden serving her husband's "strong and magnetic
personality" in order to serve herself.

If one accepted that the stress of perpetual loving service was
to be contained under pressure within the home, and *home* had
become synonymous with *house*, then it followed that personal
freedom seemed to lie outside, across the threshold. One relief for a sense of entrapment, at least for J.A.T., was gradually to move as far outdoors as she in conscience felt she could
go, and that wasn't very far. In 1905 she'd written that "there
cannot be too many things attempted at once. The line must
be drawn pretty close to home when three babies are in the
enclosure." With nine, the prohibitions were even more
stringent.

Porches, the intermediate area between interior and exterior,
had always seemed a blessed breathing space to her, a kind of
neutral zone where pleasure, simple and shaded, was allowed:
quiet times reading aloud to children after lunch, everyone a
little drowsy, rocking; late afternoon lemonade; and long
leisurely evenings with my grandfather. Her early diaries glow
with contented passages like: "Such a lovely evening. Henry
read and I sewed. It was too ideal for anything, and I forgot all
about being happy and just was." Or: "Such a happy hour on
the piazza late in P.M. Henry and self talking and reading.
Children about the place happy and good. Breeze simply
delicious. One of those ideal breathing spots in life."

"I said to my Heart, 'I am sick of four walls and a ceiling, / I
have need of the sky.'" This snatch of verse quoted in *House*

Beautiful dramatizes a turn-of-the-century yearning for open space, verandas, loggias, piazzas, pergolas, terraces—all those variations on the popular, characteristically American porch. One critic suggested that the porch was actually "the most notable" difference between the American and the European house. An architect complained that what he was being asked to produce was not a house but a huge porch-of-all-work with a few bedchambers attached.

Gradually, however, American tinkering and a penchant for home improvement intruded, and with the addition of screens, then storm windows, then radiators, many porches were reabsorbed into the body of the house, to become redomesticated as "sun porches." When this happened to the piazza at Lindum, J.A.T. was forced farther outside. She developed a sanctuary in her garden that was—at last—truly her own, her private space. Vines soon grew over her small gazebo, transforming it into a green cave, very like the early nineteenth-century "meditation huts" built by the Harmonists, a Pennsylvania sect described by Dolores Hayden in *Seven American Utopias*. J.A.T.'s hut was her place to be alone, to think.

In sociable moods she would invite an honored child, or she might entertain special adult friends, transforming meditation hut into ceremonial teahouse, a miniature version of the Oriental fantasy built by Mrs. O. H. P. Belmont, she who was also Alva Vanderbilt, on a bluff fifty feet above the sea in Newport. On one of the lacquered surfaces of the dowager's aerie appeared the following legend: "A woman of strong character is said to be a hero among women."

J.A.T.'s green hut provided her with a snatched solitude that was partially restorative, and more and more she found the time to express herself directly on paper, rather than indirectly through her house and her family. Around 1915 she was writing a number of short, sentimental verses. They are in the ladylike style of the period, and in mood light-years removed from the work of another "housewife poet," Anne Sexton, whose writing-in-residence decades later was as fiercely stark as J.A.T.'s was determinedly uplifting. The poems ranged from

"Home Free" and "Our Barn's a Bully Place," written obviously for children, to "Ambition," a document of personal
renunciation that makes me ache for her. Two of her poems
were published in *Town and Country* (women's magazines then
regularly featured a selection of mild verse), signed androgy-
nously with initials that gave no clue, as if one were needed, to
the sex of their author.

J.A.T. soon realized that a comparatively reclusive existence
as a suburban poetaster was not enough to satisfy her needs.
Between 1910 and 1920 she gradually developed a more
extroverted approach. Instead of moving, alone, out into the
garden, she would simply extend the walls of the house itself,
and her clear role within them, pushing them farther and
farther out until a whole segment of the town was embraced
within them.

In 1908 she had, as was the fashion, started a tiny Sunday
school class in her living room at Lindum. The deeply devotion-
al atmosphere of its first meeting was repeatedly shattered by
the insatiable lust of her two-year-old son who kept leaping up
to kiss a neighboring worshipper. The Boy Scouts of America
were founded in 1910, the Campfire Girls in 1912, and that
same year J.A.T. saw to it that her class metamorphosed into a
young persons' group, the Lindum Club, which was co-ed, its
aim "unselfish, straightforward Good Comradeship." By the
1920s the club was her major outside interest. Its membership
was to reach about six hundred, with an organization and
rhetoric almost Masonic in its combination of social and
"ethical-spiritual" purpose. Regular programs ranged from
dances to boxing matches, from Good Friday meetings to
hayrides. Since there were no provisions for elections, the
leader or supermother for twenty years was always J.A.T. (She
preferred to call herself the Club Helper, adopting her euphe-
mism for "servant.") Let other women organize Town Improvement Associations or Fortnightly Clubs, stage amateur
theatricals, or discuss the novel. She knew her own sphere of
influence, and like Napoleon she firmly grasped the crown and
set it on her own head.

In the career she invented, she was a self-made woman. One way or another she had managed to remain true to a pledge she made to herself early in her marriage: "Do not let anything hinder you from the deep satisfaction of knowing something, doing something, being something, of which you can say to yourself [*and other people*, a phrase she crossed out] 'I am this.' "

Louis Auchincloss has written of his mother that she was "not a talent or a personality that should have been confined to a family and a handful of friends. She played the role in life that she felt she had to play. She cramped her natural personality to fit into the box that always seemed to be opening in front of her." J.A.T. ingeniously enlarged her box, but in her early forties a sense of rebellion against cozy entrapment still boiled up in her from time to time. She, like so many housebound women before and since, longed to run away, even for just a few innocent, random hours. "If only I could drop everything—pick out someone who suits the mood of the moment, and go, go, till, oh well, till I just dropped laughing & tired & satisfied & replete with nonsense & variety & understanding, and ready . . . to take up life again. Go where? It will not matter much so long as there was space, breeze, sky, freedom. . . ."

One late March morning in 1920, a month before her twentieth wedding anniversary, when she was forty-five, she stood at a front window of Lindum watching her husband and her three eldest sons set off together for a day in the city: "Heavy fall of great soft flakes of snow. As I looked through starched white curtains I felt like something prized but placed, poor thing, in dainty tissue paper—surrounded by layers of soft white cotton. Above, an exquisite gray lid. How I longed to KICK off the lid!"

 FOUR

Good Housekeeping, 1920-1930

Six tons of pitchblende, a glow in the dark, a wife and husband working side by side, the widow in white lab coat valiantly continuing alone, confronting the mysteries of science unescorted: the romance of Marie and Paul Curie captured the imagination of America during the first two decades of the century, each of which was marked by a Nobel Prize, the first in 1903 to the couple, the second in 1911 to Madame Curie alone. Middle-class American women responded to both plot and characters in the Curies' story, and in 1921, as the third decade started, President Warren Harding presented the indomitable widow with one gram of radium, a gift "from the women of the nation."

In her long-lived monthly column for *Good Housekeeping,* "Letters from a Senator's Wife," the tireless Frances Parkinson Keyes reported the event to the homebodies who hadn't been included in the ceremony. Women readers like J.A.T. were as awed by the scientist herself as they were by science in all its mystery. Often it was the most impulsive and emotional amateur who identified with the trained, rational professional. J.A.T. pasted Madame Curie's picture in her diary, with such strange bedfellows as the late Czar Nicholas, Lloyd George, and Abraham Lincoln. Years later she was to lend me her copy of Eve Curie's biography of her mother, perhaps hopeful that I would be drawn to science and away from movie magazines.

The twenties were to witness the wildly popular accession of domesticated science, or technology in the home; but as early as 1900, women's magazines beamed at the middle class had regularly included "scientific" articles of one kind or another. The discovery of the common household germ, the pesky bacteria whose magnified linecut portraits stared out from the pages of *House Beautiful* like the faces of the Wanted on a post office bulletin board, had alerted the housewife to the physical menace crawling toward her children. One still takes certain dangers on faith; I've never recognized either a bank robber or a streptococcus. In one article called "The Unwholesome House," the writer warned women that they might themselves be unwitting carriers, introducing into their homes conglomerates of typhoid, diphtheria, and tuberculosis "germs," stowaways clinging to the hems of their street-sweeping skirts. "The home beautiful must be the home sanitary," exhorted another voice, suggesting that even a country residence was not safe, especially if it had shade trees, which could foster within the house the damp, malarial atmosphere "where disease germs thrive and multiply to destroy modern life."

The menace might be overdramatized, but the dangers were real, not bogeymen. We who now sit in vinylized pediatric waiting rooms, impatiently flipping through tattered back copies of *Parents' Magazine* or *American Baby* while our children nervously await their routine shots, forget how recent are the immunizations and antibiotics my grandmother might well have sold her soul to obtain in, say, 1915. I have never lost a friend to death in childbirth—she lost several, including a particularly close girlhood chum and, later, a daughter-in-law. No one in my immediate family in my generation or among my friends has had a child stillborn or die in infancy—her diaries were chilled repeatedly by small tragedies like "Bess's little boy came day before yesterday but went right away. Oh how my heart aches for her." Late summer's polio epidemics and winter's mastoiditis and pneumonias and lingering strep infections were indeed no joke. They were frightening possibilities few were foolish enough to haze over with wishful thinking or blind faith. A housewife had to be prepared to turn her house from a museum of artful home feeling into a field hospital at a moment's notice.

While construction proceeded on metropolitan New York hospitals—Mt. Sinai (1905) and Bellevue (1908)—J.A.T. out in suburban New Jersey was developing a pediatric clinic in her own house. The skills she'd begun to learn in her brief career as a nurse's aide were taken out of mothballs. Preventative medicine became her obsession, for with a flock of young children, one sniffle could portend an epidemic. Even an assortment of minor ailments could fill her makeshift wards, and was almost more demanding than an epidemic, in which each patient at least had the same prescriptions and regime. In January 1915, J.A.T. wearily entered in her diary one medical floor plan of Lindum: "Bill in back south room with mumps; Jim in back north room with cold; Sister and Patty in front north room with colds; John and Henry in nursery, teeth and colds; and this A.M. Fred bruised knee cap and has to keep still." Three weeks later she wrote triumphantly with an extravaganza of exclamation points: "Everybody well!!!!!!"

Once she listed "some of the ills which come much less often to even a large family if the one On Guard searches in time for causes. [They include] appendicitis, thyroid trouble, heartburn, kidney trouble, mastoid, bad teeth, eruptions, antagonisms, neuritis and other nerve disorders, toe bothers, fallen arches, tuberculosis." This dismaying assortment of the ridiculous and the sublime challenged her ingenuity, and she produced rigorous courses of treatment that called for stoicism from both nurse and patient. For example, the treatment of "grippe" (our flu) involved frequent mustard footbaths, chest rubs with mutton tallow, the burning of Cresoline lamps to combat night coughing, bedpans, Dr. Hamill's fever pills, milk or broth administered every two and a half to three hours, alcohol rubs, and tonic for ten days after the illness seemed licked, at which point the burning of a formaldehyde candle officially decontaminated the sickroom. Then, as likely as not, she started all over again with some new medical emergency.

Some of her nostrums seem today to belong to the eye-of-newt school of naturopathic medicine—cocoa butter rubs, almond oil, syrup of figs, lettuce lozenges—but she had faith in their efficacy and continued to administer old favorites even unto her grandchildren. I remember all too well my own dosing with tablespoons of the amazing elixir Beef, Wine, and Iron Tonic, or the steamy incense of tincture of Benzoin emitted by a vaporizer near my bed. Excessive as some of her therapies might have seemed to the small laboratory animal, she never lost a patient to illness or accident, a proud record.

"A house should bear witness in all its economy that human culture is the end to which it is garnished," wrote Ralph Waldo Emerson. Human culture in the literal sense, like horticulture, requires hard, dirty work, doing battle with bugs, and the expenditure of reserves of physical energy during seasonal emergencies. J.A.T. sometimes drove herself into the red emotionally, but she expected no less dedication from others. In a passionate letter to the Summit *Herald* published in July 1916 she exhorted the mothers of the town, the Home Guard, to give the last full measure of devotion "to save the children of our town" from the polio epidemic that had already afflicted 555 in New York City. She was not afraid to mount the barricades, but she admitted that "the strain is a trying one, for one hardly knows *which* direction to guard in." One solution, in that era of quarantine, was to isolate infection within afflicted houses; another was to confine healthy children and keep them from contamination in public places. Germs would never hop in over the garden gate.

The energy that drove such mother/nurses was fear, pure and simple, and no accumulation of mother-hours by the bedside of a sick child was considered excessive. Efficiency of method was not the issue; the outcome alone was important. In one siege, J.A.T. noted afterward, she didn't take off her stockings for three days.

In even the most plague-ridden households, daily life had to go on. For my grandmother, servants saw to that. Constance got the dinner on the table at the regular time and Ellen bathed the well children and tucked them into bed, while Florence Nightingale, the lady with the Cresoline lamp, the formaldehyde candle, performed in the ward. Servants, if not actually transformed into orderlies and nurses' aides when home became hospital, could—if one was lucky—be depended upon to take up the slack. Without them, how would one have managed? Child and maternal mortality statistics in the slums of the period would suggest a grim answer.

J.A.T. was not always lucky. My assumption that the mere fact of having help in the good old days implied a smoothly functioning household machine was rapidly disproved by her diaries. Early in her marriage, cooks, maids, and childtenders came and went with unsettling frequency. One parlor maid described as "warranted to turn your hair white" apparently made the whole family so nervous they could "hardly speak a straight sentence." When discovered soothing her hands with kerosene after having washed out a few of the baby's clothes in straight ammonia, she was instantly expelled. One cook, poor woman, was found passed out, flat on the kitchen floor. Actually, flat is an inaccurate description, for she was very pregnant at the time, as was J.A.T. I picture one rotund figure trying to help the other to her feet, a scene reminiscent of either Lewis Carroll or a game of *boules*.

Since the end of the nineteenth century, the obtaining of competent household help had been an issue among housewives, the Servant Problem much discussed over the teacups and examined in magazines. J.A.T. herself recommended as "a great help" an article in a 1904 *Harper's Bazaar,* and in 1977 I scurried to the Boston Public Library to read it. Its author confirmed that the perfect maid is "almost extinct . . . a domestic Dodo." She then asked why women have "incessant personal difficulties with their employees, and men do not? . . . Here in the one department of life entirely our own, we have failed." Wistfully she compared the uncomfortableness between a mistress and her domestic servant to the brisk impersonality and effectiveness of her husband's business relationships with his employees, and pointed to the need in the home for a more rational approach based on "honest wages, in exchange for faithful service, under right conditions."

With each year of the new century it became more of a seller's market, as the number of women willing to work in domestic service decreased and the number of housewives seeking help increased. In 1910 there were 1,851,000 servants and 20,300,000 households, 92 percent of which had no live-in servants at all. By 1920 the gap had widened to 1,411,000 outside workers in what I must assume was an even smaller percentage of 24,400,000 households. A housewife's interests were served by making sure she stayed out of the market by working out a long-term *modus vivendi* with any helper she might have. Gradually J.A.T. did succeed in assembling and training a small loyal nucleus in her staff that stayed with her for years, and in two cases for the rest of their lives. The nurserymaid who cared for my father, and occasionally for me, is buried in the family plot.

But much of the time, in the intimacy of an ordinary household, not a vast baronial establishment, the situation was an impossible human paradox. "The best of maids will at times drive one to a point of frantic distraction for which there is no simile," J.A.T. once wrote. Even the most competent servant or sympathetic mistress had faults and human needs, "blue days" and blind spots.

The personnel policy of a caricature Victorian bully like Mr. Boffin in Charles Dickens's *Our Mutual Friend* was defensively aggressive: "Scrunch or be scrunched." By 1925 *Good Housekeeping* described both parties in the confrontation as having been victimized under the old regime. Often it was the mistress, "afraid of her cook," who was scrunched.

One exemplary egalitarian alternative offered its services in
1925. It was an organization called Scientific Housekeeping,
Inc., which boasted a woman president and women directors
and offered to mediate between employer and employee on
business matters, such as schedules, the organizing of duties,
hours, training, and other basics open to negotiation. Scientific
Housekeeping hoped to eliminate the personal element, "the
uneasy sense of obligation on either side because of favors
asked and favors given."

The system was sensible enough, but it was an idea out of
sync with the times. The issue in the twenties was essentially a
shortage of personnel, not the improvement of management
techniques inside some hypothetical household business. Scientific Housekeeping could not clone servants or produce robots.
If any of the techniques of the man's world could be applied to
housework, they were not those of business but of industry. The
housewife would come to think of herself more as the foreman
in a factory rather than as an office manager or junior executive.
The era of household technology was upon her. Servants could
not be mass-produced and purchased. Machines could be.

And they were. All through the twenties, the new and
improved household machines rolled from assembly lines into
the kitchens and laundry rooms of America. A departing
Bertha, muttering imprecations, might be dragging her suitcase
down the back stairs at the very moment a delivery truck
bearing a new ABC Electric Laundress was pulling up at the
curb in front.

Between 1919 and 1929 Americans' consumer outlay per
capita grew at a greater rate than in any other comparable
period from 1889 to 1957, writes Heidi Hartmann, an economist
specializing in women's work. The emphasis turned to the
buying of so-called consumer durables (that is, big, heavy, and
subject to mechanical breakdown): the washing machines,
ironers, refrigerators, and stoves that were to repopulate the
homes the servants were evacuating. The champ in the decade's
popularity contest was the refrigerator, whose sales increased
by 276.8 percent, but significant contenders were toasters,

waffle irons, and stoves. Around 1920, says Siegfried Giedion in *Mechanization Takes Command,* the idea of equipping a house as one would a private factory or laboratory captured the imagination and "aroused the acquisitive instinct of the public to an astonishing degree."

The traditional early-nineteenth-century rural home had contained in the most literal sense a cottage industry, in which a whole family—not only wife, but also husband and children—was expected to participate in subsistence activities, arduous perhaps but certainly comprehensible. In order to eat vegetables, one gardened; in order to drink milk, one fed the cow. A woman's sixteen-hour day might be misleadingly but accurately described as "promiscuous industry." Her work was indeed a heterogeneous mixture of sewing quilts and underclothes, making candles and soap, weaving, drying fruits and vegetables in a preoccupation of today's "crafts." She was, of course, also responsible for daily tasks like cooking and washing. The family worked closely together, but "often the sense of drudgery, of wasteful routine, overpowered the feeling of affection." The usefulness of the tasks might be undeniable, but, as *House Beautiful* observed, the "limit of the educational value of any one of them is soon reached, be it stoning raisins, paring quinces, or even that delightful process which in the minds of some . . . seems to be the epitome of domestic bliss and family welfare, frying doughnuts."

With the development of the single or "family" wage economy, a system in full swing by my grandparents' wedding day in 1900, the middle-class husband left home to go to work elsewhere for the money with which to buy the goods and services the family had formerly provided for itself. By then, large corporations were producing two-thirds of all manufactured goods.

The new housewife continued promiscuous activities that increasingly took on a more ladylike demeanor, for if her husband prospered, she was helped and accompanied by the servants who replaced family workers. Any efforts toward efficiency of labor concentrated on enhancing a maid's performance: the effect on the life of the mistress tended to be indirect. The "new suction cleaners" of 1910 were touted as being light enough for a maid to carry from room to room. An ad for Witt's Corrugated Pails pictured a fully uniformed young girl emptying with vicarious pride her mistress's beauteous pail into a matching trash can.

With comparatively abundant help, household standards could afford to be mandarin in unnecessary refinements. A simple daily task like making a bed was a labor-intensive production: mattresses were turned twice a week, and each day mattress pads, sheets, and blankets were removed and thoroughly aired. Why? Often it was simply because that was the way it was done, hardly an answer. Dorothy Rodgers remembers her mother's linen closet as "a housewife's pride—all the cloths and centerpieces on separate rollers, so there wouldn't be any creases, and tied with bands of pink silk ribbon and lace." Her explanation is that her mother loved linens, which is certainly easier to understand than the imperatives of "that's the way it's done."

A 1903 *House Beautiful* did admit that a few concessions to efficiency and reason were legitimate: "In an establishment of two maids, ironing of dishtowels is a non-essential." Such cutting of corners was in order, for doing the laundry was a Herculean labor that could take up about half the week. On Sunday night the washing would be put to soak; on Monday fires were started and the boiler made ready and the laundry launched; Tuesday was devoted to ironing. There were drying racks and lines, and heated metal closets that could speed up natural processes. There were fluting irons, heat, steam, aching feet, red hands, and frayed nerves.

"In simply ordered houses [that is, those where dishtowels were not ironed] the mistress should be both able and willing to lend a hand in times of stress, setting always the example of cheerfulness and patience, a manner which should be assumed if one is not fortunate enough to assume it naturally." J.A.T. was able but not willing, and in 1907 she for one was sending her laundry out.

In magazines of the period, debate continued *ex post facto* on the effects of such removal of "household industries" from the home. Proponents cited as arguments: increased housewifely independence; the improved quality and low price of mass-produced items; the new professionalism of laundries, ready-to-wear manufacturers, and bakeries. Opponents, those of the home-fried doughnuts school of moral philosophy, feared that the spiritual education of the nation's children would suffer if character-building chores were dispersed into the outside world. Here again "character" was equated with self-suppression in a doubtful cause, work whose justification was often some Puritanical spin-off, like self-discipline or that terrible word, *duty*. Understandably the moralists' stern pitch was drowned out by more alluring street cries, such as "Send it to the laundry!" Housewives learned that "modern laundries have become laundresses for you"—sanitary engineers, in fact, who rid linens of even "invisible impurities."

By the 1920s the housewife saw an opportunity for compromise with honor. Through the miracle of modern technology and materialism (better *things* for better living), she could retain in her home her self-respect and her laundry, without sacrificing herself to washday drudgery. *Drudgery* was a newly popular word, much invoked. Freedom from it, through various surrogate servants, became a new life goal. The verb *to drudge* derives from two sources, the more familiar one meaning "to labor in mean offices with toil and fatigue, to suffer, endure," and the other "to serve as a soldier or assistant." With a Simplex Ironer, a woman could be freed "from the eternal drudgery of ironing," could "leave toil and fatigue behind." Not only that, she would be promoted from the ranks, would be the commander, if only of a corps of noncommissioned machines. George Bernard Shaw was more pessimistic about ultimate freedom for women. He wrote: "We ourselves throw the whole drudgery of creation on one sex." Creation is certainly a responsibility hard to delegate, especially to a machine.

One ad in a 1920 *Good Housekeeping* dramatized a prevailing fantasy, that of gaining public recognition of administrative know-how in the private sector. In the back yard of a cozy bungalow, laundry on a line is ostentatiously flapping. Around it stand no less than seven women, presumably every neighbor on the block, all of whom seem positively stunned with amazement. The spectators, a veritable Greek chorus, murmur in unison, "How does she do it? . . . 'n' it's only 8 o'clock." Meanwhile the gracious housewife is on her front porch shaking hands with a departing benefactor, who happens to be a humanoid numeral eight, more or less masculine (for raw sexuality he's about on a par with Reddy Kilowatt). This selfless robot represents the Cataract Washer, "with its magic figure 8 movement."

The Cataract was only one of the many variations on the cylinder washer that had been invented as early as the 1850s (as had, also in principle, the vacuum cleaner) but whose mass production was put off until twentieth-century electric power and technology. There were in the twenties, among others, the Rotarex, the Gainaday, the Laun-dry-ette, the Voss Sea Wave Washer ("staunch as a lighthouse on a storm-beaten shore . . . a beacon to the port of easier washday"), and, my favorite, the Geyser. This infernal machine outdid Old Faithful: dirty garments were lulled into a false sense of security by warm water, a gentle motion . . . then *suddenly*, without warning, a mighty blast of hot sudsy water would erupt, the geyser itself, an irresistible thermal force that would blast impurities, seen and unseen, right out of the clothes and into oblivion. Who could resist such a machine, then or now? In all my latterday sophistication I have been a sucker for far less spectacular natural phenomena—the Whirlpool washer, for example— ones that did nothing but churn around, drain, and occasionally ingest a particularly succulent sock.

When no-nonsense technology strode into the home, it went right to the kitchen and got to work. By the end of the 1920s, the most *gemütliche* kitchen of yore—with its crackling hearth, gravy-spotted checked tablecloth, and a resident mouse who nightly helped clean up crumbs left on the floor—that most tolerant and hospitable of rooms, might be transformed into a modern laboratory of domestic or applied science. The fumes of Lysol mingled with the aroma of Mom's apple pie.

In 1920 the ordinary American kitchen still looked like a room with furniture in it, like the kitchen in a doll's house as a matter of fact. Appliances were disparate, not built in or together, except for a double-drainboard, porcelainized sink, wall-hung, either with legs or without them, that might stand alone, probably under a window. The icebox might be in a separate pantry. The more up-to-date and refined stoves stood on four legs, often cabriole like a Queen Anne sideboard, with their ovens raised up to eye level. Older ranges were cast iron, black and behemoth and squat. Movable kitchen dressers and cupboards, cabinets like armoires, some with counters at their waistlines, stood primly apart from each other, often separated by a mere six inches or so.

During the decade the classic kitchen table stationed in the middle of the room was drawn to the wall by the centrifugal force gradually distributing cabinets and appliances around the perimeters of the room. This arrangement prefigured the now universal base cabinet, counter, wall cabinet combination of units featured in experimental kitchens as early as 1929 but which really "came in" after World War II. The L- or U-shaped counter arrived in the late twenties and early thirties, often accompanied by "the breakfast set," a small table with flanking high-backed benches that was designed to fit into "a breakfast nook."

By 1930 the home laboratory was essentially equipped. In an article titled "It's Brains not Brawn that Runs a Modern Kitchen," the Good Housekeeping Institute summarized the features of a "mechanized kitchen": ovens with heat regulators, stainless and rustless linings, insulation, automatic timers; the electric beaters, mixers, slicers, and grinders that constituted the housewife's "mechanical arm"; an automatic refrigerator; dishwasher; electric fan; with a vacuum cleaner and electric polisher in the broom closet. The institute released a policy statement *ex cathedra:* "We are beginning to think of equipment in the kitchen as made up of various units rather than as separate pieces of equipment." Mechanization, except for a few items like the garbage disposer and the food processor, was complete at a much earlier date than I, for one, had supposed.

If the kitchen was rapidly evolving during the twenties, the bathroom was modernizing itself even more expeditiously. Mass production of cast-iron porcelainized fixtures with standard fittings took place early in the postwar period; and by 1930 the flush toilet without a tank—the one-piece "water closet" (as my grandmother and *Good Housekeeping* both delicately referred to it)—was a gleaming reality. Tiled, streamlined, relentlessly white with accents of chrome, the typical bathroom in 1930 suggested a public facility or a surgical scrub room rather than a sybaritic Roman bath. The amputation of such vestigial organs as the ball-and-claw foot on the tub or the chain on the overhead thunderbox had taken a mere ten years.

The concept of the mechanized house, the home laboratory, injected more adrenalin into the psychomotors of the average woman, already quivering with the imperatives of motherhood and home feeling. For advice on how to achieve a smoothly running machine and that awesome goal of the 1920s, modern efficiency, she turned to women's writing in the reference library of contemporary home economics, a social science domesticated. The tradition of women questioning and being counseled by more experienced women may have begun at Eve's knee, for mothers (and mothers-in-law) have probably always been tempted by the irresistible apple of advice-giving. The Dear Abigails of Victorian America were not concerned with such 1970s queries as whether or not one's thirteen-year-old daughter should go on the Pill, or "What About" geriatric sex, or how to cope with a husband's yen for the babysitter. The great nineteenth-century American advice-givers had focused on less intimate matters in their many books written for other women on the management of the home, in all its daily minutiae. As Virginia Woolf pointed out in 1928, though men wrote voluminously about women, women did not write about men. They wrote about women, for them, and at them, and they still do.

Mrs. Lydia Maria Child, author of *The American Frugal Housewife* (1836), a detailed and, to me, extremely eccentric if not positively dangerous little witch's handbook filled with directions for various household potions suitable for cauldrons and spells, was an advocate of the most literal variety of home economics: "The true economy of housekeeping is simply the art of gathering up all the fragments, so that nothing be lost. I mean fragments of *time*, as well as of *materials*." According to James Marston Fitch in *Architecture and the Esthetics of Plenty,* Mrs. Child's Utopia was "aggressively small, thrifty, and domestic," but her writing had "that air of crisp infallibility which has marked women's magazines ever since."

Catharine Beecher's first book, *A Treatise on Domestic Economy, for the Use of Young Ladies at Home and at School,* appeared in 1841, but *The American Woman's Home,* in 1869, written with her sister, Harriet Beecher Stowe, was her most popular and influential work, possibly because, in Dolores Hayden's words, it seemed to give "agile definitions of female dominance in the home." Women, according to Beecher, ruled over a small Christian "commonwealth," doubling as "the minister" and "the skilled professional," one role reinforcing the other. Though Beecher is fashionably viewed today as either a kind of proto-architect or closet feminist, in Hayden's view she was in her way as conservative as crabbed Mrs. Child. Her innovative redesigning of the interior plans of conventional mid-nineteenth-century houses and her rational approach to women's work and their equipment were attempts to reorganize the home through simplification and logic and restructuring, but only so that housewives might better perform their God-given mission. Her improvements reinforced the prevailing middle-class ideology and, as Hayden points out, served to make "an obsessive standard explicit."

The American Woman's Home was a kind of pattern book imbued with a spiritual message, a set of practical instructions for home demonstrations of the Protestant work ethic. "Free" time for women was neither the issue nor the outcome of the reorganization. The result, according to Hayden, was a "terrifyingly complete enclosure for family life . . . an environment remarkably similar to standard American suburban housing today."

During the latter half of the nineteenth century other attempts to keep one's eye on the sparrow and yet use common sense and intelligence to solve housekeeping were made by a variety of women. Both trained technicians and amateurs saw in some kind of collectivism a practical way out. The Cambridge Cooperative Housekeeping Society in Cambridge, Massachusetts, was Melusina Fay Peirce's contribution. The drag of daily meal preparation, then as now inefficiently duplicated in single-family kitchens up and down Brattle Street, was the sort of wasteful chore against which she inveighed in her writings published in the 1870s and early '80s. For a time the society sponsored a central kitchen from which "take-out" meals were delivered to various member homes. This arrangement was, however, closer to the cop-out of convenience foods or Colonel Sanders's traveling chickens than to the radical idealism that had produced truly communal kitchens in such early- and mid-nineteenth-century Utopian communities as the Amana Colony in Iowa. Such deeply innovative group endeavors challenged basic social assumptions, whereas the cooperative housekeeping associations simply tinkered with the jalopy to make it run better, and like Catharine Beecher accepted as a given that womanpower alone fueled the engine. Nonetheless the Melusina Peirces were questioning accepted mandarin practices and trying to use their heads to conserve time and labor from waste in the name of appearances or convention.

Also in Cambridge and at almost the same time, Ellen Swallow Richards (who had graduated from Vassar and in 1873 from M.I.T., the first woman graduate of that or any school of science in the United States) published her first book, *The Chemistry of Cooking and Cleaning* (1882). Her manual was a popularization designed to instruct isolated housewives in the general principles of science as they could be applied to domestic tasks. It was in the helping-hand tradition of Child and Beecher, but more professionally informed than either. A remarkable woman, Mrs. Richards had a broad world view that expanded the ordinary dimensions of "home." The world is "everybody's house," she said, and its care is everyone's responsibility. Good housekeeping in the noblest sense would be the practice of environmental science or, as she called it, *oekology*. In 1892 her word metamorphosed into *ecology*. Some oekologists splintered off in 1908 and affiliated themselves with the home economists.

The National Household Economics Association had grown out of the Women's Congress at the Chicago Fair of 1893, the one and only World's Columbian Exhibition. The level of women's concerns had certainly risen since the Centennial Exposition in Philadelphia in 1876, when the women's exhibition had featured sculpture by female artists in a medium readily available to them—butter. "He" might chisel away at Carrara marble, while "she" worked in butter, which is, I suppose, slightly more dignified than working in lard. What better symbolized the ephemeral nature of much of women's work than a masterpiece in butter, exhibited on a hot July day?

For some years early in the century, Ellen Richards wrote for the home economics column in *House Beautiful*. She and forward-looking science sometimes shared space with art and architecture in the person of Joy Wheeler Dow, celebrator of the past. An index to the relative popularity of their fields was the fact that Dow was featured in the front of the magazine, while Richards was relegated to the back.

Nevertheless home economics was steadily increasing in status. It was then considered to be a reform movement and progressive, rather like Naderism today, and not, as I saw it in its twilight in the 1940s, dowdy occupational therapy for academically uninterested high-school students, who were shunted off from the mainstream of college preparation to sew lumpy dirndl skirts, bake carrot cakes, and memorize the Basic Seven Foods Essential to Good Health. As an indication of

Mrs. Richards's reputation as "the mother of home economics," when Madame Curie made her first trip to this country, her only speech here was given at Vassar under the auspices of a series of monographs honoring Ellen Richards.

More or less parallel to the phenomenon of home economics in the early nineteenth century was the home efficiency movement, whose metaphor was the home as professionally managed factory, rather than as scientific laboratory or hospital. Heidi Hartmann, in her recent analysis of the evolution of women's work in the home during the pivotal period 1900–1930, examines its relationship to the exigencies of capitalism. According to her, one establishment goal in comparing home to industry was to convince middle-class women of the "professional" challenge of unpaid work *inside* the patriarchal home, to divert them from any impossible dreams they might have of paid work *outside* it, jobs that would distract them from their primary social responsibility, motherhood.

A leading advocate and popularizer of domestic efficiency was Christine Frederick, who trod the boards on the Chautauqua circuit, speaking to large and eager audiences of women, and who also wrote for the *Ladies' Home Journal.* Her magnum opus, *Household Engineering: Scientific Management in the Home,* appeared in 1915. A training manual for the housewife, it applied the techniques of the assembly line to housework, and instructed the woman to function professionally as the "family purchasing agent."

One illustration in Frederick's book featured a woman dressed not unlike a Civil War nurse, in long skirt and little white cap, who was engaged in experimenting with the relative merits of short- and long-handled dustpans. Christine Frederick herself, as photographed in her own kitchen, as bare and spare as any convent's, officiated in robes that seemed inspired by the habit of some obscure order of nursing nuns. Her cap was as chastely white as her free-falling ambiguous garment, either smock or shroud. She spoke to women like herself who were not mere maids demonstrating improved household items or techniques, as in the era of Witts Corrugated Cans, but were the ladies in charge, wielding their own dustpans, dramatizing their roles with rather theatrical uniforms. A footnote: forty years later the dustpan experiment had still not been concluded once and for all. Lillian Gilbreth's *Management in the Home* (1954) depicts two researchers, two dustpan styles. Though the long-handled pan again is proved the winner in the lab, it has still not made it in the world. How many households today have the sensible tool? I don't know one. Apparently certain objects consistently arouse an irrational and stubborn resistance.

Reeling under an unaccustomed barrage of instruction by experts, women by the twenties might well have begun to feel unequal to their multiple mission. For a sense of duality, if not schizophrenia, was corroding the psyches of good housekeepers. Could one really coordinate discerning executive judgment with the almost automatic motions of someone on the assembly line? Could one simultaneously be middle-class administrator and proletarian worker? Social considerations demanded that a woman's collar seem to be white, though she obviously knew that, out of sight, its lining had a bluish tinge. I think the domestic neuroses that were to cloud women's minds in later decades began to develop in earnest in the 1920s, as women tried to internalize their new roles as their own servants, tried to function as the family toilet scrubber while simultaneously maintaining the genteel social image of the lady. John Kenneth Galbraith has defined these dual personalities as "wife-servants."

Somehow the ideal of efficiency seemed to imply that it was necessary to maintain a facade of effortlessness and of distance from sweat, grime, and dirty fingernails, as if women's work occurred in some pristine, abstracted laboratory of industrial chemistry, some neat and pure line where precision instruments were assembled. A superior housewifely expert might declare in a patronizing tone, "Why, my dear, housework is simply a matter of organization, of having certain standards and the proper equipment, and a clear head." A parallel would be to say that building a house is simply a matter of imagination, of good taste in details of design, carpentry tools, and a sense of space. If Joy Wheeler Dow's fantasies of Anglo-Saxon home feeling and its resuscitation in new houses were romantic, they were no less so than the phantom goal of housework easily organized, with the help-less housewife combed and smiling calmly.

A family is a pulsating organism, whose rate of growth and internal organization is unpredictable under the best of conditions. The ordinary twentieth-century single-family house is, as I well know, poorly designed as a laboratory and can try the soul of any well-intentioned Dr. Jekyll who tries to maintain in it optimal developmental conditions. And Mrs. Hyde lounges in waiting, bitchy and undisciplined, ready to take over the good doctor and undermine the system.

Like Christine Frederick, Frank and Lillian Gilbreth pursued a long career based on the theories of Frederick Taylor, pioneer in the study and standardization of industrial workers' motions so that humans might produce as efficiently as machines. From 1910 until Frank Gilbreth's death in 1924, Gilbreth Inc. was nationally prominent in the new field of scientific management and motion study. The partnership also demonstrated a certain efficiency in the production of a famously economical complement of children. *Cheaper by the Dozen* (1948), written by a son and a daughter, was a humorous and affectionate elegy to Frank Gilbreth and his presence in the family's home life, while its sequel, *Belles on Their Toes* (1950), focused on Lillian Gilbreth's own emergence into the foreground as a working widow, one as indomitable in continuing a joint life work as Madame Curie herself had been.

"Housekeeping is an industrial process," Mrs. Gilbreth wrote, and "Homemaking is housekeeping plus. The plus is the art, the individual variation, the creative work. The housekeeping is the science, the universal likenesses, the necessary activities which must be carried out in order that one may have more time and energy for the rest."

These quotations are from *The Home-maker and Her Job* (1927), a book I can enthusiastically recommend even now, over fifty years after its publication. It is a model of common-sense attitudes toward domestic work and is delightfully irreverent about sacred cows, major and minor. "Let gravity work for you," she suggests, by gaily pitching your bundles of laundry down stairs, rather than doggedly and respectably lugging heavy baskets down, step by step.

Lillian Gilbreth was gently contemptuous of housewifely possessiveness ("Why not ask of each thing we do, 'Does it really mean more to the family because it is done by me or in the home?' ") and of waste of time or motion or anything else ("Waste of energy is the cause of drudgery in work of any kind"). She constantly emphasized that the end of efficiency in housework was to provide more time for the humane aspects of family life, for fun and companionship, and she felt no qualms about enlisting the help of her large family in what was patently a common goal.

In the twelve commandments of Taylorism as interpreted by Christine Frederick, "Common Sense" was only the second item. The first was "Ideals," my grandmother's specialty. Chock-a-block with them, her diaries, like Catharine Beecher's journals, were destined to become "private writing for public consumption," and in her fifties, when her children had left home, she went back to her records of hectic home life like an anthologist. Unfortunately she tended to select the more high-flown bits, literary or medical or philosophical, and omitted many simpler, touching entries like the one for August 17, 1900: "From experience. *Watch all the time* not to turn economy into fussiness or let little or big house perplexities stay with you when the time comes to think of the one you care most for. *Try hard.*"

Ellen Richards revamped her home in Jamaica Plain, Massachusetts, into the model of a healthful house, hospitable to sun and air. Christine Frederick institutionalized hers in Long Island, calling it the Applecroft Experimental Station. A few miles from Summit, in Montclair, New Jersey, Lillian Gilbreth used her ample suburban house as a *de facto* school for scientific management, her family as research assistants. And J.A.T., the determined nonprofessional, had turned Lindum into a greenhouse in which children were cultivated and grew. Her contribution to the literature of woman-to-woman advice injected the perspective of the veteran gardener who'd been through it all, as she transformed her domestic experience into two books directed to younger women, beginners.

Though Flappers & Co. might flout the standards of the older generation, other young women of the twenties, the readers of *Good Housekeeping*, for example, hardly represented flaming youth and would still take direction. In issues of the magazine published in the decade, illustrations for both fiction and ads repeatedly featured the Wise Older Woman dispensing good counsel. The Ethel Barrymore figure leans forward in her wing chair, fingering her pearls, to console and advise the distraught young wife on the other side of the tea table; or apple-cheeked Aunt Jenny bustles around the kitchen, showing the giddy young social butterfly how to make flaky pie crust. Amazingly, the young persons actually seem to be listening.

J.A.T., the elder, served as author, editor, publisher, and promoter of her books. The first, bound diffidently in Quaker gray, was *Mother's Note Book,* dedicated to "Our Splendid Young Mothers of 1932," among them mine. Indexed for quick reference like a personal telephone directory, the book began with *A* for Adipose and ranged through *F*—Footbath to *J*—Joy, *M*—Mumps, *P*—Philosophy of Life and Pimples, to *V*—Vomiting. In her preface she wrote, "Perhaps *Mother's Note Book* may not be able to help you one bit—it's only now and then, you know, that a friend may give a 'back-up' over the wall—but at least what is here is my best, and at your service."

Her second volume, *Home Fires,* was essentially a revised edition of the first, and was a far jazzier production, with its all-American red, white, and blue jacket. When I was about eight, she took me to Bamberger's department store in downtown Newark, New Jersey, to inspect her display in the book section. I was overwhelmed by the panoply of bright copies, all with *our* name on them, and felt even then the poignancy of her barely suppressed pride of authorship.

J.A.T.'s concluding advice for her readers was: "Be sure you do your loving intelligent best, and then positively DON'T WORRY." But with their new responsibilities as human engineers and family purchasing agents added to traditional ones, women were worrying. The rising urge to fill the interiors of houses with the latest equipment was unnerving in its intensity, choices were multiple, investments large, standards uncertain, and outside pressures great. The new anxiety stimulated most home magazines to beef up their service departments, bring the home economists out of the back room and into the front office. Art and architecture moved over.

In 1900, *Good Housekeeping* had set up a rudimentary experiment station to test products advertised in the magazine. In 1909, it was dignified with the title of the Good Housekeeping Institute, and under the long editorship (1913–42) of W. F. Bigelow, the institute and the magazine really came into their own. They drew on a potential readership of about 22 million (the number of housekeepers, or women who had no job other than to care for their homes, as recorded in the 1920 census), and by its fortieth birthday in 1925 the magazine had a circulation of 1 million, and ten years later, 2 million. It was said to be the most successful publication of its genre during the thirties.

With its large sphere of influence and its apparently scientific pitch, the institute assumed the authority of some ivory-towered research center, in quest of abstract scientific truth, like Einstein at Princeton's Institute for Advanced Study. By notarizing products, the Good Housekeeping Seal, the institute's emblem, seemed to legitimatize them.

In its birthday releases the institute described itself as having grown out of the realization that "housekeepers all over the country were at work unconsciously solving each other's problems." Its role was to serve as the clearinghouse that disseminated the discoveries of each individual housekeeper into the homes of all. Mutually beneficial institute reports appeared on "The Blues in Bluing," "The Art of Starching," or how to oil and otherwise maintain appliances.

A 1925 photograph of the institute's dedicated staff at work
is, as a group portrait, a minor masterpiece. Four Madame
Curies in white lab coats and two gentlemen in black business
suits, dressed either as mad scientists or as morticians, are
seated behind a refectory table and against a book-lined wall.
The solemn task at hand is coffee-tasting. In front of each judge
is a single cup and saucer. The weight of responsibility seems
heavy indeed, for no tasters smile. They simply stare glumly
down into their cups.

In the twenties the dynamic duo of mass production and mass
marketing produced advertising as we have come to know and
love it. Women's magazines were the logical medium for it.
Radio was new (the nation's first commercial broadcast covered
Harding's election in 1920), and newspaper readers were a
heterogeneous and unreliable lot. Much money lay in the navy
blue calf purses of housewives who read the magazines that one
commentator, Ruth Schwartz Cowan, regards as an index to
their place in society: "Middle-class women were defined as
actual or potential readers of the better-quality women's
magazines, such as the *Ladies' Home Journal, American Home,
Parents', Good Housekeeping,* and *McCall's.*"

These were the women who could afford to buy but needed a
little encouragement, who doubted their ability to make
informed choices. Advertisers would step forward and advise
the ladies, who seemed willing to ignore the obvious, that such
advice was bound to be loaded, though a certain gentle cynicism
protected them against total gullibility. On the other hand, they
were unaware, I think, of how unconsciously susceptible they
were to the role model that ads held up to them in the twenties
(and thereafter) of, in Dr. Cowan's words, "the woman who
cheerfully and skillfully set about making everyone in her
family perfectly happy and perfectly healthy."

Heidi Hartmann summarizes the view of one historian of
advertising, that its primary task was "to equate the good life
with material goods." Before World War I, the popular recipe
for the good life had called for such wholesome ingredients as
golden sunshine, fresh country air, pure sentiment. She also

points to the theory that advertising provided the connecting link between technological and social change. One intermediary task it faced was to teach modern consumers "to enjoy consumption." Those old-fashioned negative virtues of women of character, "thrift, puritanism, and asceticism," had to be purged by new negatives: weaknesses like shame, fear, vanity, guilt, and embarrassment.

Housework was emotionalized by advertising, and the teacher's pet, prissy and boring scientific efficiency, was no real match. The irrational appeal of magic was stronger than the rational alternative, science. Familiar cleaning chemicals—benzine, ammonia, alcohol, naphtha, oxalic acid—had to be replaced by ballyhooed brand-name products (probably basically benzine, ammonia, alcohol, etc.) that were more up-to-date.

Advertisers were often canny enough to speak out in a watered-down imitation of the home economists' and efficiency experts' technical language. One *Good Housekeeping* ad described its product, the Napanee Dutch Kitchenet, in the vocabulary of the time-and-motion expert. Mr. H. H. Tice is pictured, deep in consultation with two women. He has pulled out his stopwatch and pedometer and is calculating how many steps can be saved by using the Dutch Kitchenet, with its many cabinets and drawers and sluices, its central work surface. Good grief, with a Kitchenet a cook need only take 25 steps instead of 176 to make hot biscuits, and for French dressing 80 steps are reduced to a mere 5. Why does the cook need to expend even five steps when all she has to do is reach for the oil, the vinegar, and a bowl, all presumably stored in the vaults of the Kitchenet? Perhaps she is allotted a few hops up and down in place out of sheer ebullience.

The fact that the magazine was to feature in its editorial section an article titled "Kitchen Cabinets as Work Centers" is probably perfectly natural, and it would be sophomoric of me to do more than note that in women's magazines editorial and advertising content often overlapped, reinforcing each other's interests and impact.

In the thirties the Federal Trade Commission did express some skepticism about the Good Housekeeping Institute's scientific detachment, and after two years of hearings, in 1941 issued a cease-and-desist order, which transformed the Seal of Approval from what readers might assume to be a guarantee based on scientific appraisal, into a kind of trademark that purported only to be a rather general endorsement by or affiliation with the magazine.

From the end of World War I until 1929, mass production and mass marketing continued to expand, erratically and apparently uncontrollably, like some self-perpetuating infernal machine, the unnatural offspring of science and technology. Was it a friendly monster? Only spoil-sport critics would warn, "It's alive, it's coming toward you, it's entering the house. It will try to take over your life."

The Thing threw off subsidiary colonies that in turn multiplied and were fruitful. One of these was the department store, and another was the chain grocery store. In 1925 the A & P Co. opened fifty new stores a week for fifty-two weeks! By 1930 Piggly Wiggly, a franchise operation, had 3,200 stores in its chain, and an ad showing beauties with bobbed hair coming and going from its Hollywood Boulevard branch. The ad's assertion, to be taken with a dose of perhaps ⅛ teaspoon salt, was that the "women of the smart world were first to launch the Piggly Wiggly vogue. Now clever women instinctively seek out Piggly Wiggly."

Shopping for the home became a new occupation and preoccupation. Nineteenth-century household industries had monopolized a woman's time, and the man of the family was usually the one who negotiated with the outside world, making any major purchases in shops and market. With the twentieth century, however, the system gradually reversed itself, and housewives had to master a new craft, one more difficult for some than for others. Ellen Richards, in a 1904 *House Beautiful,* lamented the laziness of some trainees: "The worst sign . . . is the haunting of the bargain counter by women who do not know their business of housekeeping and house-furnishing, and who take the word of a clerk that they are receiving something of value for almost nothing in money." She exhorted the American woman to use her brain and learn no longer how to "manufacture with her fingers everything which she uses," but how to spend money wisely.

I don't believe that the housewife was intrinsically any more gullible than her husband, but she was less experienced in the realities of buying and selling. Daily life, however, would provide a crash course in adult education. Yet in 1929 a commentator Hartmann cites could say, "American business loves the housewife for the same reason it loves China—that is, for her economic backwardness."

The more places there were in which to shop and the greater the selection, the more opportunities and temptations there were to spend, and spend . . . and spend. Simple cash flow had been enough to stymie women like my grandmother in an earlier, simpler age, and it continued to do so. J.A.T.'s end-of-the-month confrontations with her accounts are a refrain throughout her diaries. In 1899 she and her fiancé "made our estimates and find it takes a great deal of money to live. Clever of us truly." In the years to follow she was, twelve times annually, "awfully worried" or "rather bothered" or had "terrible mix-ups" in her accounts. She once mused: "Is there anything so depressing as bill paying? It is my only real cross—fearing the worst at the end of the month—and generally finding it too." Distress was compounded by the fact that she was only a steward of an allotment from her husband, and felt conscience-stricken if she mismanaged his money. It wasn't until April 1938, a year after she was widowed, that she wrote that at last she had ended a month in which her figures squared with the bank's. She rejoiced: "Prosaic as it may seem, is there any satisfaction *in the world* for some of us quite equal?"

The 1920s offered a newly democratized solution to an eternal problem: credit on the installment plan, with easy terms unto infinity. The rapid expansion of credit made possible for

many families the instantaneous and seemingly painless purchase of large, expensive items, primarily appliances for the
home, and cars. Heidi Hartmann reports that, in 1925, 90
percent of refrigerators and 85 percent of vacuum cleaners (all
those early Hoovers and Eurekas and now-extinct Pneuvacs)
were bought on credit. The Voss Sea Wave washer offered
"terms *so* easy you'll never miss the money." As the wicked
queen said to Snow White, "Just one bite of this beautiful red
apple, my pretty."

In *A Doll's House,* Thorwald moralized: "But seriously,
Nora, you know my principles on these points. No debts! No
borrowing! Home life ceases to be free and beautiful as soon as
it is founded on borrowing and debts."

In this case, I'm afraid I have to agree with him. Presumably I
had more sales resistance than my counterpart in the boom
years after World War I, when the new credit offered almost
irresistible temptations to householders experienced only as
mortgage-holders. Yet, sophisticated decades later, it was all
too easy for me to overextend, justifying my long-term inden-
turing to Master Charge on the grounds that my home was a
factory that was undercapitalized and needed equipment.

Installment buying might let a Voss Sea Wave crest in your
basement, but other domestic satisfactions were not so easily
achieved. Hartmann points out that an overeducation by the
stern taskmasters of home economics might foster unrealistic
standards that no human being could achieve. The failure to
succeed produced more anxiety and friction within the family.
Often the determined housekeeper, carried away by *her*
methods, her obsessive standards, would exclude the rest of her
family, untrained and loutish heathen that they were, from her
holy mission. She shrugged off human help, and revved up her
machines. She'd escape drudgery, at least in the sense of no
longer being anyone's assistant. She'd be in charge, alone.

Frank Gilbreth, when asked how one should use time saved
by efficient practices, humanely answered, "For work, if you
love that best. For education, for beauty, for art, for plea-

sure . . . for mumblety-peg, if that's where your heart lies." In 1954 Lillian Gilbreth added that "Savings are meant to be spent"—that is, neither hoarded nor buried in taking on new assignments. The heart of the zealot housewife might or might not lie in her work, but she could easily squander freed time by raising her domestic standards. The horizon ever recedes. Any rewards often seemed to be purely personal, of no interest to or significance in the outside world, which could not appreciate such expertise, the solitary satisfaction of the compulsive housekeeper of the twenties or thirties or since.

The growing self-reliance of the housewife, alone with her machines in her own home, was a development that with reason worried the service businesses, like laundries. Where earlier in the century the newly servantless woman turned to a laundry for help, increasingly she became more interested in operating her own sweatshop. By 1930 the Laundryowners' National Association was getting nervous. Its public relations campaign in one sense was pathetically obvious: ads showed elegantly coiffed, ladylike users of their professional services as being "freed" to leave home and attend "card clubs." But the association did make a valid point, largely trampled under by women running to be modern: a machine will do your work in the home efficiently but, and here's the catch, someone has to be there to operate it.

While new methodologies and machines were raising traditional standards for housework itself, women were assuming new responsibilities that would eat up more freed time. Most of these chores were contained in the house, though some home-based duties did require that the housewife spin out into the world and back again like a yo-yo. Ruth Schwartz Cowan has summarized: "What middle-class women were doing was sterilizing baby bottles, shepherding children to dancing classes and music lessons, planning nutritious meals, shopping for new clothes, studying child psychology, and handstitching color-coordinated curtains." Even shopping could be done from home in those halcyon days of telephone orders and grocery delivery, standard operating procedures in middle-class households until World War II, after which only a few vestigial specialty (that is, expensive) shops offered the service.

By 1930 the transformation of the ideal of the "Edwardian" American home, middle-class, cozy, and heavily populated with children and servants, was essentially complete. In its new personality it aspired to become a fully equipped technological creation in which good housekeeping meant managing without or with fewer servants, often according to the appealingly scientific principles of home economics. The good housekeeper, the mother of fewer children but now an industrial overseer as well, was concentrating on learning how to perform efficiently, and often found herself turning to more experienced women, or experts, or institutionalized advisers, such as women's magazines, whose motives were naturally not entirely altruistic.

The homemaker's quest turned away from spiritual goals toward material means, but for many it was intrinsically no less idealistic, and its fulfillment was as elusive as ever. The way to perfect family grace, the legendary Happy Home, seemed as unattainable through works and a vacuum cleaner as through devotion and a Christmas tree. A woman's relationship to her house and its practical demands—that is, housework—had become as emotionally hazardous as artful cultivation of a resonance of sentiments—home feeling—had been earlier.

Because old chores had been retained inside the middle-class house, while new responsibilities had been added, the average housewife of 1930 seemed to enjoy no more free time or latitude to explore the outside world than she'd had in 1920. At the beginning of the decade *Good Housekeeping* described a certain anxiety: "Men have cried out in alarm, 'With all this suffrage, with all this entering of professions, with all this throwing wide of the world's doors, women will rush out of their homes.' "

This did not come to pass, at least by 1930, nor did the simultaneous prophecy of the poet Edwin Markham offered up by *Good Housekeeping:*

But Home will sweeten as the years go by . . .
When Science shall draw down Orion's band
To ease the burden of the woman's hand.

The main difference was that now for many hours of the day the housewife of 1930 was alone in her house, working more solitarily and in a different spirit than she had before. As Hazel Kyrk had already concluded in *A Theory of Consumption* (1923), "The industrial revolution had reduced housework to the work of one woman from that of several."

By 1930 J.A.T.'s life had changed as well, in a particular way that had nothing and everything to do with broad social and economic trends, The News of the Day. In 1928 my grandfather transferred his office from New York to corporate headquarters in Lancaster, Pennsylvania. As tersely as she had once announced the happy prospect of building her own house, she noted in her diary: "[Henry] has spoken . . . about selling the place." And that was that. The family moved away and bought a large fieldstone house, rather grand but built by someone else.

In March 1930 J.A.T. returned to Summit "to help close the dear old home." Her relationship with her house was affectionate to the end. She left it without self-pity and with self-respect. Later that year she wrote: "Found in Grandma's little book today, and taken as signpost for this winter. 'What could have been done more to my vineyard that I have not done it?' "

 FIVE

Our Mothers' Tasteful Homes, 1930-1950

While Lindum stood patiently, empty and unsold, my bachelor father would sometimes camp there as a house-sitter. The house lost a custodian when on Christmas night 1930 my parents were married on the spur of the moment, in candlelight amidst native poinsettias in St. Petersburg, Florida, the bride's home town. The news was a surprise to the mother of the groom, who in frozen Pennsylvania was valiantly presiding over many fewer Christmas stockings, perhaps more eggnog. (J.A.T.'s recipe was positively Yankee in its puritanical proportions: 3 eggs to 1 quart milk, with whiskey or brandy added until "strong enough," whatever that meant.)

My parents' courtship had been short, intense, to me definitively romantic. They had met that August on one of the Clyde liners that used to steam between New York and Jacksonville. My father, at twenty-six, earnest but dashing (he did after all have a mustache sort of like Douglas Fairbanks's), introduced himself to my shy, pretty twenty-two-year-old mother and her younger sister, and plied them with glasses of orange juice, each garnished with a cherry.

For years we were to stage historic reenactments of that initial encounter at sea. My two brothers and I acquired early a taste for maraschino and sentiment.

My portrait of my mother in this generational house tour may seem comparatively sketchy, but she would squirm if I—or anyone—were to skywrite her name. J.A.T. chose to go public at a certain point in her life, the risk of overexposure in the suburban heavens her own. She was perfectly realistic about her need to speak out, in print and privately, and I'm afraid her tendency to indulge in didactic self-revelation has made its way intact to me.

My mother's choice, on the other hand, has always been to be what is known as a very private person, the genuine article, not the ersatz variety like the "elusive" celebrity who teases *paparazzi*. Unlike the Janes on either side of her, she can hold her tongue. She may know best, but she doesn't need to tell you exactly how she learned. Nor does she dish out unsolicited advice on how to run a family, a house, a life. Her methods have always been supportive, unobtrusive, subliminal, and what I've learned from her she didn't teach.

But I must stop, or else I will violate my own resolve and her privacy, though the facts of our coexistence in various houses—hers and mine—will inevitably compose themselves into a miniature profile of her. I certainly don't want to hide her nimbus in her hall closet, behind all the beige raincoats and the indomitable antique Hoover upright vacuum that never heard about planned obsolescence. But if that's where she wants to stash it, that's where it's going to stay, for it's her house, her halo.

Slyly slipping in one last comment, I must add that my mother is stubborn, a trait of character useful in her eighteen-year relationship with that powerful natural force, J.A.T., who was, by the time they first met, in full matriarchal bloom. The two women shared an overriding common interest, my father, and across the three-decade, North-South chasm between them, they glimpsed each other's strengths and were respectful. J.A.T., I believe, thought of my orphaned mother as somehow legally adopted, a real daughter in law. She sometimes overdid it, as when, helping the bride set up housekeeping in the Beechwood Apartments in Summit, she inflicted a traveling exhibit of oppressive family pictures taken out of some storage barrel and dusted off for the new household. One evening when my father returned home from work (he too was a commuter), he found all those eyes in all those frames quietly turned to the wall. Enough is enough, and even a Ruth would have concurred.

Redefining individual limits within the strange new world of matrimony preoccupies most brides. Certain fixed social boundaries were still clear, however, in the first year of my mother's marriage. "In the Hope We Live Happily Ever After" was Florence Trumbull Coolidge's attempt to provide young wives of 1930 with absolute guidance. Her "Eight Commandments" included "I shall make housekeeping my career" and "I shall see that my husband has a comfortable and cheerful home and that he is properly fed." Mrs. Coolidge herself, as pictured, fingered a place setting at a formally set but foodless Sheraton table, while trancelike she stared at some ghostly guest, or perhaps just at her husband. Her eighth commandment was stern: "I shall not learn to play golf—life holds too many other interests."

By 1935 my parents had left Summit, circulated, and returned. I had joined them along the way, in Toronto in 1932, and we had continued together to Riverside, just outside Chicago. This "suburban village," planned by Olmsted and Vaux in 1868, was probably the first such community in the country, and though senior to Summit, was more progressive in layout than the upstart in New Jersey, which had simply grown and expanded as it would.

While still rootless and renting, the young couple, absorbed in each other, refused to take too seriously any of the Coolidge Commandments, their vagabond life, or even such perplexing dilemmas of contemporary interior decoration as whether or not roller shades should wear fringe. J.A.T. and other emissaries from home often checked in, to see the baby and give advice. One sister-in-law removed the fringe.

Really serious matters of home feeling were treated with proper respect, however, and in 1934 my father in a communiqué back to headquarters had described in detail his plans for adapting a Lindum Christmas to a midwestern setting. He assured J.A.T. that he would faithfully administer all high rituals: the Sequestering of the Christmas Room, the Hanging of the Stocking, and the Revelation of the Tree. What was to be in my generation an almost totally secular shindig nonetheless retained all the paraphernalia of J.A.T.'s original high holiday, if not its orthodox Episcopalian dimensions.

When finally my parents and I gravitated back to Summit, we moved into a temporary apartment on the top floor of a generously dowdy Victorian house not far from "downtown." A florid stained-glass window stands out in my memory like a single Kodachrome cropped to exclude its surroundings, a strange detached panel of colored light. When in 1936 the much-advertised new baby turned out to be twins (one came home from the hospital in a laundry basket), the hunt for a larger home, closer to the ground and permanent, became urgent. In 1937 we five moved into a compact little house on the slope of a hill, where we were to live until 1946. Bordered on two sides by tall oaks, small, white, symmetrical, and "in the Colonial spirit," the house had many thousands of cousins, but of course I couldn't imagine that there was another like it.

How small it was I didn't realize until I haphazardly returned to Summit in 1977. I had assumed that even after decades in the outside world I could still sniff my way back into town, like Lassie coming home, but I found myself muddled in exhaust fumes, tangled between gaudy old burgerways and new multi-lane highways in that most abstract and landmarkless of styles, Mussolini Interstate. Then my ears pricked up and my tail wagged, as I suddenly knew I was climbing the short hills toward the summit.

Crossing over an invisible border into that familiar small

principality—Liechtenstein, my Liechtenstein—I knew I was home again. The hilltop seemed to have zoned out time itself. There was Overlook Hospital where someone in a mask had absconded with my tonsils. There was the Lackawanna Railroad Station, daily host to dapper commuters, their wives and children, the cobblestone approach to its track as jiggly as when we had rattled down it to wait for my father's evening train. I wandered, driving dreamily past lush green lawns, down curving, deeply shaded, ruddy October streets—Whittredge, Lenox, Hobart, Ridge, Ox Bow, Badeau, Bellevue, Llewellyn, all hardly changed. The Rip Van Winkle phenomenon overcame me. Had only I grown older?

Few cars or adults were out on the afternoon streets to spoil the 1940s set. It was the four o'clock lull. Children whom I felt I recognized were walking home from school or friends' houses, carrying their sweaters and books, collecting as they went the horse chestnuts as burnished as antique furniture that I'd once hoarded until they dried and dulled. Swerving and laughing and not stepping on cracks in the sidewalk, the kids were just as Cecelia and Joyce and Gordon and I once had been. When they got home, would their mothers be waiting? Would they telephone each other immediately, as we had, to complain languidly that there was nothing to do, that it was all *"très* boring."

Ennuyant it may well have been, like playing in a large, fenced-in formal garden, but it was certainly orderly and secure. We suburban children knew what to expect: trudging to school in the morning, peanut butter and jelly at lunch, Captain Midnight in the evening, a father coming home in time for dinner and saying to a mother, "God, what a day!" and after a little homework, a bath and bed. Life was simple, predictable.

Our parents' values seemed so deeply planted, buried like bulbs, that we never thought to question them. That we, silver bells and cockle shells, all looked pretty much alike didn't seem unusual, and, pretty maids all in a row, we wanted to be even more alike rather than less.

Taking the examples at home for granted, my friends and I

studied each others' mothers to pick out the admirable ones suitable for imitation, those who would today be called role models. The range of choice, judging as superficially as we did, was not overwhelming. I remember among my friends' mothers only one woman who was divorced, and none who worked for pay outside the home.

Within their houses, however, our mothers seemed more distinctive. Just as each house had a characteristic smell—bacon or cigarettes or lemon oil or perfume or mustiness or newness but never garlic—each mother perpetuated a special mood.

Joyce's mother folded her stockings into precise squares and filed them in her brass-and-mahogany Chippendale chest. She rescued remnant waning moons of soap and caged them in a wire utensil she swished sudsily in her dishpan. She never left pots to soak. She never wore a bathing suit; she always wore a girdle. She lived among prints of Englishmen in red coats riding to hounds, and tan stucco, and diamond-paned casement windows. Her table was set with discreet white Wedgwood earthenware. Her garden was dark green, glum with pachysandra and ivy. Joyce's mother was kind, very orderly, and dignified.

Cecelia's mother came from the South, and in her formal dining room, Nancy the maid served us tiny buttery biscuits that were Hattie the cook's specialty. Cecelia's mother planned meals, wrote them down on lists (ours just seemed to happen on impulse). The house was large and its staircase reminded me of *Gone With the Wind*. The drawing room, where we never played our endless games of jacks, was brocaded and stately, and on one wall hung a portrait of Cecelia's beautiful mother. Sometimes we greedy little girls would intercept delicacies destined for the Junior League tea: buttery crescent cookies with one end dipped in bittersweet chocolate, fancy sandwiches that looked like checkerboards or slices of jelly roll but were filled with cream-cheese-and-olive or chicken glop. Everyone agreed that Cecelia's mother had perfect taste. Her garden was fragrant with apricot roses.

Gordon's mother ran her brisk and cheerful house efficiently, without much fuss. Neither too big nor too small, it was the golden mean, warm and sunny. Gordon's mother was amusedly tolerant when we spent one long afternoon jumping off the garage roof, thundering past her and back up the stairs, out the bedroom window and—Geronimo—off again into the blue. She was interested in people, even if their behavior was odd. Gordon's mother was a concerned citizen and worked consistently and hard for charities like the Red Cross and the Mental Hygiene Clinic. She was, of course, a volunteer, but she had been professionally trained as a social worker. She was busy but friendly, and made me feel as if she found me interesting.

If I was asked where else besides home I learned to be a housewife, I could answer "other people's houses." As John Russell put it in *The New York Times:* "School and college are all very well, but it is in other people's houses that we learn the complete alphabet—A through Z—of other people's attitudes." Joyce's mother's house fascinated me: such neatness was ultimately mysterious. Cecelia's mother's I admired from afar. It was Gordon's mother's house I could see myself in someday.

Summit in the 1930s and '40s was as homogeneous architecturally as it was socially. I knew no family who lived in an apartment complex or who built a new house or who lived in one that by any stretch of the imagination could be called "modern." Though the town's population today is reportedly more diverse, and certainly more transient, the style of its single-family homes is almost as consistent as it was thirty years ago. Traditional styles still reign, even in the newest sections— Tudor, Norman, Colonial, but the greatest of these is Colonial. Literal-minded, freely interpreted, impressionistic, large or small, but still . . . Colonial.

In 1977 I wheeled toward my mother's house warily, nervously. Nostalgic memories sometimes don't survive a confrontation, and I wanted to preserve mine. I turned into "our" driveway, stopped, got out, and stared at my old friend, whom the years had not altered so much as diminished. Either the rhododendron foundation planting had grown like Sleeping Beauty's bramble hedge, or the house had shrunk.

The brick front porch, its gabled roof supported by two pillars, the paneled door with its sidelights, were still properly centered, I suppose, but the pillars seemed atrophied, spindly. The white clapboards needed paint, and so did the dark green shutters. I'd forgotten that the facade above the first story was matchboarded, if I'd ever even noticed, and the windows on that level were so small and square. The one-story sun-porch wing looked dated, old-fashioned. What had happened to the house? What had happened to me? Nothing pierced me to the heart; I did not know this place.

Suddenly I was aware of the sound of tires on gravel, and turned to see a fugitive car, my cowardly Volvo, backing itself away from a direct encounter too painful to witness. By the time I'd caught up with it and this time had more firmly applied the emergency brake, another car had swished past me into the drive, and another woman, about my age, was moving toward the front steps. She turned out not to be the lady of the house, as I had assumed she was, but someone like me, slightly out of order. The ex-wife of a temporary renter of the house, she had come to retrieve a check she'd left in her children's laundry basket (baffling, but I asked no questions). She graciously invited me to join her in a little breaking and entering. Actually we didn't have to break (the back door was unlocked), but we did undeniably enter. I'd not been inside the house since leaving it behind, at fourteen, in 1946.

Feeling somewhat illicit, and therefore more of a stranger than I might have otherwise, I tried to ingratiate myself with the house, which remained unfriendly, even hostile. It seemed to hold a grudge. The dining-room corner cabinets with their many-paned doors stared at me unblinking. The oak living-room floors hid themselves under sculptured gold nylon wall-to-wall. What had happened to my mother's tasteful Orientals? Oh yes, now I remember.

The alien refrigerator in the kitchen had sharp right-angled corners; ours had been rounded off, in the sleek *moderne* of the appliances of the thirties. What had they done with my father's Rube Goldberg garbage chute, with its trap door in the floor through which we would-be bombardiers could drop the big ones right on Berlin or Tokyo? One of his most original home-handyman projects, it had been excised without leaving so much as a scar or a seam. Where was the life that late I led? And my room. Its dimensions were strangely compressed. To think that I had once suggested to my family that I divide it in four, to make a bachelor-girl apartment where I would live self-sufficiently, doing my own cooking (I could make fudge, if the weather was right) and talking on my own telephone. My parents handled the crisis tactfully, wearing me down by helping me make laboriously measured drawings of the proposed suite. Each room, it turned out, would have been about six by six feet. Mathematics suggested that secession might be impolitic. I stopped sulking and came downstairs.

In 1977 all that welcomed me, that I recognized with a pang, were the weeds thronging around the back steps, having spilled out of the flower beds, spinachy plantain with its asparagus shaft; moiling, nameless pink and blue sprigs; a few tall, dignified wild asters. No frost had chilled and killed them. They were still cheerfully self-propagating, and I *knew* them. The poets are right; there is solace in Nature, if weeds in a suburb qualify as Nature.

When I entered my grandmother's house for the first time, I was convinced that you can go home again. When I reentered my mother's house, I was equally convinced of the opposite. You can't.

Perhaps one reason my mother's house revisited was doomed to disappoint me was that unconsciously I expected to reencounter the vitality it had once contained. I didn't think I'd find my mother on her knees, pinning a slipcover on a wing chair in the living room; my father rummaging in his tool chest in the dark, dank basement from which all projects rose overnight, like mushrooms; or my little brothers, red-faced and glistening on a 92° day, blasting out of the hot-box attic where they had gone to suffer so that (small boy logic) they would feel cool when they came down. But I didn't think that the walls would be so stiff and unresonating.

The life, our life, had gone out of the house with us. We, not it, had absorbed all the free-floating home feeling, and we had carried it away with us, to cart up other similar stairs, through other similar doors.

Now I could look at the house that had held my childhood and not feel I had to protect it, justify its existence to some hypothetical sociologist of suburban life who might try to freeze it into a statistical pattern. It was, after all, just an ordinary house and not much different from all the others, all those white Colonials with green shutters. Let him have it.

My imaginary sociologist might begin on my mother's house by pointing out certain relevant facts in its generic background. In a single generation, America had almost doubled its population and further rearranged itself demographically. The shift away from both country and city continued. When J.A.T. married in 1900, 16 million households existed within a total population of 76 million. By 1930 when my mother married, the totals had increased to 30 million households in a population of 123 million. Suburbs were burgeoning. In 1900, 15.6 percent of the population lived in the middle distance, whereas by 1930, 23.4 percent were bedding down there.

Suburban growth during the 1920s was more than just steady. In some cases it was phenomenal. Summit increased only slightly, from 10,174 in 1920 to 14,556 in 1930, but its counterparts elsewhere, fashionable and upper-middle-class, expanded incredibly. For example, Shaker Heights, Ohio, increased by 1,000 percent, while Glendale, California, grew 3,000 percent! (These statistics are lifted from Dolce's *Suburbia*.) In that one decade alone the suburban population surrounding sixty-two metropolitan districts leapt from 11 million to 17 million, as places like Forest, Grosse Point, Chestnut Hill, and Philadelphia's Main Line prospered.

In the early twenties a great upsurge in the number of housing starts soon became a real boom, previously unparalleled in scale. Builders were kept busy satisfying the demand accumulated during World War I, accommodating the continuing shift of the middle class to the suburbs. Buyers blithely made the most of

newly plentiful credit. Money seemed as easy to grow as
lettuce, and a boom economy, with all its attendant realtors,
boosters, and salesmen, made it as easy to spend. Numbers
began to influence choices by sheer weight alone: "More young
Americans are . . . a million contented housewives agree . . .
this year more smart buyers are choosing. . . ."

Expressing a cheerful materialism, a newly self-conscious
"class" of young American housewives, with their checkbooks
and charge accounts at the ready, hustled after style, taste,
social status (which money probably can buy), and love (which
it can't, or can it?). Many women apparently thought—or were
thought to think—that these commodities came packed in a
new house, like a bonnet in a bandbox. Their optimistic view of
the magic of real estate paralleled their contemporary faith in
household machines.

In 1902 Joy Wheeler Dow had commented on the American
penchant for going out on a financial limb in order to satisfy
some innate national lust for home ownership: "With us it is a
case of every man his own Louis XIV. For no matter how short
of ready money the American may be the more his new
consuming passion overcomes his prudence until he is quite
ready to mortgage everything he possesses, discount his earn-
ings and business prospect to some building-loan association
. . . any way so long as he may build his . . . house."

In 1925 a *Good Housekeeping* writer dramatized the passionate rate of spending during the postwar boom: "We have
had an *annual* building budget almost as big as the total cost of
the Civil War." A lot of homeowners were perched out on a lot
of limbs—mortgaged, laden with installment payments for
household appliances and cars, and susceptible to the unthinka-
ble, a change in the weather.

A popular novel of the early 1920s, serialized in *Good
Housekeeping,* was Ben Ames Williams's *More Stately Mansions,* a sort of parable that "lay bare a wrong that multitudes of
women are practicing every day." Nancy Vane (as in *vain*) was
"very pretty and adorable" but headstrong. (The twenties and
thirties, if popular fiction and movies are to be believed,

certainly nurtured a lot of spoiled, headstrong ladies.) Nancy's plodding husband Dick was besotted and, she thought, malleable. She, though newly wed, had already grown dissatisfied with her "semi-bungalow," even before the abominable socialite Agnes patronized her taste and standard of living. When Dick proved somewhat resistant to change, she tried everything in her repertoire to inveigle him into buying her a new two-story Dutch Colonial. She invoked the architectural argument ("Its stairs suggest a certain dignity not to be found in any single-floor apartment"); foot-stamping and pouting ("Dickie, I've simply *got* to have it"); psychological warfare ("A nice house gives a man self-respect and confidence, just as clothes do"); baby talk; and even amateur investment counseling.

When Dick continued to plead poverty, she retorted, "It's not my business to tell you how to earn the money. It's your business to get it, and mine to spend it, and that's all there is to that." Poor Dick was finally driven to forge his father's name on a down-payment check. When the Pater found out, he disowned Dick and tongue-lashed Nancy: "Pretty, brainless, selfish, frivolous little ape," adding as an afterthought, "bloodsucker, leech!" Nancy, after undergoing a single dark night of the soul, emerged wise and mature. The day was saved by Uncle Mark, the kindly old realtor, the young couple adjusted to reality in their semi-bungalow, but one suspected that . . . someday . . . they'd have that new house.

The novel seems corny and simpleminded today, but skeptics of the seventies cannot overestimate the susceptibility of a Nancy of fifty years ago. Not only was a young bride in a place like Summit constantly tempted to buy more "good taste" than she could afford, but also in many cases an ambitious, newly affluent husband, unlike Dick, actively sponsored her as a grand acquisitor for his single-family domestic museum. The era was Jay Gatsby's, not Horatio Alger's.

The decade of the 1920s was a period of competitive consumption as conspicuous as that following the Civil War, but instead of latching onto anything that was new, European, gaudy, and gilded, we seemed greedy for decanted American

Heritage, for candles, crystal goblets, weathered brick. The new and enlarged class of housewives found a romanticized national past more appealing than their own individual backgrounds. Gracious living in a traditional house in Short Hills or Wellesley—a costume drama—became a typical cultural and economic goal for a young couple starting out. The successful wife would reside, and entertain, not in a cozy home just like Grandma's but in an establishment that was much more elegant, formal, and in better taste.

The healthful suburban house whose "good intentions" were defended in 1903 often became by the 1920s a pale, narcissistic show-off that disdained the hearty outdoors of Theodore Roosevelt for its own impeccable pastel interior. The fashionable new style was one that was self-conscious, conservative, formal, and concerned with appearances. If the mode had the artificiality of the eighteenth century, it could also achieve the same fragile elegance. But how strange that women who had bobbed their hair, shortened their skirts, and gotten the vote would dream of living in houses suited to aristocratic ladies in powdered wigs.

If I were to frame an outrageous oversimplification (and obviously I am about to do so, yet again), I would describe the 1920s as the reign of the large neo-Georgian house as an upper-class phenomenon and a middle-class ideal. The 1930s were to be the decade when adaptations down into the simpler, more democratic, and less costly style described by Dow as "Witch-Colonial" became the reality for which more and more ordinary American housewives settled. The phenomenon of generalized Colonial—the Early American aura of my mother's house—was a compromise on practical grounds. This moderate approach to the design of smaller American suburban houses had been initiated earlier but was not widely and popularly endorsed across the country until after the Crash.

High fashion in the 1920s was set by boomtime *arrivistes,* the big spenders, as well as by traditional tastemakers like the aristocracy of inherited wealth, from Newport to East Egg, Long Island, to California and Texas and Florida and stops in between. Passed on from the earlier age was the showcase mentality described by Joan Didion in an essay in *Slouching Towards Bethlehem:*

Men paid for Newport, and granted to women the privilege of living in it. Just as gilt vitrines could be purchased for the correct display of biscuit Sèvres, so marble stairways could be bought for the advantageous display of women. In the filigreed gazebos they could be exhibited in a different light; in the . . . sitting rooms, in still another setting.

A modern middle-class Nancy Vane, certainly less passive than her mother, might scale down her own setting, but she was her husband's accomplice now, though he still paid the bills. The implementing of couples' mutual self-promotion became, more and more, women's business, as they learned to wheel and deal as semi-independent purchasing agents. The tone of interior-decoration features in women's magazines reinforces a sense that women's function as collaborators in "displaying the fruits of their partner's success" (to quote Veblen's definition of their role in conspicuous consumption) had become more than a practical duty akin to housekeeping, but almost a cultural obligation, like piano lessons for Barbara, and a five-foot shelf of the English classics, bound in gold and maroon. If housekeeping was technology and craft, home decoration aspired to be patronage of the arts, if not art itself.

I recently asked my mother, as we sat patching together the past, if she had any sense that her friends in Summit during the 1930s and early '40s felt at all guilty about filling their days and their dining rooms with women guests for luncheon and tea and bridge and spending so much of their time dolling up their houses and themselves to that limited end. I asked her as I would have queried Lady Mary Wortley Montagu about the social habits of those frivolous others, the players of *ombre,* wearers of beauty spots, sippers of coffee. Though neither bluestocking nor puritan, my mother was perhaps atypical in that she could take a watercress tea sandwich or leave it alone.

In her luncheons and Junior League meetings she simply sought the companionship of women outside the necessarily confined limits of the stripped-down, home-centered life her circumstances dictated; she was not seeking A Social Life, with all that phrase implies.

"No, I don't think they felt particularly guilty," she answered me, "any more than they did about not working." Her explanation was Veblenesque: "They knew that their husbands were proud to be able to give them that sort of life, and so they felt perfectly free to enjoy it."

Summit was not exactly a seraglio, but there were certain similarities in the kind of freedom its women enjoyed to the existence of Turkish ladies in the eighteenth century, as described by Lady Mary herself in 1718:

[They] are perhaps freer than any ladies in the universe, and are the only women in the world that lead a life of uninterrupted pleasure exempt from cares; their whole time being spent in visiting, bathing, or the agreeable amusement of spending money, and inventing new fashions. A husband would be thought mad that exacted any degree of economy from his wife, whose expenses are no way limited but by her own fancy. 'Tis his business to get money, and hers to spend it.

In the popular imagination, self-display, historic or historic-type houses, Georgian and Colonial design, lingering Anglophilia, good taste, lineage, and culture were all mixed up together like some rich fruitcake. When national heritage, or its cruder cousin, flag-waving patriotism, entered the scene, a comic pageant sometimes resulted.

In 1941 all of us in the third grade of our public elementary school, the Lincoln School, were drafted into a peculiar auxiliary, the Junior Daughters of the American Revolution. We Junior Daughters were of both sexes, of various creeds and ethnic origins, but, in 1941 in Summit, of one color only. Our purpose as an organization seemed to be patriotic, comparable to saluting the flag in class every morning, but we pursued our noble goal obliquely by re-creating everyday events of Olden Times.

One amazing excursion into the past was an Early American taffy pull, a very sticky affair. The mothers in charge had failed to let the molasses syrup reach the proper viscosity, and pull as we might, nothing happened except that the entire third grade became firmly glued to each other and the walls in an unforgettable example of class solidarity.

Our mothers, not easily deterred, next took us to nearby Morristown where, carefully "not touching," we straggled through the historic white clapboard Ford Mansion. Since it had been George Washington's headquarters in the winter of 1779–80, it was absolutely soaked in patriotism. Our mothers were indoctrinating us in their antiquarian tastes, one way or another. But how had they been brainwashed?

The history of latterday Colonialism is a catalogue of architectural mini-revivals: the Colonial Revival of my grandmother's girlhood in the 1870s and '80s, the American Renaissance described by Dow in 1904, the neo-Georgianism of the 1920s, when our young mothers were developing susceptibilities. A subcurrent in the twenties had been a rather pedantic, literal-minded interest in authentic old houses of an Anglo-Saxon persuasion. In that prosperous era there was what almost amounted to a fad among the rich not only for the antique English style but for importing and relocating real houses as one would furniture. In Richmond, Virginia, part of a genuine sixteenth-century priory was brought from Warwickshire to be, in 1925–28, embedded in Virginia House, an imposing Tudor fantasy. Another acquisition, Agecroft Hall, a fifteenth-century manor house, was reconstructed nearby in 1926.

Other wealthy citizens of the Old Dominion chose to pack up indigenous antiques. Theoretically, a speedy Georgian mansion could have passed a medieval stone tower on the highway into Richmond. Ampthill (1732) arrived from Chesterfield County in 1929, while Wilton (1750–53) was in 1933 a latecomer.

Sometimes the issue, as in Wilton, was preservation, the moving of the house out of harm's way. But often it was simply the whim of a collector that sent a farmhouse trundling from Vermont to exurban Connecticut and a site more convenient to Wall Street. Extracts from ancient houses—paneled rooms, for example—made their way to the new American Wing of the Metropolitan Museum of Art in New York, which opened its doors in 1925 (thus prompting a whole series of adulatory articles in *Good Housekeeping*).

In Virginia some venerable houses managed to stay put, and their restorers, like Mohammed, came to them. Berkeley (1726), one of the James River plantations so admired by Dow, was restored in 1926, and another, Carter's Grove (1750–55), in 1927. Elsewhere in the state, traditional architects, like the perfectionist William Lawrence Bottomley, were building for the "conservative American class" faithful replicas of eighteenth-century Palladian houses that emulated the "romantic charm and mellowness" (Bottomley's words) of their Tidewater prototypes.

But these dreamlike, stately homes, surrounded with azalea and dogwood, new greensward and ancient poplars, were out of reach for the ordinary family, who might be doing well in postwar prosperity . . . but not *that* well. They looked at the photographs in magazines, they admired, they copied as faithfully as they could manage. A century earlier the architectural pattern books of Asher Benjamin and Minard Lafever had provided models for neo-Classical imitation. These had their modern counterpart in the White Pine Series of Architectural Monographs, whose publication of measured drawings and other source material on Early American houses, starting in 1916, "sired many Georgian houses in the suburbs."

The national real-estate boom of the twenties—when anything seemed possible, even the kidnapping of the past or its exact reproduction—reached its highwater mark early, on the gold coasts of Florida in 1925, which was the year my mother graduated from St. Petersburg High School. Its receding waters were to leave behind beached, half-finished hotels, like the roofless ruins of Ostia Antica, looking wistfully, emptily, out to sea. The boom peaked elsewhere in the nation about a year later. By the time my mother graduated from Florida State College for Women in 1929, the stock market crash was only a few months away.

"Suddenly, my easy life slid away from me," wrote Mrs. Arthur Middleton of Charleston, South Carolina, when selling herself and many points of ellipsis to the friendly folks at Chipso Soap (in whose ad she and her starched, ruffled little girls appeared). "I found myself with the care of my children . . . my cooking . . . housework, even the washing . . . to do with my own hands. O.K., Depression . . . at least you taught me to use Chipso."

Across the country, women were learning much more radical lessons in accommodation; but for those in comparatively untouched enclaves like Summit, hard times often meant only the mildest lessons in belt-tightening. As far as housing was concerned, one might remodel a passé prewar stucco and forgo a new Dutch Colonial. Perhaps one would move into a smaller, "more convenient" house. *Good Housekeeping* in 1930 headed an editorial "Time to Remodel," and referred in it gently to "these times of slack business." Rain fell quietly on Shaker Heights and Glendale and Summit. The thunder of hammers would not sound again until after World War II.

With the demand for smaller and/or cheaper houses, or simply for remodeling, the tricky matter of adapting down, in both scale and exactness, became for designers and builders an urgent practical issue, often one of survival during "these times of slack business" when 4,000 architectural firms failed and the dollar volume of their business in 1928 declined by 75 percent. Uneasily designers entered the realm of compromise, that shaky kingdom with no reassuring code of law nor even a firm body of precedent. What are the standards for adaptation? How free or how literal should a translation be? If a mood is all one seeks to re-create, why be too prissy or pedantic?

The generalized Colonialism that dominated much suburban construction during the years between the Crash and World War II tyrannized those of our mothers who anxiously aspired to Do the Right Thing, who didn't feel secure in their own taste, and who preferred to own exact reproductions of properly pedigreed originals, thereby leaving less margin for error than if they struck out into unorthodoxy.

Though the impersonal mass production of 1950s-type tract housing, which featured ersatz, deracinated Colonial motifs, was yet to come, the prevailing winds were moving middle-class households farther and farther away not only from exactitude but also from the ideal of the idiosyncratic, sentimental family nest, the cozy repository of home feeling. What tended to be left behind was a real awareness of valid, personal domestic traditions. These were exchanged by many in years to come for some Disneyland approximation of the past.

Housewives were made conscious, more than ever before, of expert authorities outside the family who were better equipped to make aesthetic choices for them. The discrepancy between Good Taste and one's own instincts, eccentric or vulgar as they might be, was widening. Women kept looking over their shoulders to see "How America Lives" (a popular feature in the *Ladies' Home Journal*). Increasingly, the housewife found security in numbers, in thinking of herself as a type, of her home as typical.

My mother's typical house was probably constructed in the late twenties as a one-shot speculation by a builder who was not likely to have used an architect. The fact that its garage is detached dates it. The rapprochement of houses and garages was usually negotiated in the 1930s. In plan and style the house echoed a prototypical small Colonial featured in a 1930 *Good Housekeeping* article written by a streamlined fellow who called himself "Duncanhunter, Architect." (I can imagine his letterheads.)

In his piece, " 'Let Me Live in a House'—On the Slope of a Hill," he traced the design process of a residence he built for Mr. and Mrs. Howard Clay in Woodland Park, a subdivision of Summit, which he described as a "community of fine modern homes, not pretentious but possessing real architectural character." Mrs. Clay had worked ahead of her architect, constructing a doll-house model in plasticine of the structure which would embody "her good taste, and her affection for the homes of her New England ancestors."

The collaboration of architect and housewife produced a final plan almost identical to my mother's house (and to how many others?): a two-story rectangular structure, bisected by a center hall, with straight stairs (great for sliding down on a mattress, I should add). Dining room and kitchen lined up on one side of the hall, and a living room took over the other side, extending the depth of the house. There was also a lavatory downstairs, while upstairs were three bedrooms and a full bath. The one-story wing in Mrs. Clay's house contained a maid's room, and in ours a sun porch. Both these small houses were adaptations, condensations of houses of the American Renaissance like Lindum, which in turn had drawn on eighteenth-century precedents. My mother's house, within its small covers, was a veritable architectural digest.

In " 'Let Me Live in a House' " Duncanhunter documents how restrictions on suburban style could be imposed by one's peers. Generalized social pressure alone didn't homogenize appearances in Summit. Taste was reinforced by a "board of property owners controlling the entire community" that had to approve the "design and construction . . . the location of the house and garage." For example, Mrs. Clay's garage *had* to be attached and entered from the rear, that is, away from the street. It was, when built, even more unobtrusive than required, hidden below grade, under the wing.

Garage design challenged architects during the thirties. Olfactory considerations, among others, had located stables or carriage houses at some distance from the dining room table, as they had been, for example, at Lindum. The earliest garages followed the horse-and-buggy custom and were typically sited at the rear corner of lots, with long driveways leading to them. But their banishment was obviously inconvenient and arbitrary, and *Good Housekeeping*, for one, in its 1930 survey of garage architecture endorsed bringing the garage into or up to the house itself, sometimes connecting it with a breezeway or some other loggia-like device. The snuggling up to houses by garages symbolizes the gradual integration of the car into American home life. The garage, like a Trojan horse, brought the car right into the family commonwealth, and the new Buick or Packard or Ford became a member, with his own little room. His care and welfare increasingly became the daily responsibility of—guess who?—his new foster mother.

Popular judgment has always awarded custody of the car to its father. Certainly there is male bonding between the two, Big Daddy and his macho machine. But though women haven't derived any particular psycho-sexual or sporting satisfactions out of doggedly serving as taxi drivers and teamsters, they have since the twenties accumulated impressive road records. After World War II, driving from home to school to mall to service station to home again was to become almost as much a part of ordinary household routine as monitoring the cycles on a washing machine.

My grandfather bought his first car, a Buick Touring model, in 1919, and by late 1920 forty-five-year-old J.A.T. had discreetly but definitively flunked driver's education. Omitting any gory factual details, she simply recorded that driving posed "too great a risk" and that she must remember where her first duty to her family lay. The accident must have been spectacular.

At thirty-two my mother felt that she had to learn to drive at last, and though her indoctrination was perhaps as eventful as my grandmother's, she persevered against all obstacles. One of them, the rear wall of the garage, which she and the Chevrolet occasionally nudged, began to open out like a door hinged at its top. Our garage was *really* detached. My father improvised a rustic log barricade, very like the borders of parking lots in national forests.

He was equally forbearing when, during my novitiate as a fourteen-year-old Florida licensee of sorts, he read in the afternoon paper that I had, like George Washington and the cherry tree, assured the police that a rear-end collision at a stoplight had been "all my fault." By sixteen I took driving for granted as a permanent if hazardous part of my daily life, and in the harried years of early motherhood it virtually replaced walking as a means of locomotion outside the house. My husband might describe me as a search-and-destroy mission, but it was I, dented but dauntless, who logged the mileage and escorted the machine to its pediatrician and orthodontist. In three generations evolution had reequipped housewives with wheels.

The location of Mrs. Clay's garage had been dictated to her by a review board whose motive has been described to me by a Summit historian as the protection of the streetscape from the limited imagination, the poor taste, of potential developers. Concerned citizens, not profiteers, would oversee siting and related matters. But a canny woman realtor in Summit has suggested to me that the prime consideration may have been the preservation of stylistic homogeneity, keeping the town architecturally pure. Zoning regulations would strain out apartment blight and commercial intrusions, but zoning boards couldn't really legislate aesthetics. And so Summit and Shaker Heights had their review boards to exclude "discordant home designs" and Palos Verdes Estates in Los Angeles employed a paid "art jury" to serve as arbiters of taste.

The first comprehensive zoning ordinance had been passed in New York City in 1916, aimed at keeping Fifth Avenue uninfected by the spreading population of the then nearby garment district. Its chief proponent inveighed against the "out of place apartment house," whose "shifting renting class . . . lacking in neighborliness and civic pride and leading an impoverished family life" would bring instability and deterioration. Apartment-phobia continued to feed housephilia, even in the sophisticated, realistic Manhattan of the 1920s.

In the suburbs the mixed blessing of zoning caught on fast, and the gimmick spread from the public into the private sector. Housing developers began to include clauses in deeds governing "the cost of building, build back, race, etc." Snob zoning of this sort by private enterprise was not exactly in the spirit of the founding fathers, whose architectural style the developers to a large degree had appropriated. Middle-class Americans in the 1920s and '30s winked at Gentlemen's Agreements, Restricted

Communities, Private Clubs, and Quotas on one social level, while they castigated a reemergent Ku Klux Klan on another. Anyway, public zoning law was perhaps the least of the worries of the would-be householder who was "different."

Developers and speculators, according to Stanley Buder in *Suburbia,* understood more fully than federal housing programmers "what Americans wanted, and catered to that aspiration." Women in suburbs in the twenties and thirties didn't want multiple-unit housing (though they were titillated by glamorous tales of the "glitter and swank" of the classy apartment houses then rising on Park Avenue). They, like their husbands, tended to draw back at a hint of collectivism. Broad social objectives weren't fashionable yet, and the woman of genuine conscience in Summit was more likely to help the disadvantaged as a Lady Bountiful or through service organizations than to want to live with or next door to them.

And yet a woman raised in such an environment might feel drawn to a limited experiment like Radburn, New Jersey, the new town planned by Clarence Stein and Henry Wright with the commonweal in mind. Though the innovative plan of the model community featured public open space and the separation of streets and pedestrian ways, it used a familiar, traditional vocabulary in Frederick Lee Ackerman's designs for its private, single-family houses. In the 1940s J.A.T. saw one of her married daughters and her family off in their move slightly to the north geographically, a tiny bit to the left ideologically. Unfortunately, the immigrants timed their arrival to coincide with World War II, when Radburn greens sprouted fences to keep the citizens out and the olive-drab trucks, tents, and G.I.s in. Eventually the nomads moved farther north and right, to an eighteenth-century inn-turned-farmhouse in rural New Hampshire, where they settled for good among open fields and thick woods populated only by crows, rabbits, and other nonmilitary forces.

It was Williamsburg, Virginia, whose restoration began in 1926, that would, from the opening of the Ràleigh Tavern in

1932, provide widely popular models for literal-minded but feasible reproduction. Its combination of historical feeling, the smallness of most of its houses and their simple formality was for many almost irresistible.

Moreover, the Williamsburg style had a satisfyingly moral dimension. Its implications were lofty, or as John D. Rockefeller, the angel of the production, described it, Williamsburg teaches a lesson about the "high purpose, unselfish devotion of our forefathers to the common good."

Like Dow before him, Rockefeller ascribed to Colonial architecture some sort of message about inherited national character or patriotism or democracy. Accordingly, the Wythe House was for the susceptible not just the restored structure in which Thomas Jefferson had once dined with his mentor but a shrine whose very mortar held lingering traces of high purpose. On a lesser plane, worthiness and good character seemed part of the Colonial style. It's hard to imagine a mean drunk in the mellowness of Raleigh Tavern.

Williamsburg's domestic architecture, building by building, was romantic enough to satisfy the average sensibility, was historically reliable, was comprehensible, and embodied right thinking. But more than that, the prevailing style was a congenial compromise in scale and mood between Georgian social pretension and the comparative self-effacement of Witch-Colonial and its adaptations.

The popular image of Williamsburg continues to be that of a miscellaneous collection of perfectly restored single-family houses, a kind of pre-Revolutionary suburb, and not of a town as planned in its way as Radburn, New Jersey, with its streets and open space and vistas thoughtfully arranged with the common good in mind. The irony is that Williamsburg's rationale so little influenced stylistic imitators of its individual houses. "The communal good" was a consideration that hardly impinged on the consciousness of the housewives who would by the 1950s be painstakingly reproducing the Brush-Everard House on small self-contained lots twenty-seven miles from

Times Square or the Loop, agonizing over whether Apollo Room Blue or Kings Arms Rose would better set off the new Oriental rug.

The expanding ranks of the small, traditional homeowners of America were joined in 1935 by my grandparents, who had returned to Summit in my grandfather's ill health and retirement and who, after a short stint in an apartment, bought Little Lindum—tidy, Dutch Colonialish, and new. Characteristically, J.A.T. overpraised it as "one of the most perfect little houses I've ever seen." Stone and shingle and dormers and shutters, it was a pleasant enough collection of familiar elements, but perfection was neither its aspiration nor its result.

I knew that friendly house well, for in 1939–40 my brothers and I spent most of the school year there. My grandfather had died, at home, of a coronary in the spring of 1937. My grandmother had to adjust to being the head of her house. Two years later my father claimed his inheritance, as he also was attacked by his own heart. Trained nurses and a fascinating hospital bed that could be cranked into contortions took over our house for months, and we three children were bundled off to grandmother's house. Incomprehensible toddler twins who spoke in a private language, accompanied by their petulant second-grader sister and simultaneous translator, we were quite a package for a sixty-four-year-old woman to accept delivery on.

Our stay with her was an impressionable period when her Palmolive soap (or was it Yardley's?) made its mark on my Proustian memories, along with the fragrance of the boxwood that surrounded our sandbox, of the lemon verbena in her garden on the other side of the hedge. Dark winter afternoons, which I spent reading Andrew Lang's *Purple Fairy Tale Book,* were scented with cedar closet, benzoin, 4711 Cologne, and the aroma of broiling lamb chops.

When our father was out of immediate danger, we three slipped back across town to our own rooms, conscious of a shadow that had fallen across us but sure that we were still surrounded by sunlight. As I grew older, I continued to shuttle back and forth, with my parents or biking it alone. In my mother's house were many mansions. My grandmother's house was one of them—not competition but a branch. Consequently, my deepest assumptions about domestic life drew on two generations. J.A.T.'s period formality merged with my parents' casual ways; her canny employment of a sometimes formidable presence complemented my mother's modest behind-the-scenes methods. I absorbed two more paradoxical lessons: a woman could run her house and seem to; or she could run her house and not seem to. But, as a practical matter, how could she be onstage and off simultaneously? I never resolved that conflict, except by attempting to do both at once, a process confusing to everyone exposed to it but particularly to me. There was, however, no confusion on one issue. Differ as they might on style and technique, both generations agreed that home was a woman's happy duty.

From my father's semiconvalescence on, our home life had special considerations. Our house was truly a shelter for all of us, a place to rest and recuperate from forays outside. Safe in it, husband and wife cared for each other—in both senses of the verb. We children came and went from a solid home base. Neither museum nor consumer center, it requested of my mother only that she invest her attention in it in a civilized, affectionate way. Her major concern, the source of her satisfactions, was family not house. Lack of pressure and simplicity were a matter of life and . . . but we didn't talk about the other thing.

Sensing that we were now *hors de combat* in the competitive arena of suburban socioeconomics—"pecuniary emulation" in Veblen's terms, "keeping up with the Joneses" in everyday cliché—I began to think of myself as a spectator, high in the stand, eating popcorn and watching the action. I fell into the habit of surveying The Way We Live Now, a pudgy ten-year-old Marquand in brown-and-white saddle shoes. And as I planned the best-selling novel called *My Future*, predictable ordinary life seemed endlessly fascinating, in all its securely earthbound detail: how I longed to be typical. My life would be a tale of realism, not romance or high adventure.

Though I was tempted to become a dress designer when I grew up, like Helen Trent on the radio soap opera (she who based her life on the optimistic premise that a woman *can* find happiness at thirty-five . . . and after), I fully expected, however, that my destiny lay in being a housewife just like my mother, then thirty-four. I had no feeling that housewifery would be settling for second best; the two alternative careers had equal status in my mind.

Prematurely middle-aged, I studied my mother's magazines, *American Home, Ladies' Home Journal, McCall's,* taking them much more to heart than she ever did. For her they were relaxing, a minor entertainment and source of recipes and dress patterns. My grandmother had, as a young woman, found them discouraging, their examples and standards unattainable, and in 1906 had written to herself: "I'd give almost anything to be a magazine wonder." For me, they were extracurricular textbooks, and I read them as gospels.

At the starchily serious girls' school I by then attended, we were both driven and lured toward academic excellence, with college dangled ahead of us. At home I mused on boys, kissing, and dancing class, but the ultimate reality that lay beyond the B.A. and marriage was my almost preordained career as housewife. No one, except magazines, was training me for that.

I worried that I had no common sense and would therefore be unfit for my job. I worried about my looks. Surely something dramatic would have to happen before I could be "a decorative hostess." The Duchesse de Richelieu ("twice an aristocrat"), Mrs. Condé Nast, Mrs. Cordelia Biddle Duke, Lady Diana Manners, and Princess Marie de Bourbon of Spain had all used Pond's Vanishing Cream. Perhaps I should pick up a jar at Woolworth's.

My anxieties were allayed by the sweet security of life in the family—not only our nuclear group but the larger one of grandmother and those of my father's brothers and sisters who lived nearby and whom we saw regularly. But, as in this passage from James Agee's *A Death in the Family,* which captures the mood of those childhood years for me, there is only so much grown-ups can do:

On the rough wet grass of the back yard my father and mother have spread quilts. We all lie there, my mother, my father, my uncle, my aunt, and I too am lying there. First we were sitting up, then one of us lay down, and then we all lay down, on our stomachs, or on our sides, or on our backs, and they have kept on talking. They are not talking much, and the talk is quiet, of nothing in particular, of nothing at all in particular, of nothing at all. . . . May God bless my people . . . those who receive me, who quietly treat me, as one familiar and well-beloved in that home: but will not, oh, will not, not now, not ever; but will not ever tell me who I am.

"Would it be correct?" asked grown women as anxious as I at twelve, sitting in my snuffly sick bed surrounded by Kleenex, reeking of Vicks Va-po-rub, poring over *American Home* and listening to Ma Perkins on my portable table radio. Shaky taste was nothing new, nor were desperate questioners like the one who wrote to *House Beautiful* in 1909 asking for reassurance that her green mercerized silk curtains, Mission rockers, oak-stained woodwork, five red-and-blue Navajo rugs, and one large coyote pelt would "go together."

The *Ladies' Home Journal* is said to have been the first magazine to feature photographs of interiors, of other people's houses. The practice provided resource material for the uneasy to imitate, and simultaneously stirred up domestic discontent. "I wish to do over my library, which has never satisfied me. . . . Since taking *The House Beautiful* I have grown to hate the whole room," wrote one malcontent in 1904. Her daughter might have grown up to be a student of the Good Housekeeping Studio, which was in the twenties and thirties the decorating equivalent of the Good Housekeeping Institute. In the magazines, advertisers like Armstrong Cork promoted their own experts. Agnes Foster Wright, for example, was "an authority on home furnishing and decoration," and her *Floors, Furniture, and Color* had, I suspect, more than its share of suggestions about the use of linoleum.

The Good Housekeeping Studio in 1930 pictured a new group of model rooms in the nineteenth-century "manner" reproduced identically in department stores in Chicago, Minneapolis, and Los Angeles, and listed the manufacturers who "cooperated" with the studio and the stores. This sort of mutually beneficial promotional tie-in consolidated mighty commercial forces against the solitary little lady at home, worrying about the aesthetic impact of white moss fringe on forest green slipcovers.

Just as the magazines reported and instructed on trends in floors, furniture, and color, they documented fashions in rooms as they came and went. By 1937 the breakfast nook of the twenties was dismissed as "that cramped innovation of fifteen years ago, where once you were wedged in you had to be pried out." A 1940 *American Home* promoted what I can only describe as a superjock room, the collateral descendant of the bookish den. Described as a "sports and hobby room," it contained golf bags, firearms, tennis rackets, fishing poles, boxing gloves, footballs, and loving cups, as well as a carpenter's bench. It certainly gave a man something to live up to.

Another more or less masculine room, newly touted, was the "rec room," described in one magazine as a place "to have the gang over for an afternoon of amateur chemistry." This was the dawn of the jolly mystique that sent adolescents scuttling down into basements to "rumpus rooms" dedicated to wholesome, bumptious fun, like Ping-Pong and a keen game of darts. Fantastical imaginations were overstimulated, as not only rooms but the emotional charge of the family activities they would encourage were advocated in detail.

One reality remained constant in the single-family house of the period: the mother continued to be, in the words of Dorothy Field in *The Human House* (1939), "the selfless mediator without her own space, who helps the others to find privacy and fulfillment." She might have her little sewing room or a corner of the bedroom for her organdy-skirted, kidney-shaped dressing table, with its triptych mirror and twin lamps. She might have a cramped planning desk dovetailed into her kitchen. But the typical house still offered no special chamber for milady, either upstairs or downstairs, no retreat where she could create a certain rumpus of her own or, more likely, sit alone, unbusy, encouraged by her setting and its privacy to follow her thoughts where they might take her, even if that might be far away from her "real" business.

My mother, in her compact house, didn't even have my grandmother's options, the large linen closet for her midnight reading or a central supervisory headquarters in a spacious hall. Neither woman, until widowed, had truly private interior space of her own, and then each had more than she wanted.

Woman's place was shared space. However, housewives didn't seem to know what alternative they wanted, really wanted, or if they did, they found their needs hard to acknowledge to themselves. All those stereotypically feminine compromises—dressing table areas and planning centers—couldn't have fulfilled their deepest yearnings within themselves. Apparently there was little demand for an intermediate stage between being alone in a house or fully accompanied. Solitude in the midst of one's family was not felt to be important enough to demand. Certainly men didn't think to provide it.

As the two Schlegel sisters in *Howards End* agreed when discussing "a room that men have spoilt through trying to make it nice for women," men didn't know either what it was that women wanted. "And never will," added the younger, Helen. "In two thousand years they'll know," countered Margaret. She may have been unduly pessimistic in her optimism, and the millennium may arrive sooner, may be arriving, though backing and filling a bit, at this very hour.

But men in prewar America were, in spite of their natural ignorance, editing the magazines that told women what they *should* want, at least in design and decor. Edward Bok of the

Ladies' Home Journal, W. F. Bigelow of *Good Housekeeping,*
and Herbert Mayes of *McCall's* were part of the continuing
tradition of male tastemakers in magazine publishing whose
influence through the years paralleled that of women advisers
on housekeeping and supplemented the work of the architectural profession, largely male. Bok even wrote an advice column
called "Side Talks with Girls" under the pseudonym Ruth
Ashmore. When the mail became embarrassingly intimate, he
abandoned his post as Miss Lonelyhearts.

But professional home decorating is "a woman's sphere if she
is properly trained," or so said a woman who was a success in
the field, in 1910 a comparatively new one. "She knows better
than a man what a woman wants, and a client feels less restraint
in talking to her about big and little things and giving suggestive
hints than she would with the eye of the professional man
decorator upon her, sizing up her knowledge." The female
interior decorator in private practice was to become a powerful
authority figure in her own right, and when she came to power
in department stores and magazine publishing she was formidable indeed.

In 1977 I perused with awe the obituary of Jeannette
Lenygon, who had just died at the age of one hundred. It was
she who selected the furniture for the Governor's Palace and
the Capitol in Colonial Williamsburg, who in 1935 had been the
head of the committee of the American Institute of Decorators
that had worked out the then official definition that would
distinguish the profession from upholsterers, painters, and
paperers: "A decorator is one who, by training and experience,
is qualified to plan, design, and execute structural interiors and
their furnishings, and to supervise the various arts and crafts
essential to their completion." And it was she who said in 1944
that no modern furniture had yet been designed as good as that
of the past. She seems to me amply to represent the *grande
dames* among the conservative, competent female arbiters of
taste whose professional influence on lesser beings—amateurs
and housewives—has been so strong in so many overt and
covert ways.

Interior decorators provided examples in magazine features such as the reports on "society homes" that housewives ogled but would never have dreamed of trying to reproduce in their entirety. One notch closer to reality were journalistic glimpses into ordinary lives (the "How America Lives" syndrome) and ordinary domestic settings, with their comforting, familiar interiors, their venetian blinds, built-in bunk beds, ruffled criss-cross curtains, drapes, bridge tables, easy chairs, divans, in maroon, cream, aqua, and peach, with touches of royal blue and crimson—the 1930s spectrum. All too real and accessible were the endless projects of minor embellishment that housewives were encouraged to try themselves in order to transform some bland corner of their houses. The efforts of such amateur artists and craftsmen often succeeded only in leaving art and craft up on the shelf, and developed a strange uninhibited life of their own.

Why not stripe your curtains in green rickrack and edge them with ball fringe? Why not fashion tiebacks of colored yarn, braided and finished with fluffy pompoms? Why not make many tracings of your hands on your bathroom walls, color in the silhouettes, and draw rippling waves in the background? But, you might also ask, why do it? The result can only turn your bathroom wall into a mural of the sinking of the *Lusitania,* another disaster, and the project intrinsically has less to do with self-expression than with occupational therapy for the relief of anxiety or boredom.

The fine ladylike handwork of the Victorian era may have wasted as much time in producing inordinate quantities of hemstitched dinner napkins and crocheted antimacassars, but at least these minor items could be filed away in linen presses. The urge for a special new brand of do-it-yourself home decoration that first raged in the 1930s tended to afflict the structure itself, like mold. Perhaps its most pernicious effect was that it fostered in its practitioners an illusion that they were signifying—oh, spare us—they were Creative. Its legacy, flamestitch and macramé and other superfluities, was to continue the tradition of pseudowork that convinced women stay-at-homes that they

were as busy as bees and as good as gold, when all they were
doing was equivalent to a bird gussying up her cage.

During this same period even real cages for real birds were
being gilded into thirties modishness. One brand, the Hendrix
line, featured a model called "The Mayflower," which was
finished in Colonial Ivory, with decorative silhouettes in black
of the great ship itself, of Governor Brewster, John Alden,
Priscilla Mullin, and—democracy at work—one Native American in feathered headdress. "The Mayflower" was, I would
guess, a more popular item than either "The Gothic" or "The
Canary Cote."

Good Housekeeping had admitted in 1921 that "no house was
ever made into a home by a chained personality, by one fighting
inwardly to spread her wings and fly to other spaces." Perhaps
my friend Joyce's mother felt herself to be a chained personality, but all indications are that she had snapped her own latch
shut—as did so many women in cages. But we little girls of the
suburbs could hardly imagine that our mothers, in their
spectator pumps and stockings with straight seams, would ever
want to fly or flee, to hit the road. We young Americans
suffered the same limited vision that George Bernard Shaw
described in the English: "If we have come to think that the
nursery and the kitchen are the natural sphere of a woman, we
have done so exactly as English children have come to think
that a cage is the natural sphere of a parrot—because they have
never seen one anywhere else."

With the nearsightedness of the inexperienced, of the anxious
child, and of a Junior Daughter of the American Revolution, I
could not imagine either my grandmother or my mother outside
of their familiar environment, anywhere but in the houses they
seemed always to have occupied in the town where they seemed
always to have lived. Nor could I imagine that inimical forces in
the world outside our sheltered life might really threaten the
way we lived.

World War II took place at the movies on Saturday afternoon, or in comic books, or in Gabriel Heatter's grandfatherly
radio news programs ("Ah, there's baaaaad news tonight"),

just as for my children Viet Nam was fighting on a TV screen or protest marches in Harvard Square. Our fathers were usually too old for combat, though some donned Halloween-costume uniforms. When V.J. Day came, it was the dramatic end to an adventure story that we both did and did not believe. Hiroshima was distant and abstract; the fact that almost as the Bomb fell, my father had had yet another series of heart attacks was more immediate and life-altering.

In the autumn of 1946 we left Summit. My father retired to Dunedin, Florida, then a town of about 2,500 that, with its plank sidewalks and straight Main Street, looked more like a set for *High Noon* than a resort. We were soon joined by my grandmother, who hoped that a change in climate might alleviate the arthritis that frustrated and angered her. She "supervised," while my father supposedly ran interference but actually oversaw the construction of her own white bungalow with its boxy screened porch in front from which she could watch the Chamber of Commerce sunsets over the Gulf of Mexico. Not surprisingly, she called her last house Lindum Cottage. My brothers built her a birdhouse, which they gleefully christened Lindum Hut. There could be no Lindum smaller.

In 1949 J.A.T. presided over one last family reunion. As she lay dying, her grown children—middle-aged and balding and spreading a little at the hips—came to say good-bye. While she dozed between visits, we all gathered under the suspicious palms (they weren't real trees like the oaks of Summit). The tall tales and jokes, the camaraderie, surmounted the sadness of those last twilights, as I hope she realized.

We five moved into Lindum Cottage, which J.A.T. left to my parents, but a year later my father also died. Soon my brothers and I left home for boarding school and college. My mother was to remain alone, in my grandmother's house. Gradually, imperceptibly, it has become truly hers.

J.A.T.'s Pearl Bucks and Mary Roberts Rineharts and John Gunthers still line the bookshelves of that Colonial outpost in Florida, though some volumes are spotted now from years of tropical humidity. The archives of three generations fill the attic, a jumble of souvenirs as helter-skelter and often as comic in their juxtapositions as the homely accumulation known as daily life.

Below, J.A.T.'s anachronistic Colonial mantelpiece serenely frames a still-life of display logs and unnaturally bright brass andirons. Florida hibiscus blooms incongruously in the Delft vase that once held daffodils and tulips in our living room in Summit. My mother has tilted the blinds to shield antique velvet and crewel from the tropical afternoon sun, the glare that fades. Soon J.A.T.'s heirloom clock standing tall in a corner by the fireplace will somberly strike five. My husband or a brother and our assorted children will come loudly back from the beach, reeking of coconut oil. My mother will wheel in from the supermarket where she's been stocking up on the shrimp and avocados with which each spring she indulges her vacationing family. I think it's about time to have a stiff gin-and-tonic and stop rummaging around the attic in my head. We'll think about dinner later, my mother and I.

 SIX

Overdeveloping and Underachieving, 1950-1960

After lunching in the Georgian elegance of the *Ladies'*
Home Journal's executive dining room, all pale blue and pink,
crystal and brocade, roses and carnations, an editor in 1939
could then stroll out onto an adjoining terrace high in Rockefeller Center. On a clear day she could see almost forever, at least
to the World of Tomorrow of the World's Fair, with its trylon
and perisphere, Freudian caricatures of male skyscraper and
female house, then exposing themselves in Flushing Meadows.
    My own perspective on the exposition was from ground level
and distorted by nausea, the aftermath of a gluttonous roast-
beef-eating race with my cousin at the English Pavilion, which
happened also to be the site of Titania's Palace. I swayed
queasily before that largest and most glittering doll house,
crusted with gilt miniatures of fantastic royal appointments.
The tininess of the detailing of the fairy queen's house was
almost curative, totally engrossing, and in its way more realistic
than the plastic World of Tomorrow over at the American

exhibit. The U.S.A. had brashly scheduled Tomorrow for arrival in 1960, and such a projection was as irrelevant to me at age seven as the twenty-first century.

In 1950, halfway to tomorrow, I arrived at Smith College sporting the new charcoal-gray pedal pushers from Peck & Peck I hoped might update my rusty Summit bike. The preceding June, wearing white and carrying American Beauty roses, roped off from doting, snapshooting families and the rest of the world by a genuine daisy chain (we'd picked every damn blossom in a hot, buzzing New Jersey meadow), my boarding school classmates and I had ended a chapter. Unlike my grandmother and her friends at eighteen, we neither regarded ourselves nor were regarded as completed, as they were supposed to have been by their "finishing school." We had been prepared in our "prep school," certainly not finished.

For how many years had my teachers readied me for this remarkable, epochal September day? At last I was—how poignant and ironic a term—a freshman.

If I'd approached Northampton, Massachusetts, by air, the panorama below would have duplicated John Updike's weathercock's-eye view of his essential New England town, Tarbox, spread out in *Couples* like "a living map." Northampton also had its hosiery mill, its stores and parking lots, its seventeenth- and eighteenth-century survivors, its "peeling Federalist cubes" and Victorian "gingerbread mansions," its "middle-class pre-Depression domiciles with stubby porches and narrow chimneys and composition siding the color of mustard and parsley and graphite and wine," its speculative subdivisions eating away at woodland. In the words of the town's bicentennial historian, "Nearly every American style and building fad from early times right up to today is mirrored along Northampton's streets."

Architecturally the college echoed the town's heterogeneity. Its Grécourt Gates opened onto an anthology of styles: Greek Revival, Charles Addams's High Victorian Gothic, Modern Academical Functionalist. Cozy converted houses and formally monumental buildings nodded at each other politely across tidy greens. Universities in MGM musicals, places like Goodtime U., might be all of a piece, institutions constructed to play institutions, but Smith College was an amalgam, a gradual accretion. On the other hand, we students pushing our pedals around the campus looked almost G.I. in our conformist tweed, flannel, and Shetland.

Smith's earliest buildings tended to be late-nineteenth-century somber, with elaborate brickwork, polychrome effects, towered asymmetry. College Hall, the administrative center that loomed unavoidably by the Grécourt Gates, had been completed in 1875, the year of the college's opening and of my grandmother's birth. It was designed by Peabody & Stearns, the Boston firm which also produced in a similar style Alumnae Gymnasium in 1890, a date certified by a stone plaque ornamented with carved swags of greenery, with crossed racquets and bowling pins, the icons of the genteel female sportiveness that occurred behind its Victorian deadpan facade.

A huge copper beech separated Alumnae Gym from the broad front porch of its contemporary, the graceless brick dormitory christened Lawrence House, to which I'd been assigned. Actually, we never referred to a dormitory as one. We spoke of "our house." "Which house are you in?" was the standard opener to the shy stranger from Omaha sitting next to you in History II.

Though the infinite variety in the styles of the houses seemed somehow eccentric, if not downright tacky, after Summit's consistency and especially after the omnipresent aura of half-timbering at my boarding school there, one familiar human element made me feel at home. Each college house came equipped with a resident housemother. Moreover, College Hall contained somewhere in its oaken corridors, in some hallowed chamber, the mother of mothers, Alma Mater, who stood (as the disciplinary code avowed) *in loco parentis.* Though our president was a man, a dignified fellow we saw largely on ceremonial occasions (when, like my grandfather, he would emerge from his remote office), our psychological great-grandmother, the progenitor whose gift had originally founded the college, was a woman, dour Sophia Smith, whose unsmiling countenance would have impressed even the most bubble-headed promtrotters among us with the seriousness of our inheritance, as well as warned us of the agony of spinsterhood.

My first housemother, Miss Mary Stuart Rae, a cross between Queen Victoria and Miss Jean Brodie, had long before determined that Lawrence House would be a bastion of gracious living, and she stared us into compliance through invisible lorgnettes. She alone was totally unconfused by the ambiguous social status of her "gells." Our house was in fact subsidized housing, though official terminology defined it as "cooperative." All sixty-four of us received rake-offs on our room and board, residential grants that augmented our tuition scholarships. Miss Rae's mission was to see to it that though we had less money, we'd have higher standards than "the others" and would take pride in our supposedly sterling characters.

Theoretically we "cooperated" by sharing household chores, but since World War II had lured away all but the very last of the maids from institutions like Smith as well as from single-family homes, the college as a whole had swept its own halls, waited on its own tables, and made its own beds. We coopera-tors actually did little more housekeeping than any New York debutante or midwestern heiress whose daddy paid the full freight. Our slight sense of being set apart in a worthy ghetto was what really differentiated us, and the college has since realized this and retired the cooperative fiction.

After Miss Rae finally permitted her own retirement, she was replaced by a musical lady who often treated wincing bridge players to her own thundering afternoon renditions of Beetho-ven piano sonatas. She found the social identity of cooperative house girls to be somewhat baffling (but no more than we did) and once committed the gaffe of declaring in public, at one of our diligently gracious after-dinner coffee hours, that she loved living in the house, that it was like having "sixty-four wonderful maids." The visiting czarina of scholarships, through clenched teeth, corrected her. "You mean sixty-four *wonderful people.*"

The housemother fluttered and stammered, "Oh, yes, yes, that's what I mean. Sixty-four wonderful people."

The Quad, a complex of dormitories built in 1926–36 at the opposite end of the campus from Lawrence House, was more in the madcap MGM charlestoning daughters tradition than our responsible Victoriana. Relentlessly Georgian Revival in detail and mood, the Quad's overall effect, according to Professor William MacDonald, was of "a miniature Georgian suburb with ample lawns and fine trees."

To us whose self-images often bordered on the Dickensian, us Wonderful People, the Quad buildings seemed to be absolute hothouses of cashmere sweater sets and Yale pennants and fraternity pins, seemed to embody in every red brick both popularity and money. Our illusion contained only a salting of fact, and I for one extrapolated wildly from my past experience, leaping directly from architectural style to social identity. As in the real suburbs, I assumed, traditional boxes contained the genuine pearls and gold circle pins of affluence and acceptability.

Boarding school had accustomed me to the realities of sharing living space with assorted women. Gallons of Breck shampoo, countless dinner-table gripes and crash diets, Saturday night melancholia and borrowed clothes—I'd experienced it all before. At least in college we heard the not infrequent cries of "Man on floor!" (which then meant that a blushing, elderly plumber was heading toward the bathroom, plunger in hand) or "Man on phone!" (chorus of hysterical shrieks) or "Man downstairs!" (followed by thundering hoofbeats, descending). The fact that eligible men lived somewhere else gave them the appeal of imported cocktail delicacies, to be savored in small doses mostly at parties on weekends. We pondered and planned for our guests, as one does a French menu or a shopping list for a holiday feast, but our daily bread was our studies and the healthy indoor pursuit known as extracurricular activities, which we undertook with varying degrees of commitment.

About half of our senior faculty was male, and I sensed that the men were more active than their conscientious and competent female counterparts in the affairs of the great outside world. Each year a Neilson Professor was imported like a date for a very long weekend, for the chair was almost always given to a man, strangely enough. Pacing our paths and gracing our platforms were worldly figures like W. H. Auden and Alfred Kazin, men who were *known,* who *did* things, who had experienced the literary life, not just studied up on it.

One cosmopolitan participant in real life was Henry-Russell Hitchcock, professor of art and distinguished architectural historian. He was a dramatic presence on campus, or at least I who never took any of his courses found him so, perhaps because I confused the man himself with my own garbled images of Monty Woolley and Edward VII.

Hitchcock had, with Philip Johnson, prepared both exhibit and catalogue for the first International Exhibition of Modern Architecture in America, the great offering of 1932 at New York's Museum of Modern Art, and thus was, as he modestly put it, to some extent a minor actor on the scene. The catalogue's title, *The International Style,* came to identify here the whole European movement after World War II led by Le Corbusier, J. J. P. Oud, Mies van der Rohe, and Walter Gropius, famous abroad but not popularly known here until the year, as it happened, I was born.

Forward-looking emigrés had already made their mark in this country, particularly in California, as European modernism joined with our own. For example, in the late twenties Richard Neutra, who came here from Vienna and was for a time a disciple of Frank Lloyd Wright, had built successfully in his own manner the new sort of residence known as . . . the modern house. In Summit, when I was growing up, modern architecture, or at least its domestic variety, was on a level with spaceships. The phrase itself was usually preceded by a kind of psychic pause, as "You know, I hear she's very interested in . . . [slight intake of breath] modern architecture."

In 1937 Walter Gropius himself immigrated, to join the

faculty of Harvard's Graduate School of Design, and in 1938 he became chairman of the department of architecture, where he was to become "surely the most influential single man in planting modern architecture firmly in America." That same year he built for his family, in the authentically Colonial village of Lincoln, Massachusetts, an unusual house that had everyone talking. It was . . . modern, and looked unlike any of its neighbors.

Today, since the house has been acquired by the Society for the Preservation of New England Antiquities and so is certified as a genuine antique, it has been accepted into polite suburban society. Mrs. Gropius, who remains as life tenant, sometimes opens her home to groups of pilgrims. One recent May day, with the new breeze shifting the leaves of the apple trees and the meadow grass that surround the house, I also circled it, with the other aficionados whom I always encounter on such local junkets. Our shutters snapped, capturing for home consumption the exterior spiral staircase, the glass brick, the grapevines trained to embellish the spare white walls, the overhanging eaves that shade the large sheets of glass that once were something shocking, leaving *tout* Lincoln agog.

Inside, Ise Gropius received us, presiding from the Saarinen armchair students had given her late husband. In her tailored black pants and shaggy folkcrafted sweater, a canny accent of emerald green at her throat, she was herself decidedly modern, in spite of her age. No Whistler's Mother in a spoked rocking chair, she described with animation her house, its history, its reasonableness, its reasoning.

The widows of architects who live on in beloved houses designed for them by their husbands seem to derive some mysterious beneficial effect from their surroundings. On a similar occasion in Los Angeles in 1977 I marveled as Mrs. Richard Neutra at sunset displayed her house and her cello-playing with the same youthful enthusiasm and sense of drama as Mrs. Gropius. Are these women examples of a very special kind of architectural preservation?

Before they built, the Gropiuses toured New England,

savoring the ubiquitous white wooden Colonial houses that seemed so fresh to European eyes. Gropius particularly admired the way we Americans had adapted English Georgian styles from prototypical brick and stone into our wood, and the way our houses also accommodated the abominable northeastern climate, a natural resource less amenable than wood. He determined to combine his Bauhaus approach, his International Style, with our native one, to create a rational structure that incorporated the best aspects of the Colonial manner with the materials and the practical advantages of machine-age technology. When the house was completed, Lewis Mumford wrote in the Gropiuses' guest book, "Hail to the most indigenous, the most regional example of the New England home, the New England of a New World!"

The house itself, unlike its local forebears, is asymmetrical, flat-roofed, open-eyed, and welcomes the landscape into its interior rather than walling it out. But though it looks "modern," it utilizes traditional Colonial elements: siting that maximizes solar heat, frame construction, two stories, and white-painted sheathing, though its boarding runs vertically, not horizontally. The interior features a familiar large open fireplace, but the floor plan is also open, in the modern manner, with the definitions of the first-floor living room, dining room, and study merely suggested by a single oblique central partition, and a curtain on tracking, a soft imitation wall. A screened porch, in the American manner, is, however, not in its "proper" place at side or front but, in order to catch the prevailing breezes, sensibly extends as an ell from the rear of the house.

After her talk, I asked Mrs. Gropius why she thought we American women have for so long been hooked on traditional domestic architecture, *echt* Colonial or Georgian and their hybrid descendants. She answered that her husband often said that he thought we suffered from a Taj Mahal complex, a compulsion for white symmetry. He on the other hand, she added, responded to the asymmetry in Japanese design, and to its justification in Zen philosophy, which regards symmetry, or perfection, as the province of the divine. We lesser beings must content ourselves with everyday imperfection, stimulated by it to perpetual change, as we strive to reach an unattainable goal. American women have been, she suggested, insecure about their own taste, about their ability to decide among alternatives without reference to some established authority, some accepted style that is "right," although static. And, I thought to myself, they, or we, have certainly been optimistic about the possibility of perfectibility. As the Gropiuses noted from the first, we women have determined the development of the American house. Though historically our men have made it clear that they were in economic control (that is, they made the money that paid for construction, purchase, rent, maintenance), they turned choices in decoration and design over to the women, saying, as Mrs. Gropius put it, "Oh, the house, that's the wife's business. I just pay the bills."

Nonetheless, she continued, we seem often to have chosen to lock ourselves into a restrictive environment by falling back on historic styles that may actually decree darkness, inconvenience, leaks, and a tyranny of taste that demands unrealistic decisions, such as the choice of a creaky, small antique writing table rather than the large functional work surface with files that any household manager needs to do her work efficiently.

I have since pondered the fact that the Taj Mahal did, after all, entomb a wife. In order to qualify for residency Mumtaz Mahal did have to undergo the ultimate restriction of her "life style," though I don't imagine she chose it. We have, I'm afraid, often been responsible for entombing ourselves.

Mrs. Gropius had already pointed out to her listeners her own coeducational study as a case in point. With its single expanse of desk, as wide as the broad window above it, with its two desk chairs, two desk lamps, joint files, it was a single unit as reasonable as a bicycle built for two, and it encouraged a man and a woman to work together, or at least side by side. "My husband was really a 'woman's lib' person at heart," Mrs. Gropius explained, "though he would never have put it that way."

She recalled his belief in collaboration, shared effort, and how it informed the Cambridge firm he founded in 1946 with various partners—The Architects Collaborative, or TAC. The founders included two women (together with their architect husbands): Sarah Pillsbury Harkness (a graduate of the most distinguished school for women architects during the twenties and thirties, the Cambridge School of Architecture, which in 1938 was absorbed by Smith College and later discontinued) and Jean Bodman Fletcher (a student of Gropius at Harvard, and one of the women first admitted in the forties to the Graduate School of Design). Among the male partners was Benjamin Thompson, whose "design research" was to mold the taste of many of my generation of housewives, from the mid-fifties on.

"Any architect will tell you, if you get him in a mellow mood, that the design of a low cost, small house is the most difficult, the most financially unrewarding, and the most interesting architectural problem there is," or so said Catherine Morrow Ford and Thomas H. Creighton in *Quality Budget Houses: A Treasury of 100 Architect-Designed Houses from $5,000 to $20,000,* a book for general readers published in 1954 that included examples of the work of some of the best architects in the country, including Neutra, TAC, Victor Gruen, William Wurster, Hugh Stubbins, Edward D. Stone, and Paul Rudolph. One representative house, designed by Wurster, Bernardi, and Emmons and built in Los Gatos, displayed certain now-familiar earmarks of the popular postwar California style, the modern ranchhouse-cum-bungalow, with its large windows, redwood siding, and shed roof, whose deep overhang shaded part of a large concrete patio.

These smaller houses did encourage their occupants, who might otherwise feel compressed and oppressed, to make full use of those outdoor living rooms and kitchens called patios, or terraces, or decks, furnished with weatherproof chaises, dining tables, and barbecues. The old piazza, roofed but open, was reincarnated as the carport, and loungers who might once have stretched out for a nap on rattan and cretonne found themselves transplanted into full sun. Families now sat around eating and tanning in wrought-iron-and-canvas sling chairs, the indoor/outdoor "butterflies" then fluttering through the home-furnishing pages of *McCall's*.

By 1960, according to Burchard and Bush-Brown's *The Architecture of America,* few established architects could "afford to design private dwellings any more, not even their own, unless like Neutra they chose to do one occasionally as an Antaean stimulus." But this constriction was nothing really new. Royal Barry Wills Associates once estimated that 90 percent of the small houses built in the 1930s had been produced by real-estate operators or speculative builders without adequate design counsel. The percentage was probably higher in the fifties, when the number of houses mass-produced was so much larger. In mid-decade *Fortune* magazine boasted that the United States had 50 percent more households than in the period immediately before the war, and Martin Mayer in *The Builders* quotes one economist's calculation: between 1940 and 1956 the increase in single-family home ownership was greater than that in the previous century and a half of our history.

The mid-century housing boom paralleled that of the twenties. Though on a larger scale, some of the same factors were at work: a burst of postwar prosperity, a pent-up demand, plus spectacular population growth, the so-called baby boom. A new element had emerged, in the meantime, and that was the federal support for home ownership which had originated in New Deal legislation of the thirties.

In *Houses for Homemakers* (1945), a best-seller at half a million copies, designer and builder Royal Barry Wills summarized: "During World War II some 1,500,000 of our country-men expressed themselves as ready and eager to build a small house as soon as conditions permitted." Under the 1944 Servicemen's Readjustment Act all these veterans received an almost irresistible incentive to buy, not rent, the "house of their desire" with no down payment and a thirty-year mortgage at 4 percent. These benefits, when added to already existing Federal

Housing Administration legislation, made homeowning safe and easy for a whole huge new market.

Go-getting builders and overdevelopers moved into mass production as never before. In 1947 construction began on open land in Long Island on the first Levittown, the senior in the newest, largest generation of tract developments that was to burgeon across the nation.

Some of the new small development houses drew on the California style and mood, with informality spread out on one floor, which was open to the sun. The old high and the new low were combined in some models, and the split-level was born, a hybrid that looked as if its growth had been arrested as it rose out of the earth, a hyacinth nipped by an early spring freeze. Amazed picture windows gaped at each other across newly paved streets, newly seeded lawns. Back yards completed their socialization, transformed for family pleasures from service areas defined by clotheslines and garbage cans.

Many popular models were both miniature and derivative, small editions or anthologies of old reliable historical styles. In 1946 *Mademoiselle* published a kind of workbook-hopechest for prospective young housewives, which offered an illustrated selection of exteriors. The layout resembled a streetscape in suburban Toytown: all in a row, Cape Cod cottage; Colonial saltbox; late Georgian classic type; Pennsylvania farmhouse; Greek Revival cottage; Southwestern, Monterey, International, and Midwest Modern (based on Wright) models, as well as Ranch House and West Coast Modern. The original bungalows of around 1910, such as the high-style creations of Greene & Greene in California, had long since been adopted by the tract developer and, in the words of Professor William Jordy, represented "a generalized prototype compounded of sentimentality and exploitation."

Step right up, folks, pick a house, any house. Who will snap up this Levitt Cape Cod for a paltry $8,000? In a single March night on Long Island in 1949, according to Martin Mayer, 1,400 purchasers signed on 1,400 dotted lines, in a twentieth-century

Levittown land rush similar to the unleashing of homesteaders on Oklahoma.

For many a G.I., this postwar bargain house was his first foray into the market, and he wanted not only to make a good investment but also to have the sense of "belonging" and of "social continuity." In an impersonal, mass-produced modern object set down on what yesterday had been only a potato field, a person might well feel raw, exposed, and rootless, a human tuber. The emotional appeal of the traditional snow-covered home on the milkman's giveaway Christmas calendar had not diminished, and for some it had, under the circumstances, even increased.

As is characteristic of eclectic architecture in general, the tract development houses, with their mixture of stylistic details, "applied architectural symbols," were emotionally evocative rather than rationally self-justifying. The developer's need to call up the quicksilver associations from prospective buyers' domestic unconscious, to invoke through ornamentation if nothing else some vague endorsement of his product, precipitated a new outbreak of Imitation Colonial.

What more did the new, young homeowners really want in a house besides a traditional fanlight or broken pediment over the front door, a built-in dishwasher, a flagstone patio, and a cheap mortgage? By the mid-fifties, motivational researchers were checking out samples. The Cornell University Housing Research Center published its findings in *Houses Are For People* (1955): 1,000 men and women, interviewed separately, had said they wanted liveable houses, "rational shelter" that would reflect their particular value systems. Social prestige and formality were important to some, while others prized economy. Designs encouraging family solidarity were the choice of the child-oriented, while the inner-directed, to use David Riesman's famous fifties coinage, mainly sought privacy. Men and women differed on details, but they stood close together on priorities. Good housing was more important (particularly to women) than either nice clothes or expensive vacations, but it was certainly less important than college education for the children. These couples were not spiritual joggers or seekers after self; their choices smacked of a certain smug practicality. As developments proliferated, as schlocky design began to seem epidemic and the social ramifications of communities planned by builders could be observed, critics of all persuasions began leaping out of hedges and pointing to cracks in picture windows. It was smart to knock not so much suburbs as suburbia.

Above the fray, secluded in a Lawrence House garret, I read with morbid fascination of towns that seemed to parody the romanticized Summit of my childhood. In these terrible new places, where the land was flat, the trees spindly, and the houses blatantly ersatz, subsisted a bland population uniform in age, income, whiteness, level of education, of ambition or discontent, fenced into a soulless isolation from the past, or so I learned in a series appearing in *Harper's*, "The Mass-Produced Suburbs," written by Harry Henderson and published in 1953.

Long Island's Levittown had by then grown to 70,000 inhabitants who, Henderson said, were all waging lonely struggles to be different amid a leveling setting of standardized houses, commonly accepted opinions, Eisenhowerish inarticulateness, and uncertain taste. He noted that the "outside" person that women residents missed most was "my mother." These same young housewives pored over home magazines for motherly advice, extracting "approval-insured" touches for their own decorative schemes. Henderson marveled that he saw no two identical interiors and only one frequently repeated motif, a brass skillet hung on a red brick wall. A dominant style was the kind of bland modern design usually called "contemporary"—not Bauhaus but shopping center, with Russel Wright china, the omnipresent butterfly chair, pink kitchen appliances, geometric-print drapes—in short the genre featured almost to the exclusion of any other in the *McCall's* magazines of 1950–55 and which today seems to linger on in the waiting rooms of dentists and chiropractors. The other dominant style in 1950s Levittown was, according to Henderson, Early American, the enduring mode that seems to survive all competition.

Such banality was not for me, I told myself, and batted out an indignant, literally sophomoric essay for Miss Page's class in creative writing. In "Lilacs and Levittown" I stacked the cards for the humane eccentricities of Cambridge, which I had come to know well, and against Levittown, where seldom was seen an old house, an old person, or even an heirloom. With the same intolerance that kids of the sixties were to invoke against their parents' generation, the Establishment, I patronized the Unestablishment, the young marrieds a little older than I, for their runny-nosed toddlers, their clichéd bungalows, wagon wheels and lawn jockeys, their anxious, imitative contemporaneity.

Smug and smart and ignorant, I was unwittingly part of a certain tradition of intolerance. As early as 1905 Joy Wheeler Dow had inveighed against "the common clapboards of commerce . . . the tawdry veranda, the huddled-together suburban houses of the boom-tracts of land" as "quite the nightmares of our waking hours." By 1911 he announced that "the whole scheme of cutting up farms into twenty-five-foot lots is highly inimical to Anglo-Saxon home development, and in some cases it amounts to bare-faced robbery of the unsophisticated."

By the 1930s another tasteful traditionalist, Harold Eberlein, who also wrote for the shelter magazines, remarked that speculative builders seem to be unaware of the necessity that small houses remain simple in design and that overembellishment, even with details authentic enough in themselves, resulted in a modest cottage looking labored and pretentious, "like some overdressed small person."

The technique of adapting down, of working in a smaller scale, is tricky, often underestimated. Dow regarded adaptation as "the soul of architecture, presupposing the highest kind of talent, most extended education and artistic susceptibility." By all this he simply meant taste, and supremely confident of his own endowment in that area, he wrote, "I could not plan an ugly house if I tried."

Up to a certain point, he said, the closer the adaptation the greater the success of the house. "In the language of the stage, always procure what the play calls for; do not fake it. Build the house smaller but use brick."

This was basically the philosophy of Royal Barry Wills, who was in one sense a legatee of Dow, the aesthetician of the conservative suburbs, and in another sense the tasteful Levitt of New England's upper-middle class. His colleagues once described him, echoing Ibsen, as a true "Master Builder." Though his 1918 degree from M.I.T. had been in engineering, he was an architect at heart, and in 1925 he opened a tiny Beacon Street office as a self-taught designer-builder. He then proceeded to establish a reputation by publishing his sketches and designs in the Boston *Transcript* and similar journals, and by entering and winning various small-house design competitions. He would build his houses smaller than some, but he would use brick.

By 1945 and the publication of *Houses for Homemakers,* an extremely successful Wills had developed his popular compromise between a sensibly adapted traditional plan and a nostalgic loyalty to historic styles. He viewed the open plan as the core of modernist house design, the means by which, as he put it, "a feeling of space is injected into the small house by doing away, wholly or in part, with the individual living room, dining room and hall." He agreed that at contemporary prices no one could afford rooms that were merely decorations, as parlors once were. But, he added, most people "cleave to an up to date version of the style of their ancestors and I do not think they should be talked out of it." For the cleavers, Wills designed a career's worth of Garrison Colonials, saltboxes, Nantuckets, Bucks County stone houses, and an occasional Regency villa. Like Dow, he even tried his hand at the New England postcard church, white clapboard with a single spire.

Scrupulous about details, though he was more liberal in his accommodating overall plans, he included in *Houses for*

Homemakers an appendix with measured drawings of ornamental details, in the tradition of the early-nineteenth-century pattern books of Asher Benjamin, such as *American Builder's Companion*. Wills, basically an adaptor, not an originator, tried to be faithful both in small matters, such as hardware and moldings, and in a certain general appearance, or mood, of authenticity.

After I read about "the familiar fat chimney, the low eaves, the cheerful small-pane windows" of the Master Builder's work, I wondered idly how to go about getting into a Wills house as I put my notes aside for the weekend. On Sunday I joined my mother and an aunt (a Summit "girl" who had married her childhood friend, my father's brother) on the first leg of their October tour of foliage, friends, and relations. We chugged to nearby Marblehead and a small clapboard house whose fat chimney and low eaves seemed vaguely familiar. Its owners, Lindum Club veterans and long-time residents of Summit/Short Hills, had recently moved north in their retirement to be nearer their children and to live in a more compact house.

Logs snapped on their hearth, the walls were peacefully paneled, sherry tasted mellow, and though the mood of coziness was intense, the room was as pleasant as it was warm, as reassuring as an illustration in a children's book published in the twenties. How satisfying a link with the old order to find that the daughter of one of the most supportive of J.A.T.'s network of women had consolidated her legacy in just such a setting.

As we were about to leave, Mr. S. remarked, "You know, this is a Royal Barry Wills house." Of course, I thought, figuratively clapping my hand to my forehead. Such is the arduous nature of research, the unrelenting quest for knowledge.

Contests of the sort Wills had once so diligently entered and won were part of a long and respectable tradition. Frank Lloyd Wright had designed for a 1901 *Ladies' Home Journal* "A Home for a Prairie Town," as Henry-Russell Hitchcock has noted. The *Journal* in a 1939 series of competitions awarded a prize to a "frankly modern" house, No. 1412, designed by no less a figure than Richard Neutra. As *McCall's* sold dress patterns, so the *Journal* sold house patterns, complete building plans snapped up for a dollar each by thousands of more or less serious dreamers.

Though hardly in the avant-garde, magazines for women, beamed as they were at the "large middle ground of public taste," had in the thirties often tried to educate their readers in new approaches to domestic architecture. Not only did they act as pattern books, they also proselytized more generally, attempting to encourage open-mindedness to the new, rather than blind acceptance of the old.

Sometimes a magazine's vision of its own contribution was a little rose-colored. A 1935 *Ladies' Home Journal* pointed proudly to the Dutch Colonial house (as revived), which it had "sponsored," as its "distinct contribution to architectural progress." It also claimed responsibility for "banishing the front parlor of the gay nineties to the limbo of forgotten atrocities," and for pioneering the Garden Home (in which the conventional plan of yore was reoriented so that garage and service quarters faced the street, while living portions faced the rear garden). The *Journal* further maintained in its "1935 Platform" that it supported "functional planning" of the home and proposed that readers preplan theirs by assembling a kind of conglomerate doll house out of paper boxes, each of which represented a zone of activity.

By 1939 the *Journal* could claim that the historical stranglehold had been loosened and that the public seemed to be accepting "modified, unstylized design." A national poll quoted by the magazine had found that 42 percent of those interviewed preferred modern to traditional houses.

For decades women's magazines had been prescribing for domestic life: recommending, teaching, promoting, and advertising (and at a rapidly increasing rate, for between 1939 and 1956 the number of national advertisers increased from 660 to 2,742). In May 1954 *McCall's* launched, over the dashing

signature of Otis Wiese, Editor and Publisher, a new editorial
policy, one that on the face of it seemed simply to articulate an
outlook already implied:

> In common with all other women's service magazines *McCall's*
> has been striving to widen your horizons, inspire you to lead lives
> of greater satisfaction, help you in your daily tasks. There's
> evidence that we're winning that victory.
> *Today women are not a sheltered sex.* Men and women in ever
> increasing numbers are marrying at an earlier age, having
> children at an earlier age and rearing larger families. For the first
> time in our history the majority of men and women own their
> own homes and millions of these people gain their deepest
> satisfaction from making them their very own.
> We travel more. We earn more, spend more, save more. We
> listen to finer music, read more and better books. We worship
> more. And in ever greater numbers we enjoy the advantages of a
> higher education. . . . But the most impressive and the most
> heartening feature of this change is that men, women and
> children are achieving it *together.* They are creating this new and
> warmer way of life not as women *alone* or men *alone,* isolated
> from one another, but as a *family* sharing a common experience.
> From this day forward *McCall's* will be edited to meet the
> needs and excite the interests of all of you who are or wish to be
> partners in this way of life—the Life of *McCall's.*

There it is, the Communist Manifesto of Togetherness. To a
housewife of the seventies it seems like bland common sense.
Of course family members should share, as once they had, the
practical business of maintaining the house. (But would they
now?) Of course a woman shouldn't have to serve alone.

Somehow togetherness came to represent an oppressive
Utopian ideal, a spiritual imperative. Failure to live up to it
made men feel alternately guilty or put-upon, while women
became even more fragmented, less together within themselves, as they tried to add jolly camaraderie to their shopping
lists. Self-consciously fomenting youth fellowship, wearing
Mother-Daughter dresses, pushing Toll House cookies on all
comers, they began to wonder what was so private about life in

homes whose open plans already enforced too much companionship.

The 1950s saw the gradual institutionalization of *de facto* togetherness in that pop variation on the modernist open plan, the family room. In it, kitchen, dining room, laundry, and informal living room coagulated to form a single zoned space. Ironically, the term *family room* had been used in 1865 by Catharine Beecher to designate the very room it almost displaced, the dining room.

My grandmother seems to have spent very little time in her kitchen, which was physically and psychically set apart as the servants' private preserve. A parallel sense of a certain discreet distance between participants in the household extended beyond employers and employed in that more formal age, to relationships between parents (particularly father) and children. Though houses might contain more people, separatedness reigned in many.

When in 1934 Frank Lloyd Wright designed for the Malcolm Willeys of Minneapolis a kitchen not entirely separate from the living area, his decision seemed realistic, not subversive or a harbinger of "suffocating intimacy" in family dwellings. How could he predict such human consequences as resulted from its adaptation into informal mess-hall facilities with snack bars, blaring TV, churning laundry, and whining children under foot.

The family room was a feminine room but, like sewing rooms and laundries, it was just another place for a woman to work on the family's behalf. Not even a retreat where no one else wanted to go, the family room is as public as a piazza, reflecting aspirations toward a kind of casual democracy. *McCall's* wrote that such a room "makes friends with the family and demonstrates that it is better to live your own life in your own way than to go to all the trouble of keeping up with those pretentious Joneses."

By 1963 Betty Friedan could write that the open plan of the contemporary ranch or split-level house gives "the illusion of more space for less money. But the women to whom they are sold almost have to live the feminine mystique. There are no true walls or doors; the woman in her beautiful electronic kitchen is never separated from her children. She need never feel alone for a minute, need never be by herself. . . . The open plan also helps to expand the housework to fill the time available. In what is basically one free-flowing room . . . continual messes continually need picking up." As Peter Blake later pointed out in *Form Follows Fiasco,* "What Wright and his successors in Europe and the United States failed to realize was that the 'open plan' as developed in Japan depended for its success *entirely* upon one or both of two factors: the availability of cheap servants and/or the availability of enslaved wives."

In the 1950s Smith College was certainly not in the business of turning out candidates for enslavement, but it hadn't quite decided how to protect us against the possibility of abduction some dark night.

Probably the most famous member of Smith '55, and my Lawrence House compatriot, was Sylvia Plath, the poet whose posthumously published work has secured her early reputation. Sylvia, though hardly typical, was a historic type, as another Lawrence House resident, Nancy Hunter Stein, has pointed out in her 1973 memoir, *A Closer Look at Ariel.* I know I risk seeming opportunistic by focusing on her, but she more dramatically than I illustrates the dangerous illusion we shared, a belief in unlimited possibilities that was, I fear, closer to greed than to innocence. A liberal arts education in the 1950s tempted us transitional women to overdevelop in one way, without fortifying us against underachieving in another.

Sylvia moved into Lawrence House in the winter of 1954, after the breakdown she later described in her novel *The Bell Jar,* and we all understood why she was treated as a fragile special case. Her cooperative household tasks were even lighter than the *pro forma* garbage emptying and vacuum cleaning assigned to more stolid types. That winter term she simply delivered the housemother's breakfast tray. By spring her sunbathing sessions on the griddle-like flat of Alumnae Gym's roof became a more dazzling display of strength of will, lust to excel. *Mirror, mirror, on the wall, who is the tannest of us all?*

we asked. *You, Snow Whites, are pale and wan, but yon maiden is a golden swan.*

Like me, Sylvia had left a widowed mother at home and had a modest, white center-hall 1930s Colonial house in a fashionable suburb in her background. Strivers and smilers both, we shared other less desirable attributes and experiences, but we remained distant acquaintances who grinned automatically as we passed in the hall. Behind the Ipana smiles that were as much a trademark of the decade as jam-colored lipstick and cinched-in wasp waists, Sylvia and I aroused in each other a wary indifference. I was (in her view and my own) the trusty craftsman, while she was the artist, the individualist, and self-absorbed. I, though no slouch in the self-absorption department, was into other-directed student bureaucracy, all those councils and legislatures that were then considered to be fine preparation for a Smith woman's predestined "leadership role" in the community.

We did share one common interest: we were both serious English majors with a weakness for popular journalism in general, women's magazines in particular. For Sylvia the magazines were potential buyers for her "professional" (rather than her "artistic") writing, the short stories that throughout her adult life she sent off to the marketplace, to *Seventeen, Mademoiselle,* the *Ladies' Home Journal.* For me, they were potential employers (I had editorial aspirations by then) and also remained, as in childhood, my instruction manuals. These unofficial texts in vocational training would, I was confident, prepare me for my ultimate career of housewifery, the oldest profession, and the most populated (according to the definition of Phyllis McGinley, the writer who was to become by our tenth reunion a favorite of my classmates).

As Sylvia and I weighted our studies of Yeats and Shakespeare and Hemingway with a sense of a more commercial, glossier element in the daily life of words, we plugged away at assignments for *Mademoiselle*'s college board contest and met deadlines for *Vogue*'s Prix de Paris competition with the same dogged Couéism we brought to academic tasks. We cultivated slickness with hardly a qualm of conscience or conflict.

The winter of our senior year Sylvia worked on a pop story, "Home Is Where the Heart Is," the tale of a housewife whose family seems to be drifting out of her orbit, but who "manages creatively to bring them all back together," as she wrote home to her own mother. "Someday Phyllis McGinley will hear from me," she added.

Years later I met an actress who told me she'd once performed in a TV soap opera coincidentally titled "Where the Heart Is." When I asked her where in fact the heart had been, she pointed wryly at herself and groaned, "Here . . . me . . . I was it." She had been cast as one of those omnipresent wise women (every soap has at least one) who hang around home baking and looking simultaneously worried, sympathetic, and all-knowing.

A friend has recently reported a reference in a shelter magazine to a phenomenon known as The Heart of the House area, which is no more and no less than the "old-fashioned" family room. What does keep a house alive, the heart as occupant or the heart of the object?

Affairs of the heart also concerned me in my own idealized-housewife potboiler. Did we all try to write one? My story was called "The Toast," the tale of a little mousewife who finally receives a public accolade from the dashing husband whose choice of her had always baffled a suburb who underestimated her *eminence grise*. This Cinderella update is another example of how tentatively and indirectly we girls would approach the question of Woman's Role in the Home.

We were far less timid when we took the high academic road. Sylvia's honors thesis searched the image of the double in Dostoevski, while mine chatted of dream and reality in the ironic novels of Ellen Glasgow. Our subjects reflected our sensitivity to oppositions, for we were both aware of a certain duality in our natures. As literary critics have pointed out, part of Sylvia desperately needed to risk flying toward the sun, even with waxen, feathery wings. I can testify that part of me much preferred to hunker down, closer to home, safely tilling the soil. But there were moments, for both of us. . . .

This pervasive sense of duality, if not duplicity, in our lives was a more telling historical feature of students in women's colleges in the fifties than some of the sex-linked issues that seventies feminism has since focused upon. Inflammatory matters of the relative power of men and women, with their peripheral brushfires, certainly left their mark, but then so did aluminum foil, Ozzie and Harriet on the tube, the Russian wheat crop, and the marriage of John F. Kennedy. Our primary conflict usually stemmed from the simple contradictions of a double life and an unmatched set of new expectations added to a collection already handed down to us.

At a noon class in Seelye Hall we would be taken to the mountaintop and at least given a chance to gaze out at the world spread below. Then we would go back to our house for 1:15 lunch, wash our hair, wait for telephone calls from New Haven, munch Heath Bars, and sometimes write home. We got used to the fact that our lives as achievers took place outside the house; inside it, we regressed.

More than our male counterparts we were conscious of higher education as higher, a pretty but ephemeral white cloud in which we might float somewhere above *terra firma*. We'd touch down, and push off again. As Betty Friedan (Smith '42) pointed out, our assumption was that we were terrestrial animals, by nature.

We compartmentalized. Ornamental matters of the mind were kept in an upstairs guest room, or relegated to attic storage, while a canny ability to deal with practical exigencies worked in the kitchen. We might read Virginia Woolf, discourse on her, but we didn't absorb her counsel: we didn't, as she advised, try to "think poetically and prosaically at one and the same moment, thus keeping in touch with fact." We alternated instead of integrating, and someone should have insisted on our sorting out priorities with ruthlessness, with realism. But we weren't even aware that selection was necessary. And so we kept moving in more furniture, wherever there was space.

We would be artists *and* craftsmen. We would develop ourselves, but always keep the welfare of the group firmly in mind. We would find excitement in security, independence by affiliation. Though we'd be radically different, we'd be like our mothers, and in certain ways we already were.

In 1921 *Good Housekeeping* had described our mothers' situation: "There is no doubt that hundreds [of American college girls] are in a most difficult position. Possessing all the innate, old-fashioned, if you will, but robust and womanly reactions to marriage, a home, and children, they are also possessed of a tangled growth of theories and ideals, and a sharply critical attitude toward life and what it may hold for them." The college girl of the twenties was "a person of strangely interwoven impulses, ideas, and desires," and so were we.

In our cocky contemporariness, we were sure we would embody the progress, the evolution, that had occurred since our mothers' day. "I will be good," said young Queen Victoria. We would be better, or even the best, and the brightest. To cop the title of a popular novel of the decade (written by Rona Jaffe, Radcliffe '51), all we wanted was merely "the best of everything."

So with deadly naïveté, we proceeded to file off our burrs and sharp edges in order to become marketably "well rounded." Alma Mater helped by instructing us in the ameliorating arts and sciences, and we felt little if any sense that we were (1) intellectually inferior to our male friends or our brothers, or (2) likely to put our education to use in a career outside the homes we were destined to make. Alma Mater dismissed as beneath notice the homely industry most of us were dying to box ourselves into . . . someday, somewhere.

We were so sure that we would prevail in a daily life where liberal arts would supplement domestic arts (whatever *they* were). In Phyllis McGinley's optimistic words, "From the raw material of four walls and a roof, a shelter over our heads," we could make "a home by force of our own personalities" and we would engage in "superior motherhood," our career outside the formal labor force.

By graduation morning in June 1955 a depressing number of diamond engagement rings glinted in Northampton's clearest light. "Oh God, our help in ages past/ Our hope for years to come," we caroled, "Our shelter from the stormy blast/ And our eternal home."

The future father-in-law of one of us had come to address us all, the engaged, the unengaged, the disengaged, and the dégagé alike. As Sylvia wrote in a letter to a friend, "Adlai Stevenson, operating on the hypothesis that every woman's highest vocation is a creative marriage, was most witty and magnificent as commencement speaker."

Actually Governor Stevenson spoke to us future handmaidens of America in a familiar style, reasonable, wry, intelligent, modestly self-deprecating, meaning so well but in his optimism misleading us so badly. He was, forgive me, our Almus Pater, our mild and liberal father.

"I think," he began, "there is much you can do about our crisis in the humble role of housewife." Nobody hissed. There we sat docilely that summer's day, about 350 of us in our black academic robes and mortarboards, almost degree-holders in biology, art, English, government, mathematics, and not quite sure what our common crisis was.

Our mission, hardly humble, would be to save Western Man—actually some particular Western man—from "the crushing effects of specialization," of collectivism and conformity, by using that "balanced tension of mind and spirit which can properly be called 'integrity.'" We could, he said, accomplish our "saving arts" with a baby on our lap and a can opener in our hand, for our assignment was "home work" and required no public forum to be effective. With our training as "intellectual generalizers" (how right he was!), we would not only rescue our husbands from the constrictions of their vocations, but we would also save our children from the blandness of being too "well adjusted."

"In modern America," he continued, "the home is not the boundary of a woman's life." We might have to overcome weariness and distraction, but surely our education had fitted us "for the primary task of making homes and whole human beings."

Finally, as in the Book of Proverbs, he assured us that when we had looked well to the paths of our houses, having not eaten our bread idly, then verily our children would rise up and call us blessèd, our husbands would praise us. I was suffused with a glorious certainty of what James Marston Fitch calls "that endemic American fantasy . . . the happy ending, which has everyone smiling."

When in September 1955 the *Woman's Home Companion* reprinted Stevenson's speech, some editor titled it "A Purpose for Modern Woman." I was perfectly willing to take up my assignment as Modern Woman, but where oh where was Western Man? I couldn't do it without him. How long would he lurk ruddily beyond the sun that set each night on the far side of the Hudson? I was to muse on this frequently as during the next few years I, Working Girl, walked back alone to any one of a series of chastely shared New York apartments, on summer afternoons, autumn evenings, winter nights, waiting for another glorious spring.

On a Fulbright fellowship in England, Sylvia wrote in her journal of her own sense of suspended animation: "Yet a life is passing. . . . I long to permeate the matter of this world, to become anchored to life by laundry and lilacs, daily bread and fried eggs, and a man, the dark-eyed stranger, who . . . goes round the world all day and comes back to find solace with me at night."

We worked away, wistfully, impatiently. Sylvia's wait wasn't very long. When in 1956 she wrote me to announce her marriage, her style was that of her submissions to the *Ladies' Home Journal:* there was "idiotic japonica" outside her window and high romance in her life. I was envious.

Though immediately after graduation I had leapt into what purported to be a career, at heart I regarded my work as "second best," to use the same words with which my grandmother in the late 1890s had denigrated her own interim occupation. New York sixty years later was a way station for underpaid, overeducated "trainees" who used their employers as cavalierly as their employers exploited them. We were editorial assistants, researchers, junior merchandisers, and we "just loved" either books-and-people or fashion.

My first job, though more prize than serious employment, was a month's stint as a guest editor on *Mademoiselle*. I then lurched through a succession of handmaidenly jobs in book publishing, but Success proved to be as elusive as Western Man. My trajectory was meteoric in the most literal sense. Do meteors ascend? In fact, pockmarked leaden lumps plummet down onto New Mexican deserts, and stars fall on Alabama. Mine dropped onto Madison Avenue, there on the East Side among the brittle glass showcases of the fifties, Lever House and all its sleek set.

At one moment seriously distrait and at another blithely insouciant, I drifted to a small inhabited island in the near West Side, to become Girl Friday to an unlikely Crusoe, a plump little literary agent who was the elderly representative of various aging liberal authors. Her office occupied one room in her apartment, where I became a kind of visiting granddaughter.

At four on smoky autumn afternoons, we would knock off work, such as it was, to sip Lapsang Souchong and talk of Nannine's clients, the Constance Talmadges and Gene Lockharts of her rather theatrical past, or today's Eleanor Roosevelt, Mark Van Doren, and other senior Stevensonians. Her agently instincts led her unselfconsciously into matchmaking, and a succession of eligible editors joined our twilight tea ceremonies. I began to feel like a foolish geisha.

Preposterously, it happened. Northeastern Man, a scout from Boston, responded to our Oriental infusions. For three years I'd been looking in the wrong direction. He and I wasted little more of each other's time and were married a few months later, in the spring of 1959. The season was right, but the World of Tomorrow had arrived a year ahead of schedule.

I had, however, been rehearsing for it all during those New York years of stop-time. Abandoned apartments dotted the city. I had invested myself in these halfway houses, transitional between my mother's and my own, with a growing intensity whose measure was in gallons of latex paint.

Mademoiselle had billeted its twenty guest editors in a women's residential hotel, a larger, urban version of Lawrence House. From there, the square marked GO, two roommates and I proceeded north to East 79th Street and high into a bland prewar apartment building where the odors of roast lamb and other wholesome bourgeois cooking filled the elevator halls, but whose squareness was as nothing when we considered the glamorous skyline glittering and spiking to north and south, our own glossy postcard view to send home to mother.

But soon two of us split off and hopped seventy blocks south, to Christopher Street in Greenwich Village and close quarters in a low nineteenth-century structure of white brick with green shutters, built around a polyhedron of a courtyard, where a few ailanthuses trembled when subways rumbled by underground. (The building was allegedly the location of the famous shaking apartment of Ruth McKenney's *My Sister Eileen,* ultimately adapted as the musical *Wonderful Town.*)

Our quarters were minuscule, almost the dimensions of the secessional subdivision I'd once proposed for my mother's house and had wisely abandoned. I hung a print of an Edward Hicks's *The Peaceable Kingdom,* framed in imitation distressed chestnut, over the teeny-tiny fireplace, while my friend fried pork chops in the teeny-tiny galley, and recorded Vivaldi or Ella Fitzgerald singing Gershwin filled the teeny-tiny room. Each night we drew the teeny-tiny chintz curtains and filed ourselves in our teeny-tiny G.I. bunk beds. We lived a teeny-tiny life in a fragile, miniature shadow box.

Next I played house in a somewhat less microcosmic but similar setting farther west in the Village, the third (and top) floor of a small commercial building. We had the use of the flat roof, where we might better have played tenement and raised pigeons in a cage than try, as we did, to create a charming roof garden. Our gritty and moribund plants gasped for air under the creaky arbor some other romantic had once improvised of urban driftwood. We finally jammed plastic geraniums from Woolworth's into our clinker-filled flowerboxes.

Downstairs, inside, the apartment gradually succumbed to my Williamsburging of it. My then roommate bore with my atavistic urges, as she watched Wythe House green and gold and white inexorably coat walls and woodwork and furniture. Once in a while our real fireplace blazed, when we could afford to buy the tenderloin-priced logs sold by a Grimm woodman across the street, who extracted them from dark and mysterious storage somewhere down among the alligators, under the sidewalks of Bank Street.

We aimed to be an oasis in the hardscrabble city, and we might have succeeded had the marigolds had the nerve, and had sharing quarters with any other woman not begun to seem silly to me. I suffered from the cumulative effect of all those nylons, hanging like Spanish moss from drying racks and dripping, dripping into the humid nights of a whole decade. I wanted to be alone, and yet not alone.

My last New York apartment, for which I happened to sign the lease on the very day I fell finally in love, was my first and only one-woman show. I saw it as in the tradition of Henry James and Edith Wharton: one lofty, elegant bare room on the *piano nobile*, rear, of a Victorian brownstone on East 17th Street. Genteel and proper, it hid its kitchenette in one closet and its bathroom in another, as if ashamed of their vulgarity. Through two many-paned windows that rose from parquet floor to high ceiling I could glimpse the stained glass of St. George's, Stuyvesant Square, which glowed from within, reassuringly, like Christmas.

I managed to exorcize the former tenant with a single sloppy coat of flat in *fin de siècle* taupe, but added little other embellishment to the place, besides a new print, Breughel's *Fall of Icarus.* I'd typed a copy of Auden's poem, "Musée des Beaux Arts," and pasted it on the back of the mounting, in order to tell the wall, I suppose, that even the fall of a boy from sky into green water made little difference, for daily life, consolingly preoccupied, went on nonetheless.

In the one closet that behaved itself as a closet should, I soon hung a wedding dress, white peau-de-soie and lace for old fashion's sake, but short and breezy for *Modern Bride*. I might have loved that last halfway house, but when I went out its door, all trailing bridal illusion, feeling a little corny and costumed, I didn't look back.

During the honeymoon, my mother and her sister carted my tatty possessions to a startled, if not outraged, bachelor apartment in Cambridge, my new home by adoption, or invasion. Two people, one address: he and I, we were an actual social unit, a veritable nucleus, and—how odd—we would be so inscribed on official documents, wills, censuses, voting rolls. A strange and happy ending, and at last a real commencement, I thought to myself, amazed at my good fortune.

And so I proceeded to, ominous phrase, settle down.

 SEVEN

The Fall of a Doll's House, 1960-1976

Storks nest on Dutch chimneys, while wood ibises homestead treetops in Florida swamps. In Cambridge, Massachusetts, I carried bits of straw and string up two flights of stairs to our sweet and eccentric apartment, an improvised duplex carved out of a tall, accommodating frame house of the turn of the century that was willing to give up some second-floor rear rooms, its attic, and two porches (or perches).

The lot fell away sharply, beside and behind. Across a chasm, the driveway like a fiord in from the street, we could wave at old friends of mine who had by chance moved into the corresponding nest next door. Gordon (whose father had been a reluctant conscript into the Lindum Club, whose mother's house had been my aspiration) and his wife (a contemporary at both Kent Place School and Smith) gave me a sense of continuum, of one life shading into another. Their gravely beautiful one-year-old daughter appraised us of the new "older generation" with huge clear blue eyes. Coincidences continued, and both families booked space for late November 1960 at The Lying-In (now known less archaically as the Boston Hospital for Women). Early on Thanksgiving morning our son joined us, his four-day-old neighbor, and all the intensely female women lying in or sitting up or shuffling around shiny institutional halls. By noon, novice father and newborn maternal grandmother, dazed by their sudden status, toped and coped at home with the slippery roast goose I'd laid in the day before. I, queen for a day, sipped champagne and listened to the final episodes of the same radio soap operas I'd followed when I was a snuffly minor being served only sickroom ginger ale. Ma Perkins shared a last turkey and assorted homilies with her extended family: Shuffle from the lumberyard, daughter Effie, me, and all the others in radioland. Our gal Sunday and Helen Trent waved farewell, and receded into history. A new age, a New Frontier, new children, a new me.

Our aerie home soon revealed itself as a clear and present danger to family life, just as the naysayers of 1902 had suspected apartments were. Our odd fluffy puppy gnawed his way out of the third-floor porch, scrabbled up the steeply pitched roof, walked the ridgepole like a Halloween cat, and miraculously slid to a rescue point. The day of John Kennedy's inauguration, perhaps unbalanced by a surge of Jr. D.A.R. patriotism, I tripped and flew headfirst down the long straight attic staircase, the baby under my arm like a loaf of French bread. Somehow flipping in midair, we landed on my feet, to no applause . . . just a hideous stillness in the apartment. Now I understand the term "a flight of stairs," and also knew the depth of a new vulnerability as I checked over my tiny son, who was gasping in admiration at Mummy's funny trick.

No more narrow escapes for us! We would buy a house of our own. Did we really feel that home ownership would exempt us from the principles of physics and other harsh facts of life?

That same winter, Sylvia Plath wrote her mother from England that she was working on a long story "about a girl who falls in love with a beautiful old house and manages finally to possess it." Sure that the theme was irresistible to popular taste, she added, characteristically, "I'll have a story in the *LHJournal* or *SatEvePost* yet." What she did have by the autumn of 1961 was her own aged, thatched-roof cottage in Devon. "The place is like a person," she reported home; "it responds to the slightest touch and looks wonderful immediately. . . . My whole spirit has expanded immensely—I don't have that crowded harassed feeling I've had in all the small places I've lived in before."

I once glimpsed the London apartment at Chalcot Square into which she, husband, and baby daughter had been compressed, and it was as small and cellular as a bee hive. In Devon, however, Sylvia had scope, and she plunged into domesticity of the picturesque rural sort. But even authentic Anglo-Saxon Home Feeling was not quite enough for a homemaker from Wellesley, Massachusetts. In the midst of it all, she again wrote to her mother, "If you happen to think of it, could you pack me off a *Ladies' Home Journal* or two? I get homesick for it; it has an Americanness which I feel a need to dip into, now I'm in exile."

My husband and I thought of our own all-American investment as, in today's jargon, "a starter house" from which we would eventually trade up. A bargain in the prematurely inflating market of 1960s Harvard-Square Cambridge, the house was priced low because it was on the shabby "wrong side" of Massachusetts Avenue, the section movie actor Ryan O'Neal when there on location for *Love Story* ungraciously described as Outer Mongolia. Our new neighborhood certainly wasn't the mellow antique Cambridge of lilacs and heritage I'd once defended against Levittown.

And the house itself wasn't "right," according to the Summit standards I tried to repress, though it did have a certain elementary rectitude that disarmed me. Straight and narrow, it was in a transitional style that combined simple Greek Revival lines with a later, Victorian touch of bracketing and double front doors with frosted and etched glass panes. It managed to shrug off most subsequent minor modernizations, remaining quirkily self-possessed. Its complexion was a decadent claret (wine-darkness that, as we were subsequently to discover, was an early symptom of senility in New England or Barn Red house paint, initially as wholesome and hearty as apple cider). From the west slope of a gabled roof facing the street protruded an odd addition, a tin-hatted, onion-domed cupola, like a minaret.

With its strong streak of what Joy Wheeler Dow called "the Jacobin," the house's exterior would not have appealed to such a purist, but even he might have been tolerant, once inside it. He had conceded that the best of the genre was "in plan . . . eminently sensible . . . the rooms square, commodious, and airy, amplified by bay windows, besides being so arranged as to open en suite." The house did have those virtues, and if it wasn't exactly up to all expectations, it was an "eminently sensible" compromise. We negotiated a 5¾ percent mortgage and made our move.

On warm sunny days I'd leave the house with perambulator and passenger. Focused in on mundane urgencies, rarely more conscious than a postman of the rich built environment of nonresidential Cambridge, we trundled past the cyclorama that is Harvard University, museum of the work of master builders and architects of three centuries, from Bulfinch to Richardson, Le Corbusier and Gropius (whose 1949 Bauhaus graduate center held its ground only a block from our own freehold).

The residential streets radiating north and west from Harvard Square were an equally remarkable survey of domestic architecture, and the mansions of Tory Row more effectively pulled at my sleeve for attention. On brisk and golden October days, the glow of that other Cambridge seemed to catch in the windows of our cupola, enhancing our house's defects and keeping them from becoming an issue.

John Updike, iconographer, has described the interior life of early 1960s Cambridge (in *Couples*) as fraught with food and furniture. We lived in "a region of complicated casseroles and Hungarian goulashes and garlicky salads and mock duck and sautéed sweetbreads," in rooms typically filled with "sharp-edged Cambridge furniture, half Door Store and half Design Research."

Design Research was then more than a store—it was a continuing local event. Launched in 1953 by architect-impresario Benjamin Thompson (a founding partner with Gropius of The Architects Collaborative, and his successor as chairman of Harvard's department of architecture), the shop was an offshoot from TAC's interior design department, which had originated to develop fittings that would complement the architects' work, not clutter it.

D/R's early promotions described it as a "center for fine contemporary design in furniture, fabrics, and accessories," comparable to Nieman-Marcus, Lord & Taylor, and Harrod's. Perhaps, but unlike any of those merchant principalities, for years D/R happened in an unpretentious converted frame house on historic Brattle Street, directly across from the site of Longfellow's spreading chestnut tree. Customers regarded D/R as a museum house, as so apparently did the decorative Noras who matched the Scandinavian wares they tended and sold. D/R was to them "like a house and we take care of it as we would our own homes."

D/R furniture, especially as displayed in this personal, domestic setting, was frank and friendly, simple and balanced. Accessories were also candid, in practical, pure materials and natural forms echoing the idealized Northern European forests of fairy tale, with their enchanted cottages, moss and lichen, tall pincs. D/R's fabrics were so arresting in their bright colors and elemental patterns that they immediately cleared palates cloyed by the pink-and-black licorice pastilles of 1950s pop modern color schemes, or the nougat pastels of department-store chintzes, toiles, and other literal-minded reproductions of fabrics from history.

The whole mood of the store was reactive: it implicitly rejected feminine conservatism, all those hope chests filled with damask, embroidered tea cloths, gold-rimmed floral china, monogrammed linen guest towels. It did so simply by offering us a chance to choose what was brighter and better, more "our" style than our mothers' and one that seemed to appeal to men as well as women. Couples shopped together in D/R on snowy Saturday afternoons.

Thompson's taste was informal, simple, and democratically unpretentious (though everyone knew, to the penny, just how expensive its artifacts really were), and it inspired those who were "just looking, thank you," as well as those who actually bought the D/R walnut table, the D/R lamp, the D/R down-filled sofa upholstered in white Haitian cotton. The Boston *Globe* described D/R endorsement as "the avant-garde's answer to *Good Housekeeping*'s Seal of Approval."

So many young Cambridge couples lived, like us, in slightly disappointing first houses, which they regarded as temporary, in a quasi-suburb denying that it was a city, in marginal neighborhoods where, as one friend put it, you felt challenged to create "a diamond on a dung heap." Anyone who thinks her image extreme has not lived among the dog-decorated, frozen slag heaps of forgotten midwinter side streets in Outer Mongolia.

We ambitious types seemed to have little choice but to forget the rolling lawns and gardens we didn't have, and to perfect the interiors we did. We entertained inside our houses, at all those Updikean dinner parties that were, in their way, of an almost Edwardian gourmandise. A more extroverted or casual style of social life—salads and fruit *al fresco*—we necessarily left to California and other sympathetic climates. We pulled our shades down, lit our candles, tasted the sauce.

Though we weren't interior decorators in our mothers' sense, out to create a consistent historic *mise-en-scène*, we were probably as acquisitive. We aimed to assemble a permanent collection of objects representing that new variant on acceptable taste, Good Modern Design. These smaller objects, housed within our largest possession, would somehow redeem the inadequacies of the present and would rise with us. They would never embarrass us or be outgrown, like the wives politicians married when young.

We learned from Thompson that what would bridge gaps and

give coherence to our collection of blue-chips was lavish
decoration from nature, masses of well-designed flowers like
zinnias and chrysanthemums and daisies and geraniums, heaps
of perfect red apples (in Swedish glass bowls.).

"Art," said Thompson "is *not* for particular people, but
should be in everything you do—in cooking, and God knows,
in the bread on the table, in the way everything is *done.*"
Elsewhere he continued, "Design has to do with our everyday
environment—the way we live inside and outside our houses. In
this abundant age, it is a reach for meaningful values in material
things—grace, comfort, pleasure—and honesty of purpose."

Our new tradition chose to see with the fresh eye of the
child—the wise child of Salinger—rather than with the apprais-
ing squint of the antiquarian connoisseur. And we younger
wives dressed for the part, in the crisp cotton paper-doll dresses
known as Marimekkos (in Finnish, *Marimekko* means "a little
girl's dress for Mary"). The line, originally a D/R exclusive in
the United States, was introduced here the spring I was married
as part of a Finnish craft exhibit at the Cambridge store. By
summer all of my new friends were wearing the witty coat-
dresses or smocks, in a spectrum of wildflower colors, in prints
that seemed to have come straight from the easels of a
particularly joyous elementary school.

The Finnish firm Printex, producer of silk-screened fabrics
used in home furnishing, had originally run up a few sample
"house coats" for display purposes and found they had an eager
market among women who found them comfortable to work in,
and cheering. One number was called Gay Kitchen—
significantly not Efficient Kitchen or Traditional Kitchen.

Armi Ratia, Marimekko's Chanel, described her design
approach as paralleling the architect's: "He makes a house for
people to live in. I make a dress for the woman to live in." And
she added, "Our clothes must be loose and express movement.
They are part of modern interiors and modern life."

At TAC, Thompson had maintained that the furnishing of an
interior is also an aspect of architecture—"You can't draw a
line between the two things." Slipcovered in the same fabric as

my sofa pillow, was it any wonder that I found it increasingly difficult to distinguish between my house and myself. Was I, like the furniture, part of the architecture of the house, or was it part of me? We were certainly growing close.

When a branch of D/R opened in San Francisco's Ghirardelli Square in 1965, Marimekkos were again the instant smash hit they had been in Cambridge and New York, and the status housedress was seen on redwood decks après-swim, or lunching at the club. What was the appeal? Did we, East and West, want to think of ourselves as doll children, or as pillows, or as the whimsical avant-garde, intelligent enough to trade convention for comfort? Or were we seeking to introduce the young, the gay, and the simple into a domesticity we sensed was clouding over, was threatening to become as grim and complicated as income taxes, politics, our busy, busy lives?

Since World War II, as never before, the business of American housewives has been busy-ness—of a special, fragmenting sort. How many multiple personalities, homely Sybils and three-faced Eves, have we confronted wearily while reading what we are or should be? Betty Friedan in 1963 did one dissection of the many-headed monster and found her to be "wife, mistress, mother, nurse, consumer, cook, chauffeur, expert on interior decoration, child care, appliance repair, furniture refinishing, nutrition, and education." Later John Kenneth Galbraith outlined her duties as the manager of consumption: "to select, transport, prepare, maintain, clean, service, store and protect" objects.

But we housewives were also supposed to be highly charged and sensitive administrators of the "intangible, emotional tasks" of the Happy Home. Our voltage transmitted itself to those we administered who shared our houses, and who might have decided in self-defense to insulate themselves against all our "planning, coordinating, assembling, supervising." Many a competent woman has begun in faith that "the managing, the being conscious of her efficiency" would in itself satisfy her, only to have uncomfortable second thoughts.

The notion of some mystical role assigned by nature to be

played by women in the home nonetheless still maintains its hold on the imagination. Woman has long been idealized, in Doris Lessing's words, as "the supplier of some kind of invisible fluid, or emanation, like a queen termite whose spirit (or some such word—electricity) filled the nest, making a whole of individuals who could have no other connection."

This particular insect queen reacted to the swirl of options confronting her as any sensible termite would. I dug my teeth into my succulent wooden house and for a number of years munched on contentedly. In retrospect, I think I found our symbiosis suitable because I honestly believed the metaphor of the equation stated by Stanley Crawford as "The house is the Marriage, and thus to maintain and keep in good repair the house, tidy and well cleaned, is to keep the Marriage too in good repair, tidy, well cleaned."

I regret to say that as a monarch I was less like Elizabeth I, patron of the flowering of Renaissance England, than her dour sister, Bloody Mary, the persecutor. Perhaps a graphic way to summarize my reign of terror over all protestants is to describe a poster drawn for me by the brother who boarded with us in 1960–61 while he chased paper at nearby Harvard Law School. During this early period of high-handed domesticity, he was often pressed into the service of the crown.

Dominating his masterpiece of ambivalence is a Joan of Arc figure in a white tunic. From her scarlet sash hangs a mighty scimitar, engraved with the legend "The Inglorious Arts of Peace." Its blade drips vermilion blood. The sainted martyr also carries an unfurled banner on which is written "Dieu et M. Clean." She gazes upward to an Olympian figure poised in a cloud overhead, a female who is helmeted like Athena but who is bare-breasted in the Minoan manner. Her uplifted right hand brandishes a paint roller soaked in more human blood.

The amazing cross-cultural tableau also includes an Anglo-Saxon coat of arms, with odd fluffy dog rampant over diapered baby crawlant. In the upper left quarter of my escutcheon are three raised paintbrushes, in the lower right a scrub bucket. A

diagonal blazon reads "Ex parte materna," followed by cautionary words, "Tread gently, she is near . . ."
The work is dedicated "To the General. What stronger breastplate than a heart untainted."

In those early innocent days I thought of myself less as a martyr or tyrant than as a kind of contemporary pioneer woman, homesteading in the wilderness, bending my little grubstake to my will. I forced the surrender of dusty-rose ceilings to three overpowering onslaughts of white, tilled the soil, which was urban fill containing mysterious whole peanuts, a clip-on bow tie, and familiar clinkers, those universal souvenirs of the coal age in home heating. I glazed broken windows and mastered the aquastat on the ancient oil-burning furnace, which was insulated by plastery bandages that seemed to swaddle some huge gouty foot.

Once I'd tasted victory, in a lust for further power over matter, I relegated serious concentration on family morale and spiritual uplift to Monday's schedule—*next* Monday, that day of hope on which all diets begin. I contracted an overweening pride in self-sufficiency, in being the sole custodian of our house. I believe I saw myself as a plainclothes version of someone like the heroine of a recent historical novel, *The Caretaker Wife*. The publisher's ad for the book read:

A honeymoon for one is what's left of Caroline Hill's marriage celebration when her husband of one night abruptly departs for the Napoleonic Wars. Left to cope with his debt-ridden estate and five young children by his first wife, Caroline sets out to become the perfect wife and mother. During the next three tumultuous years in Regency England, she battles jealous household enemies, a vengeful nursemaid, an unexpected temptation of passion . . . and finally faces the return of the man she hardly knows.

By the mid-1960s, when my husband returned from his peninsular campaigns in downtown Boston, it was I whom he hardly knew, dressed down and in drag as a handyman. With each new do-it-yourself project, I became more proletarianized. As he rose toward seniority, with his "fine clubs and expense-account restaurants," I seemed to sink in social status. Joshing with the guys at the hardware store, swapping tales of spackle and grout, lunching on leftover peanut-butter-and-jelly crusts, on an ordinary day I may have been a happy peasant but I certainly was no lady, and sometimes it was not entirely clear that I was even a woman. What *would* my grandmother have thought?

An incident at Sears dramatized how unseriously we handy-persons have been taken. A friend and I had struck a deal whereby I would help her hang her Japanese straw paper if she would assist me with my fake-burlap white vinyl. Sensibly dressed for our work in accidentally identical costumes—bib overalls, turtlenecks, with head kerchiefs—we stopped off to buy a second paste brush. As we passed a salesman emerging with his sample case, he commented, "Wow, gals, what a *great look.*" Great look! We burst into laughter. But it was evident that once again the world had viewed our work as a pose, though we were at least semi-pro.

"By its informality, its irrationality, and its cultural importance, the whole situation of the housewife stands in violent contrast to the rest of the occupational system," wrote Theodore Caplow in *The Sociology of Work.* He went on to say that housewives are the most homogeneous work force in the country, with similar goals, values, working conditions, "an identity of metier that transcends class lines and regional boundaries."

If only housewives had a tradition of guild halls where they could meet in pride of craft and enjoy a lusty camaraderie. Instead they silently pass each other in all the Shoppers' Heaven malls of America, strangers bent on urgent private business. As Gerda Lerner pointed out at a conference on housework and child care (from a feminist perspective) sponsored in 1977 by the Women's Studies Program of Sarah Lawrence College: "Real estate development which assigns to each individual family a private home on a whole or half acre, has created living solutions which are essentially privatist and non-communal. The main link between families is the shopping center—and shopping centers are not community centers."

In an article titled "Do It Yourself Takes Over," a 1955 *McCall's* summarized that division of the building trades born after World War II, which has continued to grow steadily ever since. "Never before have so many done so much—themselves," was the Churchillian comment introducing some startling statistics and a prediction that Do-It-Yourself would change the pattern of American life as deeply as had the automobile. According to *McCall's*, 75 percent of the paint and 60 percent of the wallpaper purchased in their sample period was applied by Do-It-Yourselfers, among whom were 11 million amateur carpenters using $25 million worth of home power tools. Moreover, a survey quoted showed that women "not only initiate more projects than men but actually take on more of the muscle work."

By 1970, as figures supplied by the M.I.T.-Harvard Joint Center for Urban Studies in *The Nation's Housing* indicate, 17.7 percent of total expenditures on home improvements were for owner-installed materials, and in the next five years the dollars actually spent increased by 21.4 percent, while the proportion of the total spent on do-it-yourself rose to 20 percent.

What motives generate this kind of accelerating activity in the nest? One woman interviewed by *McCall's* in 1955 still speaks, I think, convincingly: "You do it yourself to save money for other things of course. But there's something else too. Maybe it's creative therapy for the world we live in." ("Creative" in the fifties and sixties was the "artistic" of 1912, but "therapy" is totally contemporary.) In 1977, in an article titled "Every Man's a Carpenter," John Ingersoll commented, "Do-it-yourself is as deeply embedded in our national psyche as the desire to better oneself."

And each of us has her own personal motives. From childhood I connected health and handwork, for when my father was not ill, he would hammer and saw and paint and putter. Working with one's hands became a way to express well-being, optimism, even love. My brothers and I have all reenacted this family sacrament in our adult life in our own homes.

As I watched my mother sew her own curtains and slipcovers, her pursuit seemed both practical and somehow as moral as not burying the talents. She could fend for herself, without the hired help who still lingered on in the homes of many friends, as if no one had told them that by 1930 full-time servants were supposed virtually to have vanished from the middle-class household.

Actually my mother was a veteran of a few brief wartime encounters with the domestic 4F. Her help in ages past had been strange and erratic, often terrible to behold. We children were shocked to encounter poor hungover Kathleen, who had been missing in action in New York since St. Patrick's Day, staggering down Woodland Avenue toward home, one stocking ripped and dangling, coat crumpled, an eye swollen shut. And there were a few other weird sisters, who lived in and soon took off, forever.

My own brief apprenticeship as an employer, in the early sixties, had been unrewarding, frustrating. One conscientious worker ran paper Dixie cups through the dishwasher; another low-key operative spent four expensive hours cleaning (or restoring) a single radiator. In contrast, a professional cleaning service was expensive and so devastatingly efficient that, as I straightened pictures afterwards, I always felt that some great wind had blown through the house. I'd rather, I decided, do it myself. I would murmur to myself, "Well done, my good and faithful servant."

Gradually, like so many of my contemporaries, I started to internalize the role of the servants I rejected, becoming simultaneously the demanding mistress who gave orders *and* the critical subordinate who resisted them, griping.

In *Women of Crisis* Robert Coles and Jane Hallowell Coles include a long soliloquy by a Cambridge maid, who was self-righteous in her contempt for her employer, whom she saw as riddled with liberal hypocrisies as well as muddled in self-absorption. The fashionably emancipated mistress, a familiar type, although vaguely guilty about buying the labor of another woman, nevertheless continued to mouth feminist platitudes while she pulled rank. Neither woman exemplified a deeply humane tolerance, but the two did manage to maintain an ingenious balancing act. Their performance was one that began to occur daily inside my head.

On special occasions controlled schizophrenia became a dramatic *tour de force.* A do-it-yourself formal dinner for ten demands the quick changes of a Marcel Marceau. I recall a famous routine in which he metamorphoses from puny David crouching on the right of a screen into lumbering Goliath on its left, within a split second's passage behind it. I would be similarly transformed as I hurtled through the swinging door of my kitchen. Shazam! Lady Bellamy into Ruby the scullery maid, scrabbling to snatch the entree from the broiler.

My grandmother may have liked to think of herself as just another Helper, but she knew perfectly well that, no matter what, she was clearly the Mistress. My mother's ladylike informality represented a kind of leisured honeymoon when the balance between woman and house, expectations and reality, was perhaps as close to equilibrium as it may ever get. Hers was a period when the middle-class housewife had some servants, enough machines, and most relevant, retained my grandmother's sense that the culture at large endorsed her and her work in the home. My peers and I, often mistaking solitude for independence, undertook to do it *all,* and to do it all *ourselves,* even when "it" had clearly become dauntingly plural, the new piled on top of the old. We were convinced that we were intelligent enough to remain on top of things, firmly in charge of objects and ourselves, if not of family and fate.

In the third generation since 1900, the housewife's self-confidence began to waver or splinter, just as the accumulation of physical and emotional demands on her multiplied, fractionalized. Overextended, she found what joy there is in simple competency slipping away from her. Mastering the Art of Daily Living seemed to drift out of reach. Perhaps a smaller focus was in order. Mastering the Art of French Cooking was a feasible goal, and I, like many others, turned eagerly to Julia Child (Smith '34) for instruction, consolation, and a kind of motherly companionship in the kitchen. But as tension continued to grow, the effervescence of Thompson's aristocratic simplicity became harder to retain. Days became flat, stale, unprofitable. And didn't we read about it?

In the mirror, in magazines and books, in the faces of friends encountered among the screws and washers in Sears' basement, I became sensitized to what Doris Lessing calls "the humorous grimace." Betty Friedan had already spotlighted the "new breed of women writers" who seemed to find solace in wry laughter prompted by a "comic world of children's pranks and eccentric washing machines and parents' night at the P.T.A."

"Smilin' through" as a survival tactic was, however, neither particularly feminine nor any newer than minstrel show cakewalks or foxhole wisecracks. In 1921 *Good Housekeeping* noted that women's writing "in the funny columns" reflected the fact that "the married, being on the inside, feel perfectly free to emphasize the petty, trying, trivial, restricting side" of housewifery. Similarly, couples with healthy kids can afford to complain about "parenting" to equally lucky friends, as they can't to a widow whose son is dying of leukemia. The angry Cambridge maid in *Women of Crisis* found her employer's own crises less than a barrel of laughs. What Patricia Meyer Spacks in *The Female Imagination* calls the Erma Bombeck-Jean Kerr-Betty MacDonald comic tradition is probably only boffo when both author and reader are securely resident within the sheltered middle class. There one may safely gripe about ants in the honey, not being in terror of tigers at the gate. In its way, the genre of housewife humor is as circumscribed and exclusive as suburban domesticity itself has been. It is essentially as middle class as much of the Women's Movement.

The persona of the smiling slob adopted by Erma Bombeck instantly appealed to her ready-made audience, from her first publication in newspapers in the mid-1960s through 1970s appearances in national magazines like *Good Housekeeping* and *McCall's*. By 1978 and her latest best-selling book, *If Life Is a Bowl of Cherries, What Am I Doing in the Pits?*, she had become a kind of female Bob Hope, a national institution, now rich and atypical but with the common touch that proclaims her "just a housewife" at heart.

In a 1971 *Life* interview, "The Socrates of the Ironing Board" observed: "Most of my readers are housewives. I'm saying 'Hey, let's look at us! We've all been there. We're all in this mess together. Let's get some fun out of it.'"

Bombeck, who in another guise is the Pagliacci of the Tupperware circuit, remains such an indefatigable good sport and so acute an observer of the absurdly evocative detail that in small doses she doesn't burden her readers with her pervasive sense of the underlying darkness, of the septic tank under the greenest grass. Her insistence on the plucky little dandelion growing there just doesn't work in longer takes, or when dramatized (as in a 1978 television version of *The Grass* that was an epic downer).

As Spacks comments, the humor of the housewife writers, and presumably of their readers, has been "profoundly conservative in its social implications, preserving the image of feminine incompetence, siphoning off anger, suggesting that if it's funny to be a bad housewife, there may be some dignity to being a good one."

Bombeck is no fool, and in 1971 she observed a change in mood: "Frankly the field is narrowing down of things to write about. There's a big problem in writing humor—so much sensitivity in so many areas." Certainly by the 1970s middle-class housewives, the occupational group that can be described as unpaid domestic labor, were especially touchy and, at least in print, appeared to be heading toward the wildcat strike long a theoretical possibility. The catchall phrase "Women's Lib" spiced up headlines and Sunday supplements, sandwiched in time between "Generation Gap" and "The Me Generation." As housewives became edgier and more defensive than ever before, the rhetoric made it easy to express a multitude of long-repressed resentments, large and small, legitimate and frivolous—without committing oneself to serious change. The chip on the shoulder became as chic an accessory as fashion boots, designer sheets. Raised consciousnesses loudly scorned "the dull manage of a servile house."

Pop Lib—which must be distinguished from the equal rights movement—made *kvetching* the Mah-Jongg or bridge of the decade. The safety valve on the pressure cooker provided by housewifely humor ceased to function with total efficiency.

"Liberation," by definition, promised emancipation of the slaves, or at least commutation of a lifetime sentence to domesticity. In a speech delivered at a seminar, "Homemaker: Career in Transition," Bombeck herself recently described the Movement as signifying for some "a ticket out of the kitchen." The seminar was sponsored by the *Ladies' Home Journal* and that unsung patron of feminism, Kentucky Fried Chicken (which, though I hate to admit it, has probably liberated as many woman-hours as all the cooperative housekeeping societies since Melusina Peirce).

On both sides of the Atlantic (as British sociologist Ann Oakley testifies in *Housewife,* published here in 1974 as *Woman's Work*), the same deeply self-deprecating dialogue was taking place:

Q. What do you do?
A. Nothing. I'm just a housewife.

Any one of us who has ever given that answer knows perfectly well she's been doing something. But we answer, Nothing. No thing. At least no thing of value.

Q. But what *is* valued?
A. Work.
Q. But what then is housework?
A. Housework is not work, it's labor, and labor is not valued. Labor is menial, manual. You do it with your hands, not your head or your heart.

In her introduction to *Women in Architecture,* Susana Torre concisely summarizes various writers on the distinction between *work* (which is "permanent and synonymous with the public realm") and *labor* ("impermanent and synonymous with the private realm"). Our world clusters *labor* with organic *nature* and with *dwelling*, where growth and other natural processes occur, sheltered. In contrast, *work*, which takes place outside the dwelling, has status because it contributes to *culture*, one of whose artifacts is *architecture*.

"These differences," Torre emphasizes, "are made plain by the importance given to creative and esthetic pleasure, as opposed to the toil of survival or even the satisfaction of material desires." A woman can scrub her fingers off or shop like a veritable Duveen and still say with a straight face, "I need to get a job. I want *to work*."

Certainly among us laborers in dwellings of the late sixties and early seventies low morale was not raised by international affairs or politics, or by the hot news that the young were demonstrating against the Establishment, against convention, against *us*. If our friends' teenage children were rejecting the ideal of the family who gathered 'round the hearth to pop corn, then maybe our toddlers would someday do the same, and if so, what was the use of all our nursery school fund-raisers, laundry, and vitamin pills? Were our busy lives mere exercises in futility? "I believe that what a woman resents," Anne Morrow Lindbergh was to say at Smith, "is not so much giving herself in pieces as giving herself purposelessly."

Under stress from outside the beleaguered little castles and demoralization inside them, Home Feeling twisted into contagious neurosis. No one knows exactly why Palladio's sixteenth-century Villa Foscari was nicknamed "La Malcontenta," but it was no mystery why discontent was permeating the dry walls of imitation Palladian villas across the suburban landscape during the years of the Vietnamese war, purposelessness in action, or of the Nixon descent.

Physical diseases in children had been exchanged for psychic afflictions in their mothers, among whom rampaged an epidemic of such exotica as agoraphobia, "fear of the marketplace and public places." The Housewife's Disease (also a name for ordinary depression) was said by 1977 to affect 2.5 million Americans, 85 to 90 percent of them women. Agoraphobia had its perverse variation in another lesser panic I think of as the Horse in the Burning Barn Syndrome. A Cleveland doctor recounted that "sometimes a woman would tell me that the feeling gets so strong she runs out of the house and walks through the streets."

In *Runaway Wives* Anna Sklar quotes the abandoned writer-husband of one fugitive mother, who put on her Levi's and T-shirt and really took it on the lam, leaving her family for the "free" life of an itinerant, counterculture potter. As he reconstructed events, "When I started working on my first book in the house, Cathy just freaked. I had invaded her domain. . . . I think the walls began to crowd in on her and the house became a symbol," a symbol perhaps of the ultimate insult, his ability to work where she had merely labored.

Other women took advantage of their daily privacy to conceal less dramatic escapes. Germaine Greer in *The Female Eunuch* (1971) describes nagging, overweight, and premature aging as the outward signs of misery, of women's creative energy turned inward, transformed into self-destruction. The housebound committed mini-suicide by Oreo cookie or Fudgsicle, or they popped Valium, or they hit the vodka. One Ivy-and-Junior-Leaguish ex-alcoholic interviewed on a Boston TV documentary explained, "My house was my bar," a very private bar from the time the family went off to work and school until the legitimate cocktail hour.

We read novels to distract ourselves, to gain perspective, but often found ourselves looking in a glass darkly. In *The Wapshot Scandal*, John Cheever told us the pathetic allegory of one Gertrude Lockhart, who hanged herself in despair over the aftermath of the defection of one household appliance after another:

In the meantime, the gas range went and she had to do all the cooking on an electric plate. She could not educate herself in the maintenance and repair of household machinery and felt in herself that tragic obsolescence she had sensed in the unemployed of [her town] who needed work and money but who could not dig a hole. It was this feeling of obsolescence that pushed her into drunkenness and promiscuity and she was both.

A more resourceful character in the same tale did find some solace in her house. It succeeded in distracting her from the pain of her affair with the grocery boy, "her golden Adam," even more effectively than booze. When at three in the morning she found calm in planning the renovation of her kitchen, Cheever turned to us and asked, "Was this some foolishness of her or of her time that, caught in the throes of a hopeless love, the only peace of mind that she could find was in imagining new stoves and linoleum?" No, no, I might well have answered, it is a shared foolishness: we all redecorate a house with hope. It can be changed, with mere paint and putty and a charge account, and then may in gratitude change us.

The fall of 1962, Sylvia Plath, her marriage having collapsed, the thatched cottage abandoned, saw a good omen in the London apartment she found for herself and her two small children in a house that, according to a blue historic marker over the door, had been the home of the poet W. B. Yeats. Sylvia set to work, ferociously, desperately, to paint the walls white, to arrange a bouquet of holly in a pewter vase, to reconstruct her life. She would do it herself: be a supermother, nurture a literary salon all her own, write verse that would dazzle all skeptics. A fresh start was all she needed.

As winter closed in, her letters grew bitter, as she turned on her anxious mother and easy magazine optimism in general with "Don't talk to me about the world needing cheerful stuff! . . . Let the *Ladies' Home Journal* blither about" happy marriages and "birdies still go[ing] tweet-tweet." She had already manufactured *The Bell Jar*. A potboiler she called it and used a pseudonym. But the poems she was then writing obsessively were in her own reckless voice, not calculated to please, though they were in fact to make her reputation.

London froze to a halt, that winter of 1963, and roofs leaked, pipes clogged, children coughed and cried, and mothers gave way to despondency. Sylvia could no longer write to keep herself warm, alive. In February she turned on the gas in the oven and, in her kitchen, died. The cold hopelessness of a winter eternity can take a toll of even the sturdiest soul. Cabin fever is an acute problem in Alaska, and consultants on the new state capitol planned there, as quoted by David Littlejohn in a 1978 *Atlantic*, defined the scourge as "the effects of isolation and confinement . . . associated with darkness and the long winter. Boredom, a lack of motivation, decreased ability to concentrate, excessive use of alcohol, intense need for privacy, anxiety, tension, marital and parent/child conflict leading in extreme cases to child abuse and other acts of family violence, mental and physical breakdown, including suicide, are common signs of cabin fever."

During the years following the November 1963 birth of our second child, a supremely cheerful presence in herself but no guarantee of immunity from hostile elements, I managed to create my own Alaska. My cabin was protected from melodrama, so my major symptom was only a colorless affliction. Raynaud's disease, probably psychosomatic, short-circuits the thermostats in the hands and feet of, mainly, middle-aged women, so that the extremities overreact to cold, turning greenish-white and numb as if frozen. Most of the medical specialists I saw simply advised, "Stay inside your house whenever the temperature goes down toward zero." One doctor forbade me to type, sew, or play the piano, and prescribed hard liquor at every meal, including breakfast, a regimen that threatened to turn me into a Cheever character before I abandoned it.

During those winters of my discontent, I often stationed myself at a window, the children tussling behind me, to ruefully observe the February wind whip the leaves of my rhododendrons, leaves rolled inward by the cold, furled as tight as dark green cigars. I was a shut-in, tricked or trapped by nature, haunted by a sense of underachievement, just as, I was to discover later, my grandmother had been, locked into position by the limitations of her society, the imperatives of her own idealism. She, however, had turned to imperialism; I chose isolationism. I shivered in "The Coldness of Private Warmth."

Richard Sennett, in his essay of that title, has written convincingly of the sustaining public life of the eighteenth-century city, with its openness to pleasures randomly shared with strangers in coffee houses, in marketplaces in crowded squares, in an inclusive society that simply happened outside of the domestic in-group, the family. When in the nineteenth-century "the terrors of the industrial system sent worker and bourgeois alike in search of a refuge," within the family or outside the city or both, protectorates like Summit were gradually formed. But today, Sennett continues, it is increasingly clear that "something must change, because this celebration of intimate life and the virtues of warmth, openness and sharing is denying us a large part of our humanity."

Cabin fever and agoraphobia are demoralizing home sicknesses, but nostalgia is perhaps the most insidious. The word comes from the Greek roots for *home* and *pain,* and as Anthony Brandt has also pointed out, has historically been regarded as a form of melancholy. One traditional antidote was a Stoic cosmopolitanism in which "every land is the brave man's land."

White middle-class Protestant writers have not been famously stoic, and in their nostalgia have mourned the loss of a psychic home, yearning, in Joan Didion's words, "after some abstraction symbolized by the word 'home,' after 'tenderness,' after 'gentleness,' after remembered houses where the fires were laid and the silver was polished and everything could be 'decent' and 'radiant' and 'clear.' "

In the sixties, when inflation meant only "a joyous expansion of discretionary income," many of us Boston-based burghers, admitting that daily life in our suburban houses was less than radiant or clear, undertook as our antidote a larger dose of the same old medicine. We bought second houses, in the gentle countryside an hour or two or three and a half from the core city: rural Vermont farmhouses or ski lodges, wind-swept cottages on Cape Cod or the Vineyard, leafy refuges in the Berkshires. We were not alone. Elsewhere across America, affluent women packed up station wagons for the weekend at the lake or the mountains or the beach, any place that might provide an illusion of pre-industrial pastoral. *House & Garden* and its advertisers, celebrating the trend and hoping to accelerate it, spun off a glossy periodical called *Second Home*.

In 1962 there were about a million vacation homes scattered around the United States, and growth at the rate of at least 70,000 a year was predicted. By 1973 the latest census figures gave 3 million as the total, and the annual building rate was estimated to be 150,000 a year. About a third of the nation's refuges from "the cares and tensions of everyday living" were in the Northeast.

But wherever they were, all those redwood A-frames or deck houses with fieldstone fireplaces, bunk rooms, sliding glass walls, pine or spruce paneling, and exposed beams constituted a new Intra-national Style. It was one that combined modernism with nostalgia, and updated the candy cottage of Hansel and Gretel, those innocent babes in the woods we wished we still were. Vance Packard has suggested that the furbishing of a second home appeals to women as a chance to play bride all over again. I think the urge is to go even farther backwards, to childhood's good old summertimes, filled with fishing poles, picnics, dreamy afternoons in the sun.

The suburbs seemed to move out in a ring widening from the center, as if someone had thrown a stone into a stagnant frog pond. In 1968 my husband and I, each in our own way, invested ourselves in an unpretentious, slightly overgrown farm in Gloucester, Massachusetts, thirty-eight miles north of our first home in Cambridge. We stored revived hopes in its century-old house and hung our melancholy reveries out to dry on the beams of the weathered barn that was a partial relic of an eighteenth-century house on the site, one that people said had burned down. I transferred my print of *The Peaceable Kingdom* to a wall papered in stenciled pineapples.

The medicine proved to be no wonder drug. Winters still came, furnaces still failed (but now in pairs), and dyspepsia lingered. In 1971–72 we tried an entirely new climate and continent, spending a year away on a sort of sabbatical. In temperate, mellow Rome the strain of American nostalgia from which we suffered gave way in the sun to a lively sense of the past as vital presence, a source of pleasure in the morning, not of respect in the afternoon or yearning in the twilight.

I found that, though a transplanted housewife still has her chores, trundling my shopping cart past Palazzo Farnese toward Campo dei Fiori—a field of flowers, fruit, and vegetables paved in city cobblestones—and treating myself to a morning *cappuccino* by the Bernini fountain in Piazza Navona, was not mere labor. It was work: a useful cultural experience out in the world. Our Roman experiment in international living, if not in stark realism, centered in the expansive public places of the city, outside the expatriates' apartment we sublet, with its Art Deco posters, glossy forest green enameled walls, leopard-spotted Parsons tables.

When we returned to America our city house and our country house squeaked for primary attention, sibling rivals. Oh, God, I thought, a plague on both my houses. (Elizabeth Taylor and I had just turned forty, and I too was beginning not to give a damn.) Nothing had changed, but me. Nixon was reelected— same old Nixon. The dishwasher choked and nearly died—same old dishwasher.

Even in 1971, electricity rates in Rome had been astoundingly high, which explained why the only appliance in our apartment had been a midget refrigerator. We supplemented it with a human-powered carpet sweeper and several pairs of potholder-like slippers designed for polishing marble floors. The children and I would don our square mules, and twisting and turning hilariously would shuffle off to Buffalo.

I won't say that I wasn't glad to reencounter my retinue of

American machines that more or less did it themselves, and I justified time once again spent waiting for the rinse cycle or for repairmen by contrasting my situation with that of an average Italian housewife, or even *Mamma mia* or *Nonna,* my mother or grandmother way back when. I'd remind myself of the hours wondrous technology saved me, as I tried to ignore the shade of Gertrude Lockhart that still haunted the house.

In fact, though my generation of housewives spends less physical energy on housework, we may actually use up at least as much, or more, time than the previous one. According to a 1969 report in *The Journal of Home Economics,* homemakers surveyed in 1926–27 spent 7.3 hours per day on housework, less than the 8.0 hours of their counterparts in 1967. Although food preparation and clean-up time had declined over the forty-year period, the woman-hours used up in marketing, record keeping, and general management had increased.

Another survey, published in *Scientific American* in 1974, compared the 52 hours per week spent by a nonemployed housewife in 1924 with the 55 hours per week of the 1960s. The "fortunate" women of the sixties were those who held full-time jobs. Presumably logging 40 hours a week outside the home, they added to that only 26 more hours per week of work in it. Though a 66-hour week is no joke, they did spend less than half the time on housework recorded by women who had no other job.

The working wife does have a moral advantage over the stay-at-home in soliciting help from her family, and she also learns how to strip away nonessentials. But I find that the most revealing explanation of the discrepancy is the author's contention that the unemployed wife makes work for herself, hoping that the *duration of the process,* not the *task* itself as accomplished, will justify her existence and prove to her family that she too makes a contribution in labor as significant as her husband's single wage. Veblen might well have called this phenomenon "conspicuous contribution."

In other ways my illusion of stasis proved false, as I discovered while doing my arithmetic. Like so many Americans of the 1970s who suddenly felt a need to analyze unbelievable totals, we bought a transistorized Japanese calculator, a cold little black beetle whose memory bank is never affected by emotion. With the masochistic dedication of Bob Cratchit, I computed the small change left at the end of each month of oil embargo, recession, inflation.

Fatalistically I subtracted and subtracted, but I did hold the line in one area. I was no longer willing to accept passively the personal cost of living in a house that was behaving like an extortioner. One way I retaliated was to exploit it as a business proposition, with no love lost—much as a madam uses her girls. I rented out half the garage and converted the third floor into an apartment for a succession of tiptoeing students, as well as seasonally leasing out the whole shebang as a rent-a-commune during the summers we retreated to Gloucester.

Eager-to-please landlady rapidly became slumlord. Why wax, polish, and paint when the conglomerate known as "the kids" would be moving in next month, with their Pepsi empties, stalagmites of old newspapers, pet dust kitties. Rubbing my hands together and cackling, I made minimal repairs on the cheap, with chewing gum and bad intentions. No longer had I a vestige of a craftsman's pride! "Fast and sloppy" was the motto now.

One evening as I sat at a jerry-built formica counter, culling out all the soft news from the morning *Times,* the hanging lamp overhead (which I'd wired myself) popped and burst suddenly into flame. Though I swatted out the fire immediately, a smell of burnt Bakelite lingered on in the air. Or was it brimstone? Had I received an overture from some household devil? Had he come out of the woodwork attracted not only by sloth and gluttony, but by envy as well?

The years 1972–76 may be described as my green period. I obsessively kept track of the public achievements of women I'd once known. For example, according to my research, of the twenty of us who were *Mademoiselle* guest editors in 1955 at least 20 percent had made it in the world. Joan was a critically acclaimed writer of fiction, essays, screenplays; Gael a popular columnist in a national magazine; Adri designed clothes I couldn't afford; while Jan combined college teaching with a career as a novelist. But where were we of the silent majority? Lost? Locked in at home? Still stuck in traffic on the very bridge these other Transitional Women had already crossed?

My personal energy crisis even dimmed the lights on *Tannenbaum.* One gloomy holiday it was a low-voltage lady indeed who grudgingly served pasta for Christmas dinner and carted mother, husband, and children off to a five o'clock show of a Woody Allen movie. That afternoon I knew we had to evacuate the house for a few hours. The fragrance of spruce, triggering homesick memories of other Christmases, made my eyes water.

During these years the more tangible costs of home ownership were not just rising. They were blasting off. Between 1970 and 1976 they went up more rapidly than both the cost-of-living index and family incomes, as the M.I.T.-Harvard Joint Center has reported. Monthly ownership expenses increased by 73.4 percent for an old house like ours, and by 102.3 percent for a new one. In contrast, consumer prices for the same six-year period went up only 46 percent.

Middle-aged, middle-class families like ours were used to living comfortably in the single-family homes they had come to take for granted. We were all entitled. By the mid-seventies two-thirds of the total number of households in the United States were in fact living in homes they owned. When the proportion of their income allocated for shelter began to expand and press them hard, many homeowners tried to compensate much as we did. They scrimped on discretionary outlay; they rented out parts of what was then no longer a single-family home; and, backed to the wall, they Did-It-Themselves, not as creative therapy but grimly, simply as a way to avoid maintenance and repair bills. If they had two houses, they often divested themselves of one or the other.

The final solution for many more women than ever before was to stop being housewives. It was not just a yen for independence or fulfillment, nor was it a matter of feminist principle that catapulted them out of their houses—it was the cash. One literary note is relevant. A 1906 introduction to an American edition of Ibsen's *A Doll's House* reveals that the Nora of the real-life episode on which the play was based had committed forgery not to get the money to take her husband to Italy for a convalescence that would save his life, but to subsidize the redecoration of her house.

In 1950 only 23.8 percent of married women worked. By 1975 44 percent were on the job, and the great divide was crossed in 1978, when slightly more than half the wives in America were working outside the home. The old-fashioned housewife is now a member of a new minority.

By 1977 the traditional American doll-house family like mine—working father, cooking mother, and two eating children—represented only 7 percent of all intact marriages. As the divorce rate rose, the birth rate fell. Today a typical doll house may well be deserted from breakfast to supper, except for the plush dog locked into the kitchen, keening through the lonely day.

In Florida in April 1977 the St. Petersburg *Times* covered an astounding household disaster in a nearby town. The headlined story read:

SINKHOLE SWALLOWS
DELAND MAN'S DREAM HOME

R.H. Lawson heard creaking and popping noises coming from the walls of his new dream house. Then he walked to his garage and saw a big crack in the wallboard.

"I knew I was in trouble," he said, and he was right.

It was Easter Sunday morning and a sinkhole was opening up to swallow Lawson's four-month-old home in a DeLand subdivision.

The sinkhole, 70 feet across and 100 feet deep by some estimates, began to form about 8 A.M. and continued to grow during the afternoon, taking with it the home of Lawson and his wife, their two cars and virtually all of their possessions. . . .

Geologists say sinkholes form when the water in underground
limestone caverns is decreased so much that the earth above is
no longer supported.

The water table continues to fall as Florida land is recklessly
overdeveloped. Sinkholes are my tragicomic metaphor for the
cost of living beyond one's resources, for the limits of growth.

As dream houses sank out of sight, my husband worked on a
poem he finally called "The Fall of the Dolls' House," in which
all four of us appear as a doll family. These lines of his describe
another of Nature's warnings, ours far gentler than Mr.
Lawson's:

> In a more recent snap, my wife and I . . .
> wear casual clothes but strike a mannered pose.
> I slouch eccentric, while she smiles, protecting
> the children underneath a cherry tree.
> We'll leave the house, I think. The leaves are falling.

That cherry tree had been no higher than the living room's
bay window when we moved into the house in 1961. Each
spring for over a decade its blossoms grew more spectacular,
and when their white petals drifted off, they lightheartedly
parodied winter. By 1976 the tree had overextended itself.
Though it now reached the peak of the roof, its branches had
become too top-heavy for the trunk to support. It split in
several pieces, and though the tree surgeons wired it back
together, its leaves began to yellow, wither, and fall. That last
June the birds could find only a few stunted cherries to steal.

By September we had once again rented to strangers, and
were engrossed in our own urban renewal. A year later, in
1977, we sold the house to the nearby women's college which
had gradually expanded up the street toward us like a rising
tide. When we moved out, the house would not only cease to be
our home; it would, after more than a century of service, be
retired as a dwelling. Rehabilitated into an administrative
building, it would shelter file cabinets, typewriters, Xerox and

coffee machines. Teachers and students would confer over transcripts in our bedrooms.

For three sweaty late August days after papers had been passed, the family packed, sorted, and sifted, relentlessly efficient as we threw out weird old Halloween costumes, outgrown toys, half-empty cans of paint. I was exhilarated, like the priestess of an exorcism, casting out devils with the detritus of the years. The second day, en route to the trash cans I noticed a trapped Monarch butterfly fluttering against the screens of the back porch. I tried to shoo it with a broom toward the open door. It wouldn't go.

I majored in English: I know a symbol when I see one. Strangely detached, I observed that other me try to sweep out the butterfly, which by now was flapping suicidally. I couldn't stand it. We, that housewife and I, dramatically joined forces, and together we wielded the broom like a lance. The rotten mesh rent easily; the butterfly flew off toward Somerville. What did I care if a great swatch of screening lay in shreds. Let *them* worry! My house was no longer mine.

EIGHT

A New Lease

I sit on a rock, a massive granite boulder seemingly cantilevered out of the wall in our duplex apartment's living room. Or should I call it master bedroom, or study, or living-dining area, since it is all of these? Through a strip of window above the rocks, I look down on the confetti crowds of summer drifting across Waterfront Park, our front yard six stories below. Small sailboats dart and zag on Boston Harbor, past freighters and historic wharves.

The Stonehenge aspect of our quarters is structural, not some heavy-handed decorator's whim. The six irregular quarry stones that protrude at waist-height across the exterior wall are the counterbalancing interior ends of the cornice blocks along the roofline outside. The public halves of the stones have been civilized into duplicate units, skillfully carved, matched, and joined to form a single classical molding. Our private sector of each megalith is rough and individualistic, as irregular as nature and the quarrier conspired to make it.

I'm here alone, as usual during workdays since late summer of 1976 when we left historic Cambridge for ultrahistoric Boston. In the three years since the Bicentennial we've almost forgotten all the superfluous pewter and red-white-and-Windex popsicles in which we overindulged. But the house we abandoned, the place where all four of us grew up, is as piercingly familiar as a dream, when we happen to think about it. I still cringe when I look at the stark snapshots I took of its emptied rooms that last funereal morning.

Now I'm musing on one unit in America's third century—a single year, or to be precise, a single year's lease. Should we sign on here for yet another hitch? Our experiment in alternative housing has become rather longer than originally scheduled. What has it proved?

I had wondered if we could all adjust to high compression in multifarious space. Would we get the bends? Lillian Gilbreth once observed that "there is a type of mind that rebels at 'three in one' apartments, that can sleep only upstairs in a bed that doesn't fold and that has elaborate coverings, that can eat only in a dining room from a table that is used only to dine on." Happily, our home research proved that we could take the pressure most of the time. We functioned here as if, on some excursion from real life, we were crewing a compact yacht, like those anchored across the street at Lewis Wharf.

One visiting teenager insisted that my husband and I must find a convertible sofa-bed "a bummer," a possibility our contemporaries are too discreet to suggest, but we have grown used—or perhaps simply inured—to it and all the other quick changes needed to transform our L-shaped room into its sequential functions, its zones. Our daily routines respond to the sky above the two large skylights in the sloped ceiling. Sunrise over the harbor: bed becomes sofa, table changes to desk; sunset's afterglow: desk reverts to table, sofa unfolds again. Eternally vigilant, I censor out all but essentials. There is no room for driftwood in our shipshape cabin.

Nor is there room for rampaging individualism. As a family we have had to dovetail essential activities, in negotiations that have tended to make us, teenagers and adults alike, slightly more tolerant of each others' rights, and wrongs. When in high dudgeon, the children can retreat upstairs to their separate bedrooms, their personal hi-fi's, and drown us out with music. Downstairs we mature adults struggle to compromise. We tiptoe, keep one light low when the other is out; we even grumble quietly.

In 1976 architect John Sharratt, whose large mixed-income housing complexes in Boston I admire, both architecturally and for their social premises, finished transforming for private developers Gridley J. F. Bryant's 1857 ships' chandlery. He had renovated a derelict gray elephant into the dramatic showplace later honored by the A.I.A.

The Mercantile Wharf Building, shaped like a monumental granite shoebox, first attracted me because it looked so much like the sternly symmetrical *palazzi* of Rome. The Roman originals are much more hospitable than they look from outside, and many of them have always accommodated a variety of occupants of all ages and classes, housed in a common atmosphere of sound and aroma. Sharratt's American adaptation is in that sort of Renaissance tradition.

Most of the old commercial buildings on Boston's renewed waterfront have been rehabbed within the past dozen years into fashionable apartments. And most of them contain burghers as prosperously homogeneous as those of any affluent suburb. The apartments are, with few exceptions, condominiums—city cousins of the outlying, detached single-family house.

Reurbanized older couples (the prototypical empty-nesters) compete for space with singles, or double singles, or two-income working couples, "childless by choice." The chic new waterfront is, as a place to live, about as receptive to children as Gucci or Studio 54. Apartments that rarely have more than two bedrooms don't attract families. Kids do, however, materialize daily in the playground in the park or flock from the subway station there toward the Aquarium.

The working-class Italian neighborhood of the North End, celebrated as a triumph of vital nonplanning by Jane Jacobs in

The Death and Life of Great American Cities (1961), abuts the renewed waterfront, and the Mercantile Wharf, chartered as public, mixed-income housing, must be responsive to its needs while remaining "open" to other ethnic, racial, and economic groups. Consequently, though Lithuanian surnames do not figure largely on our bell list, we are in fact an assortment that satisfies the requirements of the Department of Housing and Urban Development in Washington, D.C., as well as state and city agencies. With funding from both public and private sources, the project incorporates bottom-line self-interest and a certain democratic idealism as well as ethnicity without exclusivity. No wonder its identity seems elusive.

The exterior of the building divulges nothing about the airy garden inside, our private park. After scooping out the dark, fire-damaged core of the original structure, Sharratt created an enormous central atrium, ringed on the ground floor by shops and on five upper ones by balconies. From planter boxes on each balcony droop fronds from perhaps the nation's largest extant display of the long-suffering species *Philodendron scandens*. Below, the tiled central plaza is geometrically patterned with planter-beds of ferns and *ficus*. Above, the roof is one sweep of skylight.

Around the balconies in single file march 121 rental apartments of varying numbers of bedrooms and baths. Units in each category are allocated among three groups of tenants: low income (heavily subsidized), moderate income (some subsidy), and "market" (unsubsidized, but with an upper limit on annual income). An early prospectus announced that market apartments would be equal in number to subsidized ones, but by 1976 when we and others in the first wave of tenants arrived, the proportion had gone down from a half to a third, and by mid-1979 had slipped even further—quietly and a little mysteriously—to less than a quarter.

On the sixth (and new seventh) floor are the triplexes and duplexes like ours, stacked into what was originally lofty space under the roof. The old beams and timber trusses live on throughout the building, and exposed brick walls marking the bays now define the width of each apartment. These private partitions extend right out into the public balconies, culminating in arches that form long Piranesi perspectives on every floor.

The atrium provides a change of scale, as refreshing as the view of a lake from a cottage high on shore. The void also gives a sense of breathing space, of not living in uncomfortable intimacy with your opposite number across a conventional narrow hall. The chasm here does, like a moat, reduce the wariness level.

Certain public areas lend themselves to brief, noncommittal, random encounters among tenants: the small entrance lobby by the mailboxes; the two laundry rooms, scene of Susskindian open forums to the rumble and applause of the dryers; and the twin glass elevators where, in full view of the world, passengers feel free to exchange travelers' clichés.

Large empty rooms next to the laundries were designed as "function rooms" (a requirement of public housing that sounds alarmingly physiological). These would-be common rooms ordinarily remain locked and empty, or unlocked and empty, sporadically coming to life for residents' council meetings or a series of disco-dancing lessons or the mortification of the flesh of one short-lived women's exercise class, an experience that convinced me of a truth the Army has long known: the sit-up promotes democratic attitudes. Welfare mother, veteran Saks charge customer, single working girl, young and older, we groaned as one, we fell back gasping and laughing, together. Nature has equipped women to share ridiculous experiences with more easy good humor than she seems to grant to men, perhaps also enabling them to withstand better the idiosyncrasies of communal and city life.

Perennially the best-attended event in the building, the false fire alarm is presumably unplanned, but has served to provide the living drama that unites an audience. Supersensitive smoke detectors in each apartment are regularly triggered by oven broiling to emit loud electronic whoops ("Wolf! Wolf!" in effect, for by now no one thinks of evacuating the building).

Weary troupes of Gilbert & Sullivan firemen, complete with
prop axes and catlike tread, grudgingly entertain us, the curious
in bathrobes, who hang over the balconies to watch like human
philodendrons at the theater.

At moments like this, when we let down our guard and focus
on a common crisis, any sense of community we have is at its
spontaneous best. After all, chance alone determined who
would be living here together, and few of us disparate folk are
ready to think of ourselves as a cohesive group. We come
together as an impromptu collection, like a small crowd that
gathers around a village green or in a public park to hear the
band play. Actually, we are a kind of small village within the
city, not *sub urbe* but *in urbe*. Though we have no more than
your average villager's concern for his neighbors, we do have
one overriding shared interest. It has four thick walls and a
transparent roof.

Jane Jacobs had written about the advantage of neighborhood streets in the city over suburban ones. Heavily populated
and busily diverse, they offer a common public scene but leave
leeway for "strangers to dwell in peace together on civilized but
essentially dignified and reserved terms." Our balcony streets,
with their occasional intersections, permit the same latitude,
encourage "a civilized public life on a basically dignified public
footing, and . . . private lives on a private footing." Even as a
relic of the WASPish tradition of fenced privacy, I have not felt
watched or threatened or imposed upon—whatever it was we
housewives thought party walls in a city "tenement" might
expose us to.

Perhaps the most powerful coagulant has been a shared
adversary position toward successive dynasties of building
management. Early on, when malfunctions, leaks, lapses in
security and maintenance plagued us all, we joined in outrage:
Don't Tread On Us! This old building might be the owners' tax
shelter, but it was our home, and we were ready to take up our
muskets.

Unsubstantiated rumors continue to circulate that behind
each leak, parched philodendron, missing security guard, or

threatened rent raise lies a sinister conspiracy. No powerful force in the city at large is above suspicion, but our volatile tenant group has proved most effective when least paranoid. Once we settled down to steady and reasonable pressure on both owners and the public agencies who are supposed to be our watchdogs, we found that leaks tended to get plugged. But we live warily in a comparatively unexciting truce. All our agitation has been more like collective housekeeping than politics.

My own behavior has frequently been retrogressive. I can't stop reverting to the instincts of a housewife. Once, after concerted but ineffective protest about a dark swarm of fingermarks on the wall by the sixth-floor elevators, I gave up and turned vigilante. Donning a flasher's raincoat under which I concealed sponge and spray can, I darted out of our apartment and furtively began my private public mission, praying no one would catch me in the midnight act.

Suddenly I heard an outraged voice at my ear. "*What* do you think you're doing?" Oh my God, it was Phyllis, one person I didn't want to find me knuckling under.

"You should have called the Housing Authority," she chided. But Phyllis, Phyllis, I didn't want to call any authority: God or the governor or my old English teacher. I just wanted a clean wall.

I'll never become visionary leader or radical activist, no matter where I hang out. Too impatient and nontheoretical. Certainly the helter-skelter community of the Mercantile Wharf doesn't demand much of its members, hardly hints at the transcendental high-mindedness of a Brook Farm or the idealism of the ambitious experiments in communitarian social-ism analyzed by Dolores Hayden in *Seven American Utopias.* About all we tenants share is a rather self-serving capacity for indignation, and our single address.

When I've felt limp and wilted, like some Ashley Wilkes after the war longing for the old plantation, I've found it consoling to think of myself as transitional, like some old and ordinary house caught between two periods, two places, two styles. I was

designed for a suburb, but here I am in a city. My windows are
Federal but my porch is Greek Revival. At least it's difficult to
date me exactly.

What did I expect from my new environment anyway?
Definition? Metamorphosis? A miracle? "Good shelter is a
useful good in itself, as shelter. When we try to justify good
shelter instead on the pretentious grounds that it will work
social or family miracles we fool ourselves," Jane Jacobs writes.
She quotes Reinhold Niebuhr's marvelous term for that particular self-delusion, "the doctrine of salvation by bricks."

If I have been saved from a sense of lonely obsolescence, this
red-brick city has been as crucial as our granite home. My
grandmother's generation fled the "disease-ridden, family-
corrupting" city; mine has straggled back from a pseudocoun-
tryside that has lost its magic and many of its elms. I for one
have come to depend on the city as a natural resource in itself,
enjoying a kind of collective consumption that has blessedly
little to do with acquiring objects or caring for them. I don't
plant the geraniums in Waterfront Park, nor do I dust the books
in the Boston Public Library.

After a solitary (but not lonely) morning in the apartment
and at my typewriter, I often crave a brief *passeggiata* next door
in booming Faneuil Hall Marketplace, the nineteenth-century
trio of buildings restored to Boston in 1976–78 by the combined
efforts of many, including Benjamin Thompson & Associates,
architects.

Under new ownership in the seventies, Design Research
gradually lost its vitality because it had settled for simply
preserving Thompson's "period" style in amber. He, meanwhile, went on to the new, more public phase of his career,
epitomized by the Marketplace. At D/R's going-out-of-business
sale in May 1979, young bargain hunters spoke portentously of
witnessing the end of an era, as if it hadn't actually ended a
decade earlier.

When I am playing hookey at the Marketplace, I jostle other
promenaders in a kind of shared activity deeply different from
the Lonely Crowd frustration and competitiveness ricocheting

around malls beside highways. I can spend little or nothing and return to my desk refreshed by the place itself, though the housewife in me still may feel slightly guilty at not having bought anything (thus having "wasted time"). Usually I find I can accept psychic subsidies of this sort, which cities can offer in abundance, with hardly a qualm of conscience, civic or otherwise.

The Mercantile Wharf represents no more than a few steps in a new direction, toward more open housing and away from the closed stalemate of the middle-class house, single-family and suburban. But the progressive motion, however halting, is in itself encouraging to anyone concerned about alternatives. A living building like this one suggests that an alternative that challenges the assumptions underlying social and sexual segregation (in urban and suburban ghettoes) is viable. It works as well as any ordinarily realistic view of human nature might expect it to.

Subsidized public housing cannot promise social salvation, which is a more complicated matter than simply storing mixtures of people in better crates. Subsidization of whatever kind offers a flash of grace, not a free ride into heaven. One slogs along by oneself toward that destination. Good shelter for those who need it simply provides a place for hope to grow, and hope is one shrub that has for too long been taken out of cities to be cultivated in healthy environments elsewhere. The smug homeowner who criticizes urban dispensations of unearned charity must remember that he has himself been coddled by government in income tax deductions granted for mortgage costs and real estate taxes: a break that even in 1975 cost the U.S. Treasury $7.4 billion. Anyone who now owns a mortgaged home is living in doubly subsidized housing.

The current public policies that make a Mercantile Wharf possible are challenging the "bourgeois individualism" of the single-family home. The Federal Housing Act of 1974, which encourages the development of mixed-income rental properties, is undeniably geared more to urban needs than to suburban taste, and not surprisingly arouses catcalls when it attempts to open out of town. One example is the brouhaha

that in 1978 greeted the developer of a certain Buttonwood
Estates in Brookhaven, Long Island, when he sought to apply
the concept of subsidized rent guarantees to single-family
houses in his subdivision.

But here and there other suburbs are loosening up, livening
up, suddenly aware of an aging population of long-time
homeowners (the young marrieds who bought in during the
fifties are now within sight of retirement and a fixed income)
and the possibility that the upcoming generation may not leap
into the giddy pleasures of mortgages with quite the alacrity its
parents did. Some "exclusive residential" towns near Boston—
Lincoln, Wayland, Newton, and others—are working on innovative alternatives to the expensive single-family house simply
in order to attract the younger people that keep a place alive
and to provide for veteran residents who may gradually find
their houses a burden, physically and financially.

One brisk but sunny May day in 1978, on the terrace of Ben
Thompson's Cambridge restaurant, The Harvest, I lunched
with a Harvard freshman. When I was first married, Polly had
been the baby-next-door, a grave little observer of adult quirks.
At nineteen, she spoke directly of how and where she might like
to live when and if she were to marry. Conditionality has
apparently replaced the settled expectations of 1955. "I know
no one who is basing a future entirely on the prospect of
marriage," she commented.

I had known her father, her grandparents, and her great-
grandparents, Summit residents all: her grandmother's home
had been one important model for me; her aunt now lives in her
late great-grandmother's house. Very timidly I asked if she
thought she might ever choose a suburb—Summit, to be
precise. I suspected what her answer might be and hated to bear
witness to a statement that would be as final as a beheading.

"Well, Summit is a place I *know* I'd never choose to live. Too
Republican." Her Staffordshire blue eyes were as deep, her
hair almost as blonde as when she was one year old. "Too
WASPy," she added.

Polly was not so much rejecting her native land or the Grand

Old Party or the faith of her fathers as she was making a statement about her own resistance to limitation, compromise, and preconception. She simply wasn't going to perpetuate an inherited style, one not of her own choosing. She says that someday she would like to live either in the "real" country or in the city, but not sandwiched in between. Young women in general just don't seem to want to be like us, their middle-aged, homebody, suburbanite mothers. According to one mid-seventies survey, only 3 percent of the seventeen-year-old girls in the country wanted to grow up to be "a housewife."

Perhaps it's a matter of terminology. Few women who already are housewives and relatively content are willing to admit it these days. Some of us are downright hostile in our defensiveness. (Helen Reddy sings in the background the silliest of lyrics, "I am woman, I am invincible!") We milder types conjure up smart answers to interrogations about our occupation (our identity), avoiding at all costs saying plainly, humiliatingly, that we're "just housewives." Erma Bombeck, perennially sassy, has replied, "Would you believe, Love Goddess?" Others toss back politely evasive job descriptions: household engineer, child rearer, unpaid domestic worker, and (with a touch of class) *factotum,* literally "one who does everything."

My favorite answer, the most humane and effective in shutting off further discussion, is that always given by a friend whose background is European. When asked what she does (a question, she says, that Europeans consider as offensively personal as asking what one's annual income is), she answers politely but firmly, "I live."

Perhaps as Ann Oakley suggests, the term *housewife* should simply drop out of the currency of the language. It is now so overinflated that it means nothing. Recently a married English-woman, Naomi James, single-handedly circumnavigated the globe in a sailboat, a 30,000-mile voyage. When she completed her round trip, U.S. headlines read "Housewife Sails Around World." Housewife! Her skill and accomplishment aside, she hadn't even been *in* a house for 272 days.

The association between houses and women has long had snickering overtones in sex-linked colloquialisms. A "house-bit" in the mid-nineteenth century referred to a paramour servant; "house under the hill' to a woman's private parts, as did "housewife" itself. The term for widow was "house to let." How long would even the least macho husband have put up with being dismissed as, for example, a "house-stud"? Would a passive, omnivorous adolescent son have stood for having his mother call him a "house-leech"? If "housewife" strikes us as a dirty word, we should not use it in polite company. I can't bring myself, however, to substitute euphemisms without feeling as silly as the Victorian women who put pantaloons on piano legs or as pretentious as the manufacturer who calls a 1979-model stove a Savory Centre. A spade is a spade is a spade.

Seeking further signs of a change of climate in the heartland dominated by single-family houses, the natural habitat of housewives, I spent three long evenings at what I thought might be a lively confrontation: the 1978 town meeting of Milton, Massachusetts, affluent, historic, and suburban. The agenda proposed a titillating change in the local zoning for single-family homes to permit construction of "single-family attached residential homes" in clusters on a former estate.

Here, I predicted, would be a classical defense of the American Home, a battle for God, for country, and for Mom. Conservative town fathers would tussle with future-oriented speculators. Sparks would fly, fireworks in the night sky.

One issue was indeed incendiary (a ballot revision sponsored by the League of Women Voters, whose organization seems in certain Milton political circles to be regarded as a middle-class female conspiracy hatched in some alleged "clubhouse"). But sweet reasonableness reigned when the zoning amendment finally came up. As if at some conference of agonized atomic scientists, the air blew cool with high-mindedness, with the sense of "responsibility to generations as yet unborn." The speakers' rhetoric was strangely reasonable in tone, and my attention wandered. But when money began to talk, we all perked up and listened quietly. Emotions started to bubble.

Clearly, the most persuasive force is no longer theoretical, neither political nor social nor vaguely moral. In Milton the realities of a stagnating tax base and assessments that had risen 100 percent in ten years constituted a clear and present danger to the citizenry, or its bank balances. Let speakers warn that "nothing can change the character of a town more significantly than multi-family building." Let others counter that Lexington and Concord already had in the works cluster housing comparable to that proposed for Milton, and that those archetypical American towns weren't worried about the fallout. Let reassurances be passed around that the new development would be, as someone put it, "in the single-family context as we know it." The vote was clearly a *fait accompli:* the sense of the meeting was unmistakable long before balloting, perhaps even before the call to order. Multi-family housing moved smoothly into Milton, and I saw not a tear nor an apoplectic countenance among the members of the town meeting, who with stoic calmness bowed to the inevitable.

Elsewhere the trend I like to think of, optimistically, as a gradual evolution toward a less rugged individualism in housing is proving to be almost perversely slow, as if the country were sleepwalking. Simple common sense might explain any of a number of responses but this passivity in the face of elementary economic facts of life that we read every morning over coffee. Families continue to migrate from the city or to it, from Northeast to Southwest, or simply from one suburb to a better one, still clinging to the idea, if not the old soul-grabbing ideal, of home ownership. Statistics state that only the richest quarter of the population can reasonably afford new houses, but a much larger fraction persists in enrolling themselves in the growing ranks of the house-poor. It's not as if they weren't warned.

Young wives complain to the Boston *Globe* that in their shiny applianced homes "there are no kids, no nice furniture. Everything goes to the house," and they must go on working and postponing children in order to "support a mortgage," as an addict supports a habit or a man supports a wife. As one economist asked his *New York Times* interviewer: "If you're not going to have four kids or three kids or even two kids, what's the point of living in the suburbs?" Children, after all, have always been a major justification for adult sacrifices for a house in the suburbs.

The housing industry, especially its energetic superbuilders, is not taking the lead in moving toward a new "context." Why should it? Plenty of people are still hooked on the single-family house, on gas-guzzlers, and other established American prerogatives. Fox & Jacobs, a Texas giant, continues to mass-produce conventional residences plonked onto individual but ever-smaller lots, boasting, "We can't build [them] as fast as we're selling them." An eager market continues to snap up houses with trade names like Today, Accent, and Flair that could as easily be nationally advertised brands of felt-tipped pens. Martin Mayer has quoted a visiting representative of French builders: "In France the home is the patrimony, it is what a man will leave to his children, it is immortal. In America, a man's home is a consumer good; he uses it like other consumer goods and buys a new one when he is tired of this one."

A cold-blooded, acquisitive attitude toward houses as very large objects, comparable to Cadillacs, dominates some markets. If a car doesn't have a "moral dimension," why should a house? Often homeowners who must immolate themselves economically on their houses would never think of justifying their choice on sentimental grounds, as being dictated by irresistible Home Feeling. Many individual speculators regard their houses simply as blue-chips or piggy banks. They invest pennies that they fully expect to shake out, with interest and appreciation, before long. More and more families who are periodically transferred by large corporations use a third party, like Homerica or the other nationwide real-estate and relocation agencies, to sell one house and choose another for them—to arrange the divorce and the remarriage. In Summit, for example, such matchmaking is now common practice.

Why can't I, who invested too much diffuse emotion in my house, have learned by now to be more tolerant of casual contemporary ways? Why should I be such an intractable prude and continue to draw away from people who don't choose to marry but just have brief and mercenary affairs? I've considered taking a position in favor of serial monogamy, but have abandoned the idea. My current theory is that probably women should attempt to confine their relationships with their homes to simple friendships, balanced and reciprocal. The limits of friendship allow just enough space for common sense and rational behavior to thrive, unlike the open-ended, often sacrificial demands of some impossible passion. Women's emotional energies should be saved for those central relationships that compose married life rather than squandered on mere symbols of them. But the line is hard to draw. Who can say when homemaking becomes housekeeping?

In a century where so often quality has given way to schlock, distrust of change is understandable. *Novelty* has come to mean "cheap and tawdry." And resisting change seems to be logical and responsible, like historic preservation.

Of all our styles of domestic architecture, the Colonial single-family house is the most formalized, most unchanging, and therefore the most consoling. Preserved or reproduced, it still represents enduring national values and family virtues, balance and reason, security and taste and success—in short, all the qualities Joy Wheeler Dow extolled at the turn of the century. In today's uncertainty, when so many tried-and-true assumptions are wavering, it is not surprising that, clinging to the familiar, we are now in yet another revival of enthusiasm for all things Colonial. The current American Renaissance is as emotional, literal-minded, and concerned with objects as any of its predecessors. Sentimental materialism lives on.

And as before, the latest Colonial Revival is good carriage-trade business. *House & Garden* publishes a guide called *American Tradition* with features like "How to Decorate, Remodel & Build Using the Best of Our Heritage," and offers "Colonial House Plans You Can Order." Colonial Williamsburg's mail-order catalogue (if a volume bound in maroon imitation leather and stamped in gold can be called a catalogue) features $8,000 breakfronts in reproduction as well as $3.50 boxes of beeswax tapers. And *House Beautiful*'s new quarterly *Colonial Homes* is often indistinguishable from the full-color magazine sent to members of the National Trust for Historic Preservation. Long out of print, the White Pine Series of Architectural Monographs, whose original publication in 1915 sparked the neo-Georgianism of the twenties, is back on bookstore shelves once again in facsimile editions.

"What will follow the Colonial?" *House Beautiful* asked in 1904, and briskly predictive, then answered itself, "[The Colonial] has come to stay for the next century or so, and with the time beyond we need not concern ourselves."

But of course we do need to concern ourselves with the future, if not the length of the season in which the Colonial style will be in fashion. Single-family houses may have become ritualized in style and concept, but at the end of the seventies the mature women who already occupy them are changing in spite of themselves.

Historically we housewives have been suggestible, eager and willing to act out the expectations of family and popular culture. We have shown little consumer resistance. Lacking confidence in our own individual taste, we have welcomed standards and fashions imposed by authorities, whoever they might be— mother figures, magazines, or local customs. Our conservatism has demonstrated a formidable staying power. In exercising all the negative virtues of conventional feminine "character," we have been good girls and have held on to, have truly *kept* the houses we were given. We have resisted temptations to sabotage a system that seemed to be endorsed by society at large, not to mention by our husbands, our families, and our friends, and we have probably been too strong for our own good.

Old-fashioned critical descriptions of *A Doll's House* as "a direct assault on marriage from the standpoint of feminine individualism" and Nora's farewell address as "a declaration of independence" have marked women like me—transitional, postmodern, neo-revivalist, eclectic, or however we choose to think of ourselves. Liberation, a century after Ibsen, demands that when we make a personal declaration, we too must, if we have any spirit at all, separate ourselves from our houses. We slam doors on the way to offices or to the divorce courts or to the bus station.

A woman may in fact be free and independent even if she turns back from her threshold and continues as a "house-dove," a "stay-at-home" in sixteenth-century slang. That's a respectable decision, one which has been amply considered and defended by Arlene Cardozo in *Woman at Home* (1976). But being a house-dove hardly eliminates the possibility of being a *femme sole*. This tidy French phrase, encountered in Ann Oakley's *Women's Work* and not in Julia Child, is a legal term for adult widow or unmarried woman, which was also applied in fifteenth-century London to a married woman liable as a single person in any craft or business that "by herself apart" she practices and "with which the husband in no way intermeddles." The woman alone undertakes the risks of failure, or success.

"Of course we would all like to 'believe in something,' " wrote Joan Didion in an essay on self-respect in *Slouching Towards Bethlehem.* We would "like to lose our tiresome selves . . . to transform the white flag of defeat at home into brave white banner of battle away from home . . . but I think it is all right only so long as we do not delude ourselves about what we are doing, and why."

We may compromise by psychically detaching from our family house a room sacred to ourselves alone. Commandeering other people's space for a feminized rendition of my grandfather's den is, I suppose, a way of redressing the balance, but it seems to me to smack more of Separate But Equal than of progress toward a deeper equality between the sexes in the home. No matter, it is currently all the rage.

As I have drifted through recent domestic history I have proceeded on the firm conviction that some sort of room of one's own was essential to self-realization in the domestic setting. After all, I'd been taught Virginia Woolf's 1920s vision of "feminine individualism." Now, after actually working on my own at home in supershared quarters, I'm not so sure that the only truly separate room needed isn't in one's own attic, in the head. Of course those of us who are welders of monumental sculptures have a special practical problem, but for most quiet white-collar pursuits, a special walled-in place is perhaps a luxury like furs, desirable but unnecessary when you already have a good cloth coat. Today, schools give all but the mothers of very small children a good chunk of the day which, if they are able to choose to be at home and are sufficiently ruthless, they can keep for their own business in a house temporarily all their own. But doing this, seizing time, requires accepting a new definition of character. It does require character to pursue a deliberate course of Bad Housekeeping when no broad cultural encouragement for putting last things first yet exists.

There are indications that Bad Housekeeping is on the increase. *The New York Times* reported in May 1979 that another computation of time spent by women on housework in 1965-75 (this published by Cleveland State University) reveals that non-working housewives seem to be devoting fewer hours, from over 50 to 44 per week. Alas, they are using their freed time to watch TV. This is progress?

My preference for time over space is not a particularly popular position, at least among those contemporaries who now proudly display segregated studies and studios, often representing more equipment than output. Certainly, acting out a new role in a professional setting does give confidence to the late-blooming ingenue, but literal-mindedness has been a constant temptation to the housewife. (We have wanted to do things in the *right* way, in the *right* costumes, with the *right* props.) Once again it threatens to divert our energies from performance to stagecraft, from content to appearances, from form to style. We don't need more female-dominated real estate—we need less.

Though no one of us has to have a room of her own, we must have a room with a view. My grandmother and I, decades apart, looked out at the snow and felt trapped inside our houses,

excluded from the variety and opportunity we felt lay somewhere else—in the city, in work. Women are no longer
excluded: we have choices, alternatives, but they do expose us
to risks. We may have to relinquish coziness, a sense of being
anchored in space by tiny roots, of achieving cumulative
satisfactions by accomplishing trivial deeds. The small interior
view of one's life, the miniature woman set in a doll's house, is
no longer necessary. We don't have to reduce ourselves to
fashionable diminutiveness in order to conform to some artifi-
cial standard of what a woman's dimensions should be. But it's
hard to remember to look away, to refocus: I have to remind
myself to take my teacup out of the kitchen and climb up on the
rocks in the apartment wall in order to look out on the city, the
planes across the water, the ships leaving and entering the
harbor.

We transitional types stand nervously at open front doors,
purses in hand, and hesitate. We wonder how far outside we
dare go. Will we lose our balance, fall, get lost? The monoliths
lodged in my wall reassure me, because they seem to represent
a solution to my dilemma. They remain unshakably themselves,
each secure in a distinctive "angle of repose," each in equilibrium between the alternatives of exterior and interior, between
public light and private warmth. On the outside they collabo-
rate as members of a cornice, but inside they remain eccentric
and roughhewn.

Men and women, we all need a little help from our friends, men
and women. But in the domestic isolation of the single-family
house, women have too often stubbornly struggled alone in
their pride to save their souls or fold their laundry. I wish I
could now, after all, help with either task. I'd like to suggest a
few menus or advocate advanced sisterhood and domestic
collectivism, but I haven't come that far yet, and probably
never will manage it. Besides, sisterhood strikes me as a
narrowing concept, implying loyalties only within a single
generation of siblings. As I look around at my contemporaries,

my pseudo-sorority, I am often overwhelmed by an urge to seek
counsel elsewhere, from mother-surrogates who are older and
wiser or from daughter figures who are younger and fresher. I
like my generation of housewives as individuals, but I don't
admire us much as a group. We're okay, like house wine, but
we're not one of the great vintages. Too many sour grapes,
perhaps. Like the Last of the Red-Hot Mamas, the Last of the
Red-Hot Housewives are a tiny bit embarrassing, glum remind-
ers of the glory that was home.

The season may be over. The vitality that infused the
single-family home from its origins up to the mid-seventies has
faded, and there seems to be precious little new under the sun.
In 1977 my mother and I, masquerading as solicitous Sunbelt
grandma and possibly relocating divorcée, cruelly raised false
hopes among the exceedingly friendly folks in sales at various
ready-made "communities" in the Tampa-Clearwater section of
Florida, now booming more than ever, sinkholes or no. We
cased Screened Lanais (porches), Leisure Rooms (family
rooms), and Master Suites, segregated from smaller or children's single bedrooms according to the popular "bi-nuclear"
style for "neo-families." We saw "adult village communities,"
"retirement communities," and "leisure communities" (where
residents are kept frantically busy at classes in belly-dancing,
lapidary work, and "Psychology for Everyday Living"). The
developments varied in size and quality, but they were all in
plan and outlook basically cloned from country clubs and built
out in the boondocks, the landscape of *The Yearling*. I
half expected to come across Jody and Old Slewfoot, carrying
golf bags and heading toward the first tee.

One "planned residential community," East Lake Wood-
lands in Safety Harbor, offered some "housing alternatives":
Country Club Condominiums (as alliterative as Karamel Kandy
Korn), Cluster Homes, Patio Homes, and Private Homes
("family sized . . . including a Florida rendition of the traditional Northern two-story homes"). All were in the "single
family context as we know it" in their respectable exclusiveness.
In nearby Countryside, 1,400 acres have been similarly devel-

oped by U.S. Home, "America's leading home builder . . . through the years over 65,000 families have purchased our homes around the country."

Home, home, home—why can't a realtor call a house a house? Though the "home"—single-family and detached—continues to garner the vote, "pluralism is the word in architecture and interior design today." So wrote Ada Louise Huxtable in *The New York Times* at the end of 1978, adding that "those who make taste tell us that there is room for every kind of taste . . . you can't argue with that; you can only hope that in the relentless process of popularization one kind of hokum will not ultimately substitute for another."

What kind of exchange is it to trade, for example, the obsessive Colonialism of the 1920s and 1930s for phony hybrids like the $200,000 superdevelopment home recently announced for construction? One typically pompous model comes with cathedral-ceilinged foyer and bridal staircase in a genuine hokum-historical style, Bavarian Tudor.

Hokum comes high these days, and so does ticky-tack. In 1978 Washingtonians protesting plans for Nelson Rockefeller's ex-property on Foxhall Road referred to the prospect of "a typical tract development, ticky-tacky houses in the $300,000 to $400,000 range." Nonetheless, the developers' waiting list numbered two hundred.

As Russell Baker has asked: Who are all the people who can afford such prices—in Houston and Beverly Hills and George-town? (They can't all be Arabs.) "Until the statisticians find out," he continued, "they will remain the phantom rich who haunt the rest of us with a sense that we are never going to make it to Newport."

Common sense tells me I shall never make it to Newport, just as I'll never be tall, or forty again, or sing Gershwin in a smoky bar, or even own a Blackglama mink. I also know—at last—that I shall never, ever, grow up enough to build the stately mansion whose plan I must have imagined in childhood but thought I had long ago set aside in favor of more rational accommodations to reality. It was the castle to which some prince would carry me off. I think I finally reconciled myself to my repressed taste for it and its practical impossibility simultaneously, on a single spring day in 1975 in Richmond, Virginia. I had reencountered my childhood friend Cecelia, whom I had hardly seen since our respective marriages years before. We met at my hotel and spent the day catching up while touring the James River plantations Joy Wheeler Dow so admired—Shirley, Westover, Berkeley. By late afternoon, an overdose of tradition—all that boxwood and symmetry—had overstimulated my emotions. I was ripe for a sudden infatuation.

Back in Richmond, we approached Cecelia's house. We passed a brick serpentine wall, turned in at iron gates, and proceeded down a long driveway, by formal gardens, through a forest of ancient trees, blooming dogwood, and azalea. Then, amazingly, there it stood, the house. Its old bricks were suffused with a heavenly glow, its flawlessly proportioned entrance centered with divine precision, and its curved Palladian wings were extended toward me, dignified loving arms prepared to embrace a good child.

This distinguished house, Nordley, was one of the earliest Palladian-Georgian Revival houses designed by William Lawrence Bottomley, who wrote to his client before beginning construction in 1923, "I want to have your house perfect in style and proportion, but at the same time I would like to give it a certain romantic charm and mellowness." His reproduction certainly succeeded in charming me. I fell for it recklessly, in full knowledge it was a love object unattainable even if it hadn't already belonged to another. I committed adultery in my heart.

I returned to Cambridge and attempted one last time to polish my house, imperfect in style and proportion, into an Old Dominion patina. The cold-creamed faces of the furniture leered back at my efforts. Then, perhaps in a foreshadowing of our departure for the Mercantile Wharf a year later, I gradually began to let go. What absurdly innocent and girlish projections of princely residences had been lying dormant until Nordley released them! And had I been counting all along on growing up to live like my own grandmother, or her grandmother before

her? In all due respect to both formidable women, I certainly
didn't want that now. Which is fortunate, given my tempera-
ment and finances.

It has become clear that unless I want a life of chronic
frustration, I must settle for simply finding, not possessing, a
certain perfection in houses. If the city taught me about
collective consumption, about enjoying public space as if it
were my own, Nordley suggested that there is a kind of special
purchase-and-sale agreement for houses that belong to others.
No money changes hands, and you are home free. You can
homestead and enjoy a building without holding its deed, and
for me that is a happy discovery which has simplified and
enriched life. It leaves the garden gate open. I will never be
constrained by having to try to live in Nordley, to be responsible for it and to it. Instead of sitting inside looking out, I am
content to stand outside looking in. Simple sublimation like this
sends women out in the spring rains on tours of other people's
houses, and on another level it powers the efforts of hard-
working preservationists.

Perhaps no one ever really owns a house at all. Strong-
minded houses, like certain old women with real character, if
they survive at all, stubbornly remain uncorrupted. Cosmetics
and the latest fashions don't affect them. "One says 'my house,
my home'" wrote Doris Lessing. "Nonsense. People flow
through houses, which stay the same, adapting themselves only
slightly for their occupants."

An elderly stranger once presented himself at my Cambridge
doorstep and introduced himself. I recognized him as a kindred
spirit, another rooter in the past. His father had lived in "my"
house at the turn of the century and had passed on photographs
of its interior as it was in 1895. The old son carefully extracted
them from a folder. "Be careful, boy," I imagined a distant
voice cautioning.

There was my living room, a sepia parlor bedecked with
Victoriana: an étagère crusted with bric-a-brac, ornate wicker
rockers, Boston ferns, satin-upholstered side chairs. It could
have been the set for the first New York production of A Doll's

House in the early 1890s. My contemporary underdressing of the same space had transformed it, but the structural identity of the room itself, its features, were thoroughly recognizable through both disguises. The windows with their outsized cornices, like beetling eyebrows, belonged to "my" house and to "his" as well. The light entering through them was the same, just as if the eighty years between the photographer's click and my own blinking gaze had never happened.

Having so far thrown snowballs at the single-family house, the word *housewife*, the building industry, a room of one's own, sisterhood, and home ownership as a creed, I would like now to dispel this aura of negativism and to reestablish my credentials as a nice friendly lady who learns from experience and tries to pass on nuggets of wisdom (like hot potatoes). Unfortunately, much of what I come up with in the advice line is as airily whimsical as my expropriation of Nordley. I can make no task force recommendation to the President on national housing policy. I can only advocate, for women in my situation, a very personal program whose goal is to find a home where the imagination may grow. It is a tender plant that needs shelter in some warm glassed-in place, out of the wind.

My metaphorical plans and elevations specify many doors and very large windows. I insist on no particular style—this sort of home may draw on memory and precedents or on aspiration alone. It can be chastely symmetrical or wildly eccentric—who cares? Its basic premise is that any object is less important than people; when the home-as-object threatens to dominate its occupants, they should remodel or move out at once. A dwelling like this can be the home base from which we start out to run for first, or to fly, and to which we may return whether we score or we strike out. How simple my Utopia sounds, but how difficult it is to build in real bricks and boards.

The Place of Houses (Charles Moore et al., 1974) suggests that what domestic architecture lacks is "heartfelt, personal convictions about what a house really should be like." Without

dreams, the authors continue, "the other two forces which
delimit choice (what we can afford and what is available) are
not, as they should be, challenges that spark the imagination.
They are simply the dreary material limits which shape our
world."

I once did step beyond the limits of literalness and into a
visionary construction—part dream, part myth. At the opening
of the new Cooper-Hewitt Museum in 1976, a show titled
"MANtransFORMS" included a—what shall I call it?—a
sculpture, by the Iranian architect Nader Ardalan and the
sculptor/painter Karl Schlamminger. The explanatory notes
posted at the entrance to the room where it was displayed were
daunting:

This exhibit explores a contemporary expression of one of the
most profound and ancient quests of design—the transformation
of the square (symbol of the temporal) into the circle (symbolic
of the spiritual) through the form of the primary unit of
architecture, the room—the sacred idea of room.
    It is based upon the golden mean measure of man and one of
the fundamental growth principles of nature, the helix.

Elsewhere in the literature I carried, it was described as "direct
emotional experience of light and space."

Sacred indeed. Holy Moley. I entered skeptically, to say the
least. I found myself alone in a space defined by what seemed to
be shimmering rain and a shaft of sunlight, in a cube whose
walls were flickering, descending streaks of light organized
around a central axis that was a single strong beam. This
glowing geometry of squares and circles, with helixes spiraling
from corners to center, was encased in blackness. I had entered
a mandala: I stood at the center of symmetry. For a few minutes
I was overcome, moved almost to tears.

I soon fell back to earth from the dazzling universe of
symbolic forms, and began to examine the Plexiglas rain, to
look up to see where that sunbeam came from. Could I see the
bulb? How many watts must it be? Then I approached the

impenetrable blackness. It was cotton cloth, a little sleazy. I pushed out through an opening, and instantly the last of the magic disappeared. I stood in a rim of room, outside an ordinary curtain, in a converted parlor in the old Andrew Carnegie mansion, and next to a window. I looked out and down, to a city scene of the Ashcan School, a back alley with trash stacked, its grimy detail unspared even by the smoggy gray daylight filtering on it like dust. In an instant I had moved from transcendental vision to the gritty reality of daily life. It's a trip I've taken before. We all have.

This penchant for moving in circles, in round trips from coast to coast, into the past and back again, seems to need some final defense. I now justify these journeys as miming the helix, which when duplicated in DNA is at the heart of the growth of living things. Maybe, just maybe, I am spiraling forward, inching ahead like convolvulus growing up a white pillar, creeping toward a higher vantage point and that different perspective I've been seeking. Or perhaps, as another woman has concluded, it's simply the journey that counts, not the destination. . . .

Williamsburg was outdoing itself. The whole spring of 1978 was in blossom that one May morning. In the Palace Garden, on a bench at the center of its boxwood maze, Mary and I sat in the sun, munching on Pepperidge Farm cookies. We two old friends watched assorted waving arms and heads that appeared over the hedgetops and then disappeared, as their owners tried to scout their way into our little square of privacy.

Mary described her life in an authentic Williamsburg house, one that is "actually four joined structures that indoors and out combine in pleasing manner eighteenth- and early-nineteenth-century architectural styles." Once the youngest of her four daughters discovered a dippy lady tourist scuttling around the front porch, peering into windows. "Oh, is this your house, dear?" the embarrassed peeper asked. And then, as if to make up with flattery for her gaffe, she added, "Oh, I just love it . . . it's so . . . so . . . Colonial!"

We reminisced about Smith classmates, inevitably about Sylvia Plath, and talked of each other's work, of Mary's research on Emily Dickinson in preparation for another book, of her growing interest in historical archaeology. She asked if I would like to fly with her to the plantation house on the Rappahannock River that she and her family had rented as a weekend getaway, where they had all been digging up eighteenth-century household shards, fragments of crockery, china, wine bottles.

When Mary said fly, she meant it literally, and as we rose high above the Tidewater in her small plane, the trees of May below seemed as green and miniature as broccoli flowerets or parsley sprigs. By the time we landed in a buttercup field behind the large white house, the sky had begun to cloud over. When we took off again, soaking cold rain was pouring down. Visibility from the air was zero. I suspected something was wrong when Mary started tapping a couple of the instruments, as if to start them, and knew it was when she said, with the steely self-possession of fighter pilots in World War II movies, "Pass me the gum."

I watched admiringly as she twiddled dials and spoke in a language of numbers and letters, in search of vectors. "Hello, Williamsburg, this is Juliet Hotel, come in, please."

She was so obviously in control, so clearly knew exactly what she was doing, that I couldn't be worried, especially after she reassured me that the instrument that told us whether or not we were flying upside down was still working properly. The possibility that we middle-aged ladies might have been wrong-side-up over the birthplace of American representative democracy was one that hadn't occurred to me.

Finally the voice of numbers allowed us to start our descent. We broke through the clouds, and there it was, beautifully functional, unhistoric Williamsburg Airport. We landed smoothly and taxied to the parking space. I jumped out of the plane, exhilarated by the flight and the hint of danger but delighted to be safely on the ground, to be home again.

For Further Reading

Most of these works have been cited in my text, and I recommend them for further reading or for re-reading.

I'd also like to thank here women who pointed me toward some of these sources or who otherwise provided light in the library on some dark winter days: Lesley Davison, Elsa Dixler, Naomi Faison, Margaret Henderson Floyd, Gunilla Jainchill, Polly Longsworth, Ellyn Polshek, Margaret Supplee Smith, Frances Truslow, Mimi Truslow, Sally Truslow, Mary Van Meter, and Wendy Weil.

Allen, Frederick Lewis. *Only Yesterday.* New York: Harper's, 1931.
Andrews, Wayne. *Architecture, Ambition and Americans.* New York: Macmillan, 1964.
Auchincloss, Louis. *Portrait in Brownstone.* Boston: Houghton Mifflin, 1962.
———*A World of Profit.* Boston: Houghton Mifflin, 1968.
———*A Writer's Capital.* Minneapolis: University of Minnesota Press, 1974.

Beyer, Glenn H. *et al. Houses Are for People: A Study of Home Buyer Motivations.* Ithaca, N.Y.: Cornell, 1955.

Blake, Peter. *Form Follows Fiasco.* Boston: Atlantic/Little, Brown, 1977.

Bombeck, Erma. *At Wit's End.* Garden City, N.Y.: Doubleday, 1967.

———*I Lost Everything in the Post-Natal Depression.* Garden City, N.Y.: Doubleday, 1973.

———*"Just Wait Till You Have Children of Your Own!"* Garden City, N.Y.: Doubleday, 1971.

———*The Grass Is Always Greener Over the Septic Tank.* New York: McGraw-Hill, 1976.

Burchard, John, and Bush-Brown, Albert. *The Architecture of America.* Boston: Atlantic/Little, Brown, 1961, 1966.

Calhoun, Arthur Wallace. *A Social History of the American Family.* Cleveland, Ohio: Clark, 1917–19.

Cardozo, Arlene Rossen. *Woman at Home.* New York: Doubleday, 1976.

Cheever, John. *The Stories of John Cheever.* New York: Knopf, 1978.

———*The Wapshot Scandal.* New York: Harper, 1964.

Child, Lydia Maria. *The American Frugal Housewife.* Edited by Alice M. Geffen. Reprint of 1836 edition. New York: Harper, 1972.

Coles, Robert, and Coles, Jane Hallowell. *Women of Crisis.* New York: Delacorte/Seymour Lawrence, 1978.

Didion, Joan. *Slouching Towards Bethlehem.* New York: Farrar, Straus, & Giroux, 1968.

Dolce, Philip C., ed. *Suburbia: The American Dream and Dilemma.* New York: Doubleday, 1976.

Dow, Joy Wheeler. *American Renaissance: A Review of Domestic Architecture.* New York: Little, 1904.

Fitch, James Marston. *Architecture and the Esthetics of Plenty.* New York: Columbia, 1961.

Ford, James, and Ford, Katherine Morrow. *The Modern House in America.* New York: Architectural Book, 1940.

Ford, Katherine Morrow, and Creighton, Thomas H. *Quality Budget Houses: A Treasury of 100 Architect-Designed Houses from $5,000 to $20,000.* New York: Reinhold, 1954.

Forster, E.M. *Howards End.* New York: Knopf, 1921.

Friday, Nancy. *My Mother/My Self.* New York: Delacorte, 1977.

Friedan, Betty. *The Feminine Mystique.* New York: Norton, 1963.

Frieden, Bernard J., and Solomon, Arthur P.; with Birch, David L., and Pitkin, John. *The Nation's Housing: 1975 to 1985*. Cambridge, Mass.: Joint Center for Urban Studies, 1977.

Gardiner, Stephen. *Evolution of the House*. New York: Macmillan, 1974.

Gilbreth, Frank B., Jr., and Carey, Ernestine G. *Belles on Their Toes*. New York: Crowell, 1950.

———*Cheaper by the Dozen*. New York: Crowell, 1948.

Gilbreth, Lillian M. *The Home-maker and Her Job*. New York: Appleton, 1927.

Gilbreth, Lillian M.; Thomas, Orpha Mae; and Clymer, Eleanor. *Management in the Home*. Rev. ed. New York: Dodd, Mead, 1954.

Gillies, Mary Davis. *McCall's Book of Modern Houses*. New York: Simon & Schuster, 1951.

Greer, Germaine. *The Female Eunuch*. New York: McGraw-Hill, 1971.

Hartmann, Heidi I. "Capitalism and Women's Work in the Home." Unpublished Ph.D. dissertation. New Haven, Conn.: Yale University, 1974.

Hayden, Dolores. *Seven American Utopias*. Cambridge, Mass.: M.I.T., 1976.

Hennessey, William J. *Vacation Houses*. New York: Harper, 1962.

Hitchcock, Henry-Russell. *Architecture: Nineteenth and Twentieth Centuries*. Baltimore: Penguin, 1971.

Homeownership: Realizing the American Dream. Prepared by Economics Dept., U.S. League of Savings Associations, Chicago, 1978.

Ibsen, Henrik. *A Doll's House, Ghosts*. Vol. VII, "The Collected Works of Henrik Ibsen," intro. by William Archer. New York: Scribner's, 1914.

Jacobs, Jane. *The Death and Life of Great American Cities*. New York: Random House, 1961.

Keniston, Kenneth, and the Carnegie Council on Children. *All Our Children: The American Family Under Pressure*. New York: Harcourt Brace Jovanovich, 1977.

Kennedy, Robert Woods. *The House and the Art of Its Design*. New York: Reinhold, 1953.

Lessing, Doris. *The Summer Before the Dark*. New York: Knopf, 1973.

MacDonald, William L. *Northampton, Massachusetts, Architecture & Buildings.* Northampton, Mass.: Bicentennial Committee, 1975.

Mayer, Martin. *The Builders.* New York: Norton, 1978.

McFadden, Cyra. *The Serial.* New York: Knopf, 1977.

McGinley, Phyllis. *Sixpence in Her Shoe.* New York: Macmillan, 1964.

Miller, Jean Baker. *Toward a New Psychology of Women.* Boston: Beacon, 1976.

Moore, Charles; Allen, Gerald; and Lyndon, Donlyn. *The Place of Houses.* New York: Holt, Rinehart and Winston, 1974.

Mudge, Jean McClure. *Emily Dickinson and the Image of Home.* Amherst: University of Massachusetts Press, 1975.

Oakley, Ann. *Woman's Work: The Housewife, Past and Present.* New York: Pantheon, 1974.

Pierson, William H. *The Colonial and Neo-Classical Styles.* Vol. 1 of "American Buildings and Their Architects." New York: Doubleday, 1970.

Plath, Sylvia. *Johnny Panic and the Bible of Dreams.* New York: Harper & Row, 1979.

————*Letters Home.* ed. Aurelia Schober Plath. New York: Harper & Row, 1975.

————*The Bell Jar.* New York: Harper & Row, 1971.

Rodgers, Dorothy. *A Personal Book.* New York: Harper & Row, 1977.

Ruddick, Sara, and Daniels, Pamela, eds. *Working It Out.* New York: Pantheon, 1977.

Schoonmaker, Ann. *Me, Myself, and I.* New York: Harper & Row, 1977.

Sheehy, Gail. *Passages.* New York: Dutton, 1976.

Sklar, Anna. *Runaway Wives.* New York: Coward, McCann & Geoghegan, 1976.

Smith, Page. *Daughters of the Promised Land.* Boston: Little, Brown, 1970.

Spacks, Patricia Meyer. *The Female Imagination.* New York: Knopf, 1975.

Steiner, Nancy Hunter. *A Closer Look at Ariel.* New York: Harper's Magazine Press, 1973.

Swerdlow, Amy, ed. *Feminist Perspectives on Housework and Child Care.* Transcript of a conference sponsored by Sarah Lawrence College, 1977.

Torre, Susana, ed. *Women in American Architecture.* New York: Whitney Library, 1977.

Ullmann, Liv. *Changing.* New York: Knopf, 1976.

Updike, John. *Couples.* New York: Knopf, 1968.

———*Marry Me.* New York: Knopf, 1976.

Veblen, Thorstein. *The Portable Veblen,* ed. Max Lerner. New York: Viking, 1948.

Weibel, Kathryn. *Mirror, Mirror.* New York: Doubleday, 1977.

Wills, Royal Barry. *Houses for Homemakers.* New York: Franklin Watts, 1945.

Wills, Royal Barry, Associates. *More Houses for Good Living.* New York: Architectural Book, 1968.

Woolf, Virginia. *A Room of One's Own.* New York: Harcourt, Brace, 1929.

Index